Attrition of Teachers in Private Schools

Problems, Causes and Remedies

Attrition of Teachers in Private Schools

Problems, Causes and Remedies

Dr. Mukti Patel

ALLIED PUBLISHERS PVT. LTD.

Noida • Mumbai • Kolkata • Chennai • Bangalore

ALLIED PUBLISHERS PRIVATE LIMITED

D-5, Sector-2, **Noida**–201 301
Ph. Nos.: 0120-4320295/2542557/4352866 • E-mail: delhi.books@alliedpublishers.com

17 Chittaranjan Avenue, **Kolkata**–700072
Ph.: 033-22129618 • E-mail: cal.books@alliedpublishers.com

15 J.N. Heredia Marg, Ballard Estate, **Mumbai**–400001
Ph.: 022-42126969 • E-mail: mumbai.books@alliedpublishers.com

No. 25/10, Commander-in-Chief Road, Ethiraj Lane (Next to Post Office)
Egmore, **Chennai**–600008
Ph.: 044-28223938 • E-mail: chennai.books@alliedpublishers.com

P.B. No. 9932, No. 15, 3rd Floor (Next to Vijaya Bank),
5th Cross, Gandhinagar, Karnataka, **Bangalore**–560009,
Ph.: 080-41530285 / 22386239 • E-mail: bngl.books@alliedpublishers.com

Website: www.alliedpublishers.com

ISBN: 978-93-89934-91-5

Disclaimer: This book is updated version of work done by the author for her doctoral thesis work.

Citation: Patel Mukti (2024), Attrition of Teachers in Private Schools: Problems, Causes and Remedies, Allied Publishers Pvt. Limited, Noida

Published by Sunil Sachdev and printed by Ravi Sachdev at Allied Publishers Pvt. Ltd., D-5, Sector-2, Noida–201 301

Foreword

Teacher attrition remains a major concern for school leaders and policymakers in many countries. People leaving organizations all the time and is not worrisome; but employee attrition is a different matter altogether. Even though the term is often used interchangeably with employee turnover, employee attrition is different from employee turnover. Employee attrition happens when employee who leave an organization for any reason are not replaced for a long time, or not ever. Attrition often results in a decrease in the size of an organization's or department's workforce because positions are not filled when employees leave. In India, teaching profession is perceived as the profession with lower salaries; and this perception is very strong among the teachers. That directly affects their motivation to teach, causes competent teachers to leave the profession itself. Low compensation is also the reason why good students avoid choosing education as their major in higher studies. The government accepts the flaws in the system and their inability to attract bright minds to the profession. To help further understand why teachers leave the profession and to inform the development of targeted interventions to tackle this phenomenon, this present study aims to understand and evaluate the problems, causes and remedies for the growing attrition rate of teachers in private schools of Anand district of Gujarat.

Tushaar Shah
Emeritus Scientist
International Water Management Institute (IWMI).
Sri Lanka/New Delhi Office

Acknowledgement

Firstly, I express my deepest gratitude to my guide Dr. S.S. Kalamkar, Director and Professor, Agro-Economic Research Centre, Sardar Patel University, Vallabh Vidyanagar, Anand for being so understanding and approachable at each phase of the study. I am indebted to him for his incredible support, care, commitment, concern, guidance and many hours of valuable discussions. It has really been a great pleasure to learn from him and update my knowledge on the topic and other relevant fields. Without his constant inputs and guidance, the study would not have been undertaken and completed in the manner it has been done. I am grateful to him from bottom of my heart for all his efforts.

I am thankful to the Vice Chancellor of our University for his support whenever needed.

I am deeply indebted to Mr. M.B. Sharma, District Education Officer (DEO), Anand District, Anand for sparing his valuable time and discussing on the present scenario of education in the district. Thanks to Office staff of DEO for providing required details about the schools of the district.

I would like to express my gratitude to Shri. B.N. Patel (Managing Trustee, Sardar Patel Education Trust, Anand) for helping me with getting appointments with management personals of renowned private schools of different tehsils of Anand District.

I am grateful to Prof. (Dr.) Yogesh C. Joshi (Director and Head, Department of Business Management, Sardar Patel University, Vallabh Vidyanagar) for being supportive and cooperative throughout the study. I also thank Dr. Raju Rathod (Associate Professor, Department of Business Management, Sardar Patel University, Vallabh Vidyanagar) for his valuable inputs in statistical analysis of the data. Thanks to all other faculty members of Department of Business Management for their valuable comments on the study. I am also grateful to external experts for making suggestions on research tools at initial process of research. Big Thanks to Mr. Kartikey Dave, Vice Principal, J.P. Thakkar High School, Anand for his support in conducting pilot survey and always being there till the end of the study.

I express my heartiest gratitude to the Management Personnel, Directors, Principals, Teachers (Permanent and Contractual) of all selected schools for permitting me and providing all required support in conducting the survey despite of their busy schedules. I am deeply indebted to all the parents and students for their active participation in data collection.

I am grateful to Dr. Dalip Kumar (Senior Executive (projects), National Council of Applied Economic Research, New Delhi) for proving secondary statistical data and other relevant literature on the research topic. I would like to thank Dr. Kinjal Ahir (Associate Professor, Department of Economics, Sardar Patel University, Vallabh Vidyanagar) for helping me with literature related to research topic. I am also thankful to all Librarians (Bhaikaka Library, Library of Department of Business Management, Library of Agro Economic Research Centre and Library of N.S. Patel Arts College) for their help in getting required literature.

I am thankful to Ms. Nandini Virmani (Principal, Swaminarayan Vidhyapith, Valasan), Mr. Kartikey Dave (Vice Principal, K.J. Thakkar High School), Mr. Dharmendra Gohel (Ex-principal, BAPS Vidhyamandir, Bakrol), Mr. Chirayu Patel (Teacher, Bavis Gam Vidhyalaya, Vallabh Vidyanagar), Ms. Razia Vhora (Teacher, Adharshila Vidhyalaya, Anklav) for sparing their valuable time in building case studies related to research topic. Special thanks to Dr. Sahdev Luhar for helping in narration of Case Studies.

I am grateful to Mr. Mahesh Parmar (Office Superintendent, UGC Section, Sardar Patel University) for his support. I thank all Ph.D. scholars of Department of Business Management for their necessary support. I am also thankful to the Office staff of Department of Business Management for providing all official documents on time.

I thank Ms. Aarti Suryavanshi and Ms. Vaishnavi Shinde for their support in designing schedules for primary data collection. I am deeply indebted to Dr. Brijen Patel, Dr. Rajesh Patel, Dr. Ajaysingh Chauhan, Mr. Moin Malik, Mr. Bhagat Patel, Mr. Kamlesh Patel, Ms. Daksha Patel for their valuable support during the phase of primary data collection. I would like to thank Ms. Rinku Rathod and her team for their help in data feeding work. I am thankful to Ms. Prachi Patel for helping me with tabulation of data.

Last but not the least, I express my deepest gratitude to my mother (Mrs. Jaya Mohan Patel) for taking good care of my infant baby and making the whole journey of this study smooth for me. I am indebted to my father Dr. Mohan Patel (Vice Chancellor, Krantiguru Shyamji Krishna Verma Kachchh University, Bhuj, Kutchchh) and brother (Mr. Praharsh Mohan Patel) for evaluating each stage of the study critically based on their vast academic experiences. I thank my mother and father in law for helping me to balance my life. I am thankful to my sister, sister and brother in law, my grandparents, my nephews and other family members of mine and my in-laws for motivating me to complete this research study. Heartfelt thanks to my husband Shri Kapil Patel and my dearest son Master Sattva Patel for not only adjusting their schedule with my requirement but also providing all necessary support and encouragement in conducting this research work.

(Dr. Mukti Patel)

July 15, 2024

List of Abbreviations

AM	:	Arithmetic Mean
BaLA	:	Building as Learning Aid
B.Ed.	:	Bachelor of Education
BPO	:	Business Process Outsourcing
B.Tech.	:	Bachelor of Technology
CAL	:	Computer Aided Learning
CBSE	:	Central Board of Secondary Education
DEO	:	District Education Officer
DISE	:	District Information System for Education
ECCE	:	Early Child Care Education
EFA	:	Education for All
ERC	:	Employee Retention Connection
et. al	:	others
etc.	:	related aspects
GDP	:	Gross Domestic Product
GER	:	Gross Enrolment Ratio
GSEB	:	Gujarat State Education Board
HR	:	Human Resources
IB	:	International Baccalaureate
i-BaLA	:	Inclusive- Building as Learning Aid
ICSE	:	The Indian Certificate of Secondary Education
ICT	:	Information and Communication Technology
KG	:	Kinder Garden
KGBV	:	The Kasturba Gandhi Balika Vidyalaya
KPO	:	Knowledge Process Outsourcing
LMC	:	Local Management Committee

MBA	:	Masters of Business Administration
MBO	:	Management by Objectives
M.Ed.	:	Masters of Education
MHRD	:	Ministry of Human Resource Management
N	:	Number (Sample)
NER	:	Net Enrolment Ratio
NPEGEL	:	National Programme for Education of Girls at Elementary Level (NPEGEL)
NUEPA	:	National University for Education Planning and Administration
Ph.D.	:	Doctor of Philosophy
PTA	:	Parents Teachers Association
PTR	:	Pupil Teacher Ratio
ROL	:	Review of Literature
RTE	:	Right to Education
SSA	:	Sarva Shiksha Abhiyan
UDISE	:	Unified District Information System for Education
UNESCO	:	United Nation's Educational, Scientific and Cultural Organisation

Contents

List of Tables

List of Maps

List of Figures

List of Boxes

CHAPTER 1

Attrition of Teachers:

Significance and Scope

1.1 INTRODUCTION

Education is a basic need for a human being like food and shelter. It is considered as an essential element to one's life. While food is required for good health and shelter is for safe life, education is for conversant mind. As South Africa's former president Nelson Mandela quoted "Education is the most powerful weapon we can use to change the world[1]". Quality of Education is a main determinant for economic development of any nation.

Education gives meaning to an individual's life as with it the possibility of one being successful in any given field of art or work becomes considerably easier and worthwhile. With education comes knowledge and with knowledge comes power. However, power that a person possesses will be dependent on how an individual uses it. It is said that knowledge is something that teaches us what to do whereas, wisdom is something that teaches us how and when to do any given activity. Basically, knowledge or we can say education can be gained but wisdom can only be acquired by a special few.

Ages before, time has witnessed incidents and stages where teacher or Guru was known to be the prime means for acquiring knowledge as well as wisdom. Hence, by looking into the ancient time, one can obtain massive information about the significance of the role of teachers in the society and how it affected the overall personality and being of any person whosoever.

Now a day, retention has been a catch word for all types of business enterprises. Various practices have been adopted to retain high performing individuals in all the types of industries. During the last two decades or so, education in India has been privatized and commercialized to a great extent and has been accepted as an Industry. There is mush-rooming of aided (grant-in-aid supported colleges) and unaided private

---

[1] Address by Nelson Mandela at launch of Mindset Network, Johannesburg 16 July 2003 (available at http://www.mandela.gov.za/mandela_speeches/2003/030716_mindset.htm)

schools in almost all corners of the country. Augmented quantity of private schools has put a big question mark on quality of education in India. That to retaining good teachers has always been an area of concern for almost all the private schools running in different parts of India. Pre-primary, Primary, Secondary and Higher Secondary Schools serve as foundation for further higher studies and the problems occurring at these levels have long term impact on education of the youths which are future of our nation.

1.2 NEED AND IMPORTANCE OF THE STUDY

With more than 1.4 million schools and more than 230 million students' enrolments, India is one of the largest and complex school education systems in the world, along with China *(The British Council, India, 2014).* With the growing time, education in modern India gained a whole new facet and so did the role and performance of the teachers in the society. Many fundamental Laws and Acts have been enacted pertaining to the improved and ongoing performance of the teachers all over the nation. But, as it is rightly said that the coin has two sides, the journey of the teachers in the private schools have also seen their share of hardships in their career in terms of their expectations to have a more stable and revised facilities from the legislation and other governing bodies including respective school management where they are entitled to work.

Education system in India is based on education provided by the public as well as the private sector having financial support from either from Central government, State Government or any local trust/funding agency. According to estimates[2], about 29 per cent of Indian rural children (six to fourteen age group) are educated privately. With more than 50 per cent children enrolling in private schools in urban areas, the balance has already tilted towards private schooling in cities. As per a Special Report[3] (2010..), even schools at the bottom of the private education pyramid are complaining of teachers being taken away by the Business Process Outsourcing (BPO) industry and other sectors of the economy. Most of the english-medium unaided schools which comprise the largest group in the private school sector catering to students from lower middle class families, are affiliated with state examination boards and charge nominal

[2] http://www.thehindu.com/features/education/school/over-a-quarter-of-enrolments-in-rural-india-are-in-private-schools/article5580441.ece

[3] educationworldonline.net

annual tuition fees, due to which they are unable to reward their teachers satisfactorily. While on the other hand, the BPO industry, which is growing at very fast rate at almost 56 percent every year and offers start-up monthly remuneration, which is almost double than that of private unaided schools, can easily attract teachers working with english-literate unaided school. So, the ultimate worry is to retain competent teachers for quality education.

The UNESCO Institute of Statistics in its report on *Teachers and Educational Quality: Monitoring Global Needs for 2015* released in June 2006 had noted that to meet the Millennium Development Goal of providing elementary education to all children by 2015, India will need the greatest inflow of new teachers in the world, more than 2 million. The government had set a target of adding 82 million school seats by 2016, but, according to the estimated of McKinsey 2012 report, needed to add 34 million secondary school seats and double the number of secondary school teachers hired every year to reach the target (*Piramal A., Hindustan Times, January 21, 2014*).

All the sectors of the Indian Economy, including education have been influenced by New Industrial Policy (1991). The educational sector has seen an invasion of too many private schools since 1991. This influx of private schools is advantageous to the country to achieve goal like 'Education for All (EFA)' set by UNESCO and thus schools have been accessible for many in India *(Chavan P., 2015)*. The country has recorded 13.67 per cent growth in students' enrolment form standard I to standard X (*Dhawan H, Times of India, January 22, 2013*). The education report reveals that there were 2532 private self-financed schools in 2009 which increased to around 11,965 in the year 2012–13 and keep it increasing. This increase in private schools has also increased the need of competent teachers.

Boyd *et al.* (2006) stated that employees play vital roles in any organization. Ultimately employees contribute immensely to the performance and success of the organization and are the most valuable resource that any organization can rely on for its sustainable growth. Employees too would like to stick to the same job for long run, as the change is actually difficult to manage with family. But in reality, many a times they are forced to leave the job due to less pay, unhealthy working conditions, conflicts with colleagues, less opportunities for betterment and also as the spouse is getting their desired job in another state. This turnover has definitely a long term impact on success of any organization, and educational institution is not an exception. It is actually becoming hard to attract, acquire, motivate and retain key Talent.

The attrition rate is around 20–30 per cent across industrial sector in India annually *(Raisinghani M., 2015)*. The cost of attrition is not just losing that employee but the cost also includes various hidden costs such as cost of recruitment, cost of selection, cost of orientation, cost of training, loss of students' classes, and so on. Few educational problems have been very prominent all over the world now a day. The most prominent among them all is the failure to ensure that primary and secondary classes are all staffed with competent teachers. Teacher training institutions are not creating sufficient number of qualified teachers to meet the demand of upcoming schools. Increasing student enrollments and increasing teacher attrition are the reasons for the shortfall of teachers at school, which is making the situation worse for unaided schools all across the world. And ultimately all these, making the quality of education to be questioned.

Gujarat ranks 9th on the Education Development Index (EDI) as prepared by the National University of Educational Administration (NUEPA). This index measures the performance of states on the Universalization of Elementary Education programme[4]. The schools supported by State Government are under Gujarat Secondary and Higher Secondary Education Board. While many of the private schools are affiliated to Central Board of Secondary Education (CBSE) and Council for the Indian School Certificate Examination (CISCE) board. During the last five years, students in Gujarat seem to be finding their way to private schools in the state, as states the Comptroller and Auditor General of India (CAG) in its 2014 report.[5] The paradox here is that private schools need teachers against growing number of students and they are finding it difficult to attract and retain competent teachers. Number of students have been increasing in Anand and therefore the study is needed to address a real problem of retaining good teachers for longer period.

1.3 SCOPE OF THE STUDY

"If you want to measure the economic development of a country then start by looking into its classrooms", said by the then President of India

[4] http://www.gidb.org/education-education-system-in-gujarat

[5] https://indianexpress.com/article/cities/ahmedabad/children-in-gujarat-finding-their-way-to-private-schools-cag

Shri Pranab Mukherjee, in November 2013, spoke at a public forum about how if we were "to attain a growth rate of 9 per cent per year, we must put in place enabling factors, most prominent of which is the quality of education". As per the data published in 2017, there were in total 722 Universities in India, out of which 47 are in Gujarat. There are hundreds of private schools running in Gujarat, particularly in Anand, which is education hub of Gujarat. In fact, there is mushrooming of private schools in almost all tehsils of Anand District.

The study is conducted in Anand district, as it is one of the most educated districts of the state with education hub like Vallabh Vidyanagar. The paradox here is that private schools need teachers against growing number of students and they are finding it difficult to attract and retain competent teachers. Number of students has been increasing in Anand and therefore the study is needed to evaluate and address a real problem of retention of teachers for a longer period. Gujarat is a state, which has witnessed the growth of almost 233 per cent in literacy rate in 2001 over the census of 1951.

The economic growth of the nation is fully dependent on the quality of education, which is in turn dependent on competent teachers. With the help of this study, causes of high attrition rate among teachers in private schools will be highlighted, which will be helpful for the schools/ management to identify where they went wrong. The study will also be helpful to suggest some remedies to handle the problem effectively. The study of private schools in Anand district can also provide reference to study 'teachers' retention problem' in the other parts of the country.

1.4 SIGNIFICANCE OF ATTRITION

A high value indicates high levels of teacher turnover which can be disruptive for the learning of students. Where teachers teach for 30–40 years, the attrition rate will be below 5 per cent in the profession. Attrition rates above 10 per cent indicate that the average teaching career lasts only 10 years throughout the career.

Shortage of teachers is a significant contributing factor that widens equity gaps in education access and learning for various classes of the society. Assessing and monitoring the problem of teacher attrition is necessary to a sufficient supply of qualified, competent and well-trained teachers as well as to their effective deployment, support and management in the teaching profession.

The study is conducted mainly to identify the reasons for heavy turnover of the teachers in private schools. Education at school level serves as a foundation for further development. In fact role of teachers at school becomes very crucial as they are the educators and creator of next generation. Major chunk of the students is with private schools in India. So, when teachers are not stable, the quality of education ultimately suffers. And students are the main sufferer as they connect the subject with the teacher teaching it. This makes a problem of attrition as the biggest worry for any educational institution and ultimately for a Country as a whole. As discussed before, with the mounting needs of the teachers, the education sector has now started facing the problem of attrition in various parts of the country as well as in different types of schools.

1.5 SIGNIFICANCE OF THE STUDY

Government of India aims to introduce revolutions in the field of education and it should be done by keeping teachers in focus. Teachers are the foundation for the creation of next generation as responsible citizens. Present status of education in India has been an area of worry, as quality of education is deteriorating day by day. When we talk about demographic dividend, the quality of young generation of any nation is in doubt if education standard of the nation is not up to the mark. Thus, it is quite possible with poor quality education; youth population dividend may turn out to be liability on the nation. The irony here is that the cost of education has increased tremendously, while quality of education has hampered due to instability of competent and qualified teachers in unaided private schools.

Teachers especially those who work in small self-financed private schools are susceptible to lack of job security and antagonistic and stringent work environment at schools. Such an unfair state of work place has led to the job dissatisfaction, depression, lack of interest in work and sense of isolation among most of the teachers working mostly in small self-financed schools. And the worst part is their situation is always ignored by the Government.

Other than exploitation, work load, minimum salary, discrimination in pay and lack of satisfaction with the profession are some persistent problems of such private school teachers. Such problems vary from school to school and cannot be generalized for all the self-financed educational institutions at any place of the nation. The recent estimates show that 25 per cent of all enrolments of students in primary/elementary education is in self-financed schools in the country (As per DISE 2006–07). Not only non-poor children study in these schools in urban areas, but children of poor households also study in such schools in large numbers. Government alone cannot handle the need of education nationwide, so it has to rely on such schools. These schools have all the sections of study from preprimary to secondary, but success of such institutions is again dependent on competent and committed teachers.

The data on District Information System for Education (DISE) reveals that in India approximately 78 per cent of primary schools had three or fewer teachers to attend to all grade levels in the year 2005, and as per DISE (2006) more than 55 per cent of the schools had 100 or fewer students. However, because of deprived quality of public schools, 27 per cent of Indian children are attending private schools. In the current scenario, self-financed schools have protection from any potential changes in political/public policy or movement to resolve teacher's protests and teachers perceived to be intimidating to their private interests are fired immediately. The Government has very little regulatory control over most functionalities of its constituent states, especially in regard to education policy. So there is no similarities in socioeconomic, cultural, and political factors within the states too.

1.6 NEED OF THE STUDY

In India, teaching profession is perceived as the profession with lower salaries. And the perception is very strong among the teachers. That directly affects their motivation to educate students, causes competent teachers to leave the profession itself and also compels good students to not choose education as major in higher studies (OECD 2009). The government accepts the flaws in the system and their inability to attract bright minds to the profession.

So, in the current research work the researcher aims to understand and evaluate the problems, causes and remedies for the growing attrition rate of teachers in private schools of Anand district of Gujarat.

1.7 OBJECTIVES OF THE STUDY

The specific objectives of the study were as follows:

1. To study pupil/student-staffing pattern in private schools of Anand district;

2. To study appointment patterns of teachers in private schools of Anand district;
3. To study problems in attracting competent teachers in private schools of Anand district.
4. To examine factors determining the healthy and positive relationship between different stakeholders (teacher-student-parent-management) in private schools of Anand district.
5. To find out reasons behind high attrition rate of teachers and its adverse effects in private schools of Anand district.
6. To suggest remedial measures to solve the problem of retaining good teachers for long time.

1.8 HYPOTHESIS OF THE STUDY

The study tries to test following hypothesis after analysis of the collected data.

1. There is high rate of attrition among temporary teachers due to job insecurity in private secondary schools in Anand district.
2. There is an effect of exit of teacher on education of students in Anand District.

1.9 LIMITATIONS OF THE STUDY

To come out with the useful findings of the research, one should consider the limitations of the study. Following are the limitations to be considered before drawing the necessary inferences.

1. Data was collected only from schools having Secondary and Higher Secondary Sections.
2. The study was conducted at the schools where English is medium of instruction.
3. The study data covers one District of central Gujarat for concrete policy formulation.
4. Difficult to contact the teachers who have already left the school.
5. Parents could not be approached easily.

1.10 SCHEME OF CHAPTERIZATION

The book is organized in to nine chapters. Introductory chapter presents the brief overview of education system, privatization of education and problem of retention of teachers, significance and scope of the study, need and objectives with hypothesizes, and limitation of the study. Chapter II present the review of past research studies conducted on the topic under study at national as well as at international level. The methodology used for present research work in presented in detail in Chapter III. Chapter IV discussed the present status of education in Gujarat having more focus on study area, i.e. Anand District. The results of primary data analysis on attrition of teachers through management perspectives are presented in Chapter V. The teachers and parents perspectives on selected topic are presented in Chapter VI and VII. The next chapter provides the experiences recorded from students about impact of leaving teacher in between in academic session. The last chapter presents summary and conclusions with policy implications came out of the study.

CHAPTER 2

Understanding Attrition with Review of Research at International and National Level

2.1 INTRODUCTION

Review of research done is necessary for extensive understanding of the topic in current perspective to establish research path to serve the pre-determined objectives of the study. It also gives the current scenario of the proposed topic to understand the research gap. Literature review is mandatory to establish background of the whole research work. Therefore, in this chapter, post work done/literature is reviewed on aspects related to attrition of teachers in India and abroad. The review of books, chapters in edited book, interviews and articles in newspapers, articles in magazines, research papers in journals, research projects, related websites, any other work or findings related to topic in India or any other country was undertaken.

Statistical findings of various projects indicate that the major problem for schools of various countries is not a shortage of teachers in the system. The actual problem is that, even in countries where sufficient numbers of teachers are trained and recruited, many of the newly graduated students choose not to go in to teaching profession at all or to leave the profession after just a few years of starting teaching career *(Cooper and Alvarado, 2016)*.

The intensity of the problem is such that none of the country is left unaffected. The problem of teachers' attrition has been prominent in most of countries of the world, whether it is developed, developing or under-developed status. There have been various researches on the topic in a particular part of the country to find out the reasons or remedies of the problem. Education can hamper at any time if teachers are not competent and stable in any part of the world. There are some recent developments in the area of research to improve quality of education through retaining qualified teachers for long and also to improve image of teaching profession in developed as well as developing countries. There are also some international organizations like UNESCO, which covers the whole world to highlight the intensity of problem in all over the world.

Direct literature on this topic is difficult to get as it is started getting attention recently. Therefore, cross literature is also considered and reviewed to understand the problems from all the possible perspective. Review of literature is classified as below:

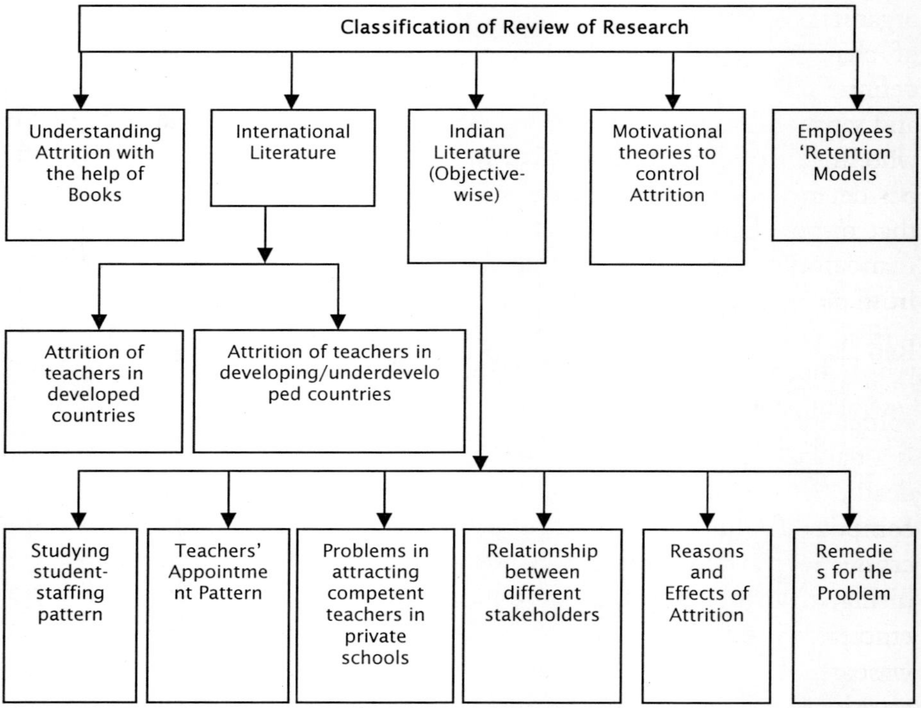

Figure 1: Classification of Review of Research

Firstly, books having chapters on attrition is reviewed to get theoretical understanding of attrition. Then the literature related to the topic is divided as international literature and Indian literature. International literature is again divided to understand the problem of attrition of teachers in developed countries and developing countries. Under the category of developed countries, literature related to attrition of teachers in the countries like USA, Australia, Canada, Singapore, and Europe is reviewed in detail. Under the category of developing countries, literature related to the topic of the countries like Ghana, Ethiopia, Kenya, Tanzania,

Nigeria, and Pakistan is reviewed in detail. Under the category of Indian literature, literature is divided according to objectives of the study. Literature related to motivational theories and retention models is also reviewed to highlight some ways to control attrition.

2.2 Understanding Attrition with Review of Books

Subba Rao (2012)[1] explains in his book meaning of employee turnover as external mobility means shifting of employees into and out of an organization due to any reason. Author again defined the term "as the rate of change in the number of employees of an organization during a definite period." Further author mentions that employees who are happy and satisfied stay for a longer period in an organization whereas employees who are not happy and satisfied in the present organization or in their current career try to search for a job at other places. Author also stated that on the other hand, when an organization cannot find any suitable and competent employee from any internal sources, it selects to get one from outside the organization.

Rao also tries to summarize effects of employee turnover on organization, it may affect positively or negatively but the effects are more negative as compared to the positive effects. Author describes that employee turnover is a natural and unavoidable part of any organization which occur due to death, retirement, layoff etc. up to certain limits and it also helps to attract competent employees into the organization, but when employee turnover crosses a certain limit, it may lead to many difficulties as higher cost of hiring, training and development, induction and placement, declining efficiency and productivity of employees, and high rate of accidents and wastages. Author strongly suggests that to reduce the negative impact of attrition, Human Resource Managers should analyze the reasons of attrition and provide solutions to the problems arising out of the turnover. He tries to focus on various reasons of employee turnover such as, better status in other organizations, dissatisfaction with the current job, getting better remuneration, starting own enterprise, family issues, continuous weak health etc. He states at the end that there are umpteen number of new job opportunities due to globalization, so employees resign from their current jobs in order to join new jobs in other organizations for better career prospects.

Memoria and Rao (2012)[2] explains the meaning of employee turnover, reasons for employee turnover and how to deal with its effects. Authors describe labor turnover as the result of voluntary resignation which is not healthy for any organization. They also summarize causes of resignation as deteriorating health, better prospects elsewhere, physical disability or getting married in case of young females. Resignation may also be involuntary when an employee is asked to resign due to his negligence of duty or serious damage to company by his actions. They further describe that the intention of resignation must be recognized beforehand and both the parties must comprehend the dynamics of resignation. The authors suggest that exit interview can help a company to understand the reasons for the voluntary resignation of the employees. They also discussed a case about Hexaware Technologies limited, which says that the company made an attempt to understand the reasons behind resignations. Chief People Officer of the company revealed that he has designed a procedure of exit interview to understand the reasons of voluntary resignation. He further added that the idea may not work always, but it is helpful. He also said that attrition has been common in all types of industries and they have implemented various steps to reduce attrition such as job rotation, opportunity given to employees to select preferred location and review of compensation scale twice in a year.

Prasad (2011)[3] reveals that employee attrition and overstaffing of employees are the biggest problems for many organizations in current time. The author is also surprised to know that employee attrition is significantly high even in those companies which are considered as the 'best places to work' by the employees, and therefore companies are coming out with retention plans and policies to reduce turnover of employees. Author mentions about the survey undertaken by Economic Times in partnership with the USA in 2009 for identifying India's best companies to work for and based on survey of 373 companies, study concluded that the companies which are best places to work have high rate of employee attrition. In the manufacturing sector, the attrition rate was 10–12 per cent in 2005 and in 2006, it increased to 12–20 per cent in India according to Business Today (July 2007).

Author segregates causes of employee attrition as employee related factors and organization related factors. Employee related factors comprise of too much future expectation, tendency of changing job frequently among young employees at the starting of their career, better career prospects in new organizations, lack of satisfaction from the present job, habit of staying at home, and desire to start one's own business. Organization related factors include faulty human resource policies and practices particularly related to compensation, poor organizational culture, conflicts between the employees and the organization, promotional strategies, poor working environment, lack of training and development, deprived leadership and supervision, unrealistic organizational goals, expectation about recognition and pay, which leads to high employee attrition. The author further describes that high rate of employee attrition is costly for employees as well as the organization. High turnover of employees indicates that there is something erroneous in the organizational practices and it must be resolved, otherwise the organization cannot be flourished. On the other hand, an organization has to bear various types of costs due to high rate of employee attrition. The cost of employee turnover includes cost of hiring and orientation, cost of recruitment, selection and placement of new employees, cost of training and development, loss of production, adverse impact on the existing employees' morale, loss of goodwill and prestige of organization in human resource market, specialization cost of new employee, disturbed teamwork and team spirit in the organization. The author concludes that employee turnover can be controlled with the help of exit interviews, effective retention strategies, attractive pay package, stay interview, retention bonus, non-monetary benefits, job designs as per employees' competencies and proper employee relationship management.

Peter and Welch (2010)[4] have explained that employee turnover is not only the problem of India but China and Russia are also facing the same problem. China is facing the problem of high employee turnover not only in Chinese but also in foreign owned companies. The major reason for staff turnover in Chinese and foreign owned company is insufficient compensation. Chinese employees change their organizations for higher salary and not for better prospects. In China, multinationals companies train their employees to make them use their machinery and instruments properly and therefore it becomes very difficult for an organization to prevent employee turnover. Chinese companies have come up with various plans and programs to retain the employees, such as employee development programs and provision of additional perquisites. Chinese employees are given better compensation to make them positive about the organization and also to retain them for long. Problem of employee turnover is also prevalent in Russia. The employees who know foreign language and have experience of working in western companies are in high demand in Russia, therefore they move freely between one organization to another for better opportunities.

Memoria and Gankar (2010)[5] describe turnover as a problem not only for the employees but also for organizations. Authors believe that labor turnover is due to resignation and they identified reasons for employee turnover such as unhappiness with working conditions, low compensation, persistent ill health, old age, and personal family problems. Author further describe that employee attrition is unavoidable up to some extent due to retirement and new recruitment, but when turnover is due to resignations and dismissals it has adverse impact on the workers and their productivity. The quality and quantity of production also gets affected. They mentions the case of The Bombay Textile Labor Committee, which has pointed out the fact that though a high rate of turnover exists in all organized industries in India, no reliable data on its extent is available anywhere. They also mentions about The Rege committee, which collected some data on labor turnover during the Second World War and found out that the labor turnover rates are legitimately high in the engineering group in Calcutta.

Khanka (2009)[6] describes in his book on Human Resource Management (text and cases) about various reasons of employee resignations, may be voluntary or involuntary depending on the reasons for resignations. The reasons for voluntary resignations of the employee are ill health, marriage, better prospects in other organizations etc. Further, turnover is advisable for the organization as some of them have been recruited wrongly for the position by the recruiter. Author also feels that a high rate of employee turnover is an alarming sign for any organization indeed. Author states that it becomes essential for the organization and the management to search and analyze the causes of employee attrition in such cases. Author strongly believes in the procedure of conducting 'exit interviews' of the employees who are leaving the organization to resolve the problem of heavy employee turnover. In his view, it may help the management to control employee turnover before it reaches a dangerous situation.

2.3 INTERNATIONAL LITERATURE

2.3.1 Attrition of Teachers in Developed Countries

2.3.1.1 *United States of America (USA)*

Keigher (2010)[7] conducted the Sixth Teacher Follow-up Survey (TFS) in the year 2008–09, on behalf of the U.S. Census Bureau, which was sponsored by the National Center for Education Statistics (NCES) of the Institute of Education Sciences within the U.S. Department of Education.

Author undertook a follow-up survey of teachers who left teaching in the year after the previous school and staffing survey data collection, including retirees and those who continue to teach. The survey was conducted with an objective to understand teachers' mobility and attrition among elementary and secondary private and public school teachers who teach in grades K-12 in the 50 states and the district of Columbia. Author completed survey by interviewing about 4,750 current and former teachers in total. Of these respondents, author found that about 2,600 teachers were still teaching at the same school; 890 were still teaching but at a different school; and 1,260 had left the profession. Author found that out of total public school teachers with 4 or more years of experience, 55.3 percent moved from one public school to another public school in the same district and 42.3 percent moved to another public school district and in case of private school teacher with 4 or more years of teaching experience, 35.3 percent moved from a private school to a public school and 64.7 percent moved from one private school to another private school. About 26.2 percent of public school teachers and 16 per cent of private school teachers changed schools because of personal life factors. Author concluded that 5.3 percent of public school teachers and 13.0 percent of private school teachers left teaching because their contract was not renewed. Findings also highlighted that 8.9 percent of public school teachers and 17.4 percent of private school teachers, out of those who left teaching were working in other occupation, including military service. Author concluded that 40.8 percent of public school teachers and 15.5 percent of private school teachers, of teachers who left teaching reported opportunities for learning from colleagues were better in their current position than in teaching.

Thomas and Hammond (2017)[8] studied why it has been important to study teachers turnover and what can be done to stop it in USA. Their study used findings of a 2016 study by LPI, *A Coming Crisis in Teaching? Teacher Supply, Demand, and Shortages in the U.S.* They also used data from the latest National Center for Education Statistics' *Schools and Staffing Surveys,* and then they tried to find out who is leaving, why, and which students are most impacted. They reported that in USA, more than 1 lakh classrooms are staffed by the instructors, who are not fully qualified to teach. They also found out that 90 per cent of open teaching positions are created by the teachers who are leaving the profession itself. Almost 66 per cent of the teachers leave the profession for the reasons other than retiring, mostly as they are not satisfied with the profession.

They mentioned that attrition of teachers in USA is about twice as high as compared to high achieving nations like Finland, Canada and Singapore.

Further, study shows that it is quite essential to address the issue, as the cost of attrition to students and the budget of districts is significant. Authors argue that teachers' attrition directly influence students' achievements negatively. When inexperienced and under-qualified teachers are hired to fill vacancies in the school, there is negative impact on learning of the students. Study estimated that each leaving teacher can cost around $20,000 in an urban district. As per their study, turnover rates are highest in the South and lowest in the Northeast parts of the country, where states tend to offer higher pay, support smaller class sizes and make greater investments in education sector. They also found out that shortages are persistent in specific subjects like Mathematics, Science, Special education, English language development, and foreign languages. Besides, turnover rates are 50 per cent higher in Title I schools, which mostly serve students from low-income households. Lastly, they could also find out that turnover rates are 70 per cent higher in schools serving the largest population of students of color.

Author reported that teachers who are alternatively certified are 25 per cent more likely to leave their schools. The other reasons of teachers' attrition are lack of administrative support, working in districts with lower salaries, dissatisfactions with testing, accountability pressures, lack of opportunities for advancement and dissatisfaction with working conditions. At the end, authors suggested to federal, state and district policy makers to improve key factors associated with attrition of teachers such as compensation, teacher preparation and support and the most importantly Teaching conditions.

2.3.1.2 *Australia*

Buchanan, *et al.* (2013)[9] conducted the longitudinal study in Australia on early career teachers' decisions to remain in or leave the profession through personal interviews, telephonic interviews and used tracking surveys as tools for data collection. They had taken in to consideration a survey of 1351 beginning teachers conducted by the Australian Primary Principals Association (APPA) which indicated that 24 per cent of teachers felt they are likely to leave teaching within 5 years (APPA, 2006). They used constant comparison data reduction methods for analysis of data collected over a period of 4 years. They mentioned that most of the teachers want to become better teachers over a period of time and they strive for appreciation. Two main factors for retention of early career teachers are opportunity given to teachers for professional learning and supportive work environment. They also suggested "Teachers Help Line" by government or school leaders can be a better way to support teachers to face challenges of early years.

Study shows that the satisfaction from the profession improves as the early career teachers gain experience as they desire for better teaching and handling of their classes. This sense of improvement contributes to their desire to remain in the profession of teaching. This ultimately reduces their turnover. Findings indicate the importance for early career teachers of resilience, reflection, responsiveness to students and the school environment, relationships and resourcefulness. They suggested teacher education programs and school leaders should focus on developing and supporting the attributes listed above in their graduates and beginning teachers for their retention. They also highlighted the fact that when they start teaching they are highly motivated, but factors like isolation, poor communication, unprofessional working conditions and excessive workloads lead to frustration. On the basis of their extensive study they believed that peer collaboration, including peer observations and feedback appear to be very valuable for new comers.

Mckinnon and Walker (2016)[10] had undertaken a study to find out ways to retain teachers for long in the schools which was funded by Australian National University. Authros reported that Australia is failing to retain the competent people in the profession of teaching. Study highlighted the facts that attrition rates are around 30 per cent to 50 per cent in the first five years of the career, which is very high. Authors opined that it is really difficult to get precise numbers of teachers leaving the profession, but as per the latest data collected from all states and territories shows that on an average about 5.7 per cent (21,404) of teachers left the teaching profession in the year 2014. Attrition rates are different in different parts of the country, but it is promisingly high in the Northern part, which is 15.94 per cent. Authros argued strongly that though the attrition rates might not be higher compared to other professions, the attrition of teachers has far reaching impact. The study came out with following implications of the attrition nationwide:

- *A huge loss of expertise:* The Australian school teachers are aging, and as per various researches the teachers who leave the jobs are likely to be replaced by even less experienced and competent teachers. They also mentioned that in South Australia, about 50 per cent of the teachers working in public schools are older than 50 years.

- *Partial loss of investment in initial teacher training and orientation*: As per research estimates, 20 per cent of education graduates do not register themselves as teachers on graduating, meaning attrition starts even before entering the education system. Most of these graduates are employed elsewhere either in non-teaching roles in the education field or still seeking for employment. So, they reported that Commonwealth spends around A$ 40,000 to train one teaching aspirants in a span of 4 years undergraduate program, when they do not join the profession it becomes a huge loss.
- *Continuous fall in the ratio of teachers to students:* they reported that population of students is expected to increase by 26 per cent by 2022 in the schools with a growth rate of 32 per cent in primary schools and 18 per cent in secondary schools, more teachers will be required to teach these increasing number of students, or else class sizes will be much larger again.

Further author mentioned that there are shortages of specialist teachers in remote and regional areas, which is evident from the case of Western Australia, where 80 per cent of teacher vacancies were for government school secondary teachers in science, english, math, design and technology in the year 2007–08, which has led to teachers being called upon to teach subjects out of their respective fields. They summarized the whole matter as loss on the part of students. They could find out the reason behind new teachers leaving and the most important among all is lack of support and mentoring. They also added that it is not because other teachers and principal are not interested but it is because they simply do not have time for any additional work than school related activities.

In the second part of the article, they highlighted the need of retaining graduates once they are in the system as all other things have been taken care of. They quoted that heavy work load is a major complaint of the teachers and that is a reason for them to leave the profession. They also mentioned that as per researchers heavy workloads, classroom management issues and a lack of collaboration and support are the problems faced by the teachers. They mentioned that the nation would continue to lose the teachers if they are not given the flexibility to be creative and innovative. To retain teachers in the profession, they had taken the example of

Finland and also compared the education system of Australia and Finland. They said that it is easier to get in to teaching programs in Australia, then why so many leave the profession. To highlight the differences between Australia and Finland, they started with the education system of both the nations. They found out that early career teachers in Finland are trained well and then given flexibility to try new things in the classrooms. On the other side in Australia, High level of administrative demands, teaching loads, pastoral care and extra-curricular activities leave too little time for teachers to practice collaboration and innovation.

Study also highlighted the need of supporting teachers by allowing them with space and opportunity to innovate and do good things in the class rooms. They strongly felt that there is a need of cultural shift to practice the said changes to retain teachers in a systematic manner and concluded that to retain teachers for long, steps should be taken as, (a) supporting teachers though mentoring, (b) flexible working conditions, (c) allowing them for innovation and reflective practice, and (d) changing the context of the education, and not only standards

2.3.1.3 *Canada*

Karsenti and Collin (2013)[11] conducted Canada-wide survey in 2013 to find out why new teachers drop out, with major objectives to determine professional aspirations to enter the teaching profession prior to quitting; to identify the main reasons for new teachers to leave the profession; and to identify the individuals to whom new teachers turn when problems arise. Two sets of questionnaires (teachers who dropped out, teachers who witnessed the dropped out) were canvassed to find out the real understanding of the issue covering 34 dropped out teachers and 167 teachers who witnessed the dropped out. Authors found that about 70.3 per cent of the dropped out teachers have five or fewer years of experience, which supports the argument that quitting happens mostly in the induction period. As per their study, the main difficulties of drop-out teachers are the amount of work to be done at home (80 per cent of respondents agreed was too much workload, 77.8 per cent of respondents agreed was too heavy). Besides, informants also agreed with drop-out teachers in terms of difficulties they faced. Study concluded that lack of support from colleagues and management is a main cause for attrition of new teachers, while low salary was not a prominent factor for drop out. Class room management, relationship with the students and their parents are main challenges for new teachers. Administrative support, University training, friendly working conditions and strategies to help them in difficulties are basic requisites for retention of new teachers. The most important need of new teachers is professional induction: mentoring, which appears to have a positive impact on professional inclusion and the reduction of attrition.

2.3.1.4 *Europe*

Basteyns (2013)[12] undertook a study on policy measures to improve the attractiveness of the teaching profession in Europe which was commissioned by the European Commission. The study was to support the work of the European Commission and the Member States in the framework of the 'Education and Training 2020' program. The study covered all levels of education from elementary to upper secondary with an objective to identify the issues relevant to the attractiveness of the teaching profession in Europe and then to map, analyze and evaluate policy measures currently implemented in Europe for attracting high quality candidates into teaching. Author gave recommendations about measures that could enhance the attractiveness of the teaching profession. Author with the help of other experts' team had undertaken the study through a literature and document reviews, an online questionnaire administered in 31 countries of European Union and field interviews with national decision makers in the education sector, which were conducted by European experts in 20 countries of Europe. Their recommendations to enhance attractiveness of the profession are as follows:

(a) *Recruitment of future teachers:* Diversify selection criteria to enable suitable candidates from other professions to enter the teaching profession and Preserve high recruitment requirements.

(b) *Retraining for teachers:* Frame and publicize assistance schemes for teachers who wish to leave the teaching profession for a different career options.

(c) *Initial teacher education (ITE):* Ensure that student teachers come into contact with the field early in their ITE and are made aware of real-life teaching requirements and provide special training for school heads, teacher educators, mentors and teachers who coach student teachers.

(d) *Early career support (ECS):* Extend ECS programs beyond the first year of teaching to the initial two or three years, Reduce the number of classroom hours for new teachers, so as to facilitate them to participate in ECS programs and Make comprehensive support programs mandatory for all new teachers.

(e) *Continuing professional development (CPD):* Ensure that CPD is compulsory and free, Provide CPD in or close to the schools or education institutions to avoid wastage of time, diffusion and inefficiency and Organize ITE, ECS and in-service training as an integrated and consistent practice of professional development during the whole career of a teacher.

(f) *Salaries:* Define transparent criteria of professional excellence and encourage instantaneous salary hikes for the most efficient teachers.

(g) *Teachers facing difficulties:* Be more intent to teachers facing problems and support them to solve their concerns. Mainly develop revised coaching for them.

(h) *Profession's image:* Communicate more about the profession that conveys values to upcoming generations and Take help of the media to foster a more accurate image of the profession.

EFAGMR (2015)[13] Education for All Global Monitoring Report and the UNESCO Education Sector at the 12th Session of the Joint ILO/ UNESCO Committee of Experts on the Application of the Recommendations concerning Teaching Personnel (CEART) in Paris had released this policy paper to address the challenge of recruiting and training quality and competent teachers, by using country administrative data collected by the UNESCO Institute for Statistics (UIS) since 1999 till the date and information from a variety of other sources relevant to the topic. The paper states that teachers are a critical education resource in every country of the world. From early childhood program that is through pre-primary, primary and secondary school, the presence of qualified, competent, well-motivated and supported teachers is necessary for effective learning of the students. What and how many students achieve in school is strongly influenced by effective teaching. This policy paper inspects international progress in addressing shortages of teachers and quality of teacher. The paper also explores the global need for more number of teachers, not just enough teachers but also good qualified teachers who are also well-trained and effective in teaching.

The paper highlights the fact that shortages of teachers remain a serious problem all over the World. The primary education systems had employed above 29 million teachers in the year 2012, out of them 82 per cent was employed in developing countries. The increase in the number of primary teaching staff was about 17 per cent from 1999 to 2012, i.e. about 4 million teachers. The increase in number of secondary school teachers was from 24 to 32 million from 1999 to 2012. The Pupil Teacher Ratio as more important indicator which indicates that between 1999 to 2012 the average PTRs have hardly changed at the primary and secondary education levels globally. The PTR improved slightly in primary education, from 26:1 to 24:1 over the period, while in secondary education, it has improved from 18:1 to 17:1 globally.

Further it indicates that the future needs for teacher recruitment are determined by current teacher deficits, demographics, enrolment trends and the number of children who are out of school in the current situation. It also mentions about analysis by the UIS in 2014 which shows that 27.3 million teachers are needed by 2030 in primary school (UIS, 2014). About 23.9 million are needed to replace teachers who retire, change occupations, or leave due to illness and death, out of the total teachers required between 2012 and 2030. It also indicates that 3.4 million teachers are required to make up the shortfall and address expanding enrolment. The paper finds out that around 190,000 additional teachers are needed to be recruited each year for a sufficient supply of teachers to assure universal primary education by 2030. The policy paper highlights the following recommendations for governments of different countries to take corrective actions to assure the equitable deployment of qualified, competent, motivated and well-supported teachers for all children:

(a) *Attract the best teachers*: The paper suggests to recruit and retain the best of the teachers from a wide range of backgrounds. It also highlights the importance of policies and strategies to ensure that teaching is attractive to highly qualified and competent candidates from diverse backgrounds, with good subject content, who are ready to get recruited in remote areas, and teach underprivileged students. The paper implies to recruit teachers from within local communities, which can increase liability, particularly in countries having history of teacher absenteeism. It also feels that local teachers are also more socially and culturally similar to the students and parents in the schools.

(b) *Get and retain teachers where needed*: The paper suggests that qualified and trained teachers should be motivated to work in areas where they are needed the most with the help of suitable working environment and an appropriate combination of monetary and non-monetary incentives. The paper is in favour of improved pay, healthy working conditions and attractive career path to retain competent teachers and maintain their commitment to teaching profession. The paper highlights the importance of the effective management of teacher deployment as if it is directed by an effective and transparent use and presentation of data, it can be helpful for equitable distribution of teachers across the regions as enrolment rates have increased over a period of time.

(c) *Improve teacher education*: The paper suggests that policies should be designed and implemented to ensure teachers have appropriate qualification and training before and during teaching career. The paper mentions that there are still shortages of trained teachers even in countries without severe shortages of total teachers. The paper suggests that Education quality can be at risk if untrained teachers who lack qualifications, preparation, motivation, appropriate working conditions and ongoing professional development are hired. The paper also brings about the fact that severe teacher shortages may prompt governments to recruit contract teachers, especially when they are forced to reduce public sector spending on education. It paper supports hiring contract teachers but they should be provided professional development to benefit from the same career path, professional programs, promotion opportunities and professional status as other permanent teachers. The paper mentions that teachers of all categories should be trained adequately in theory as well as practical exposure. The paper also highlights the need of preparing teachers to help learners with different learning needs and backgrounds, to teach reading abilities to children in early grades, and to deal with the children in the language they understand. Importance of continuous professional development for all teachers to adapt to new learning challenges and competencies is highlighted.

2.3.1.5 *Singapore*

Calvin Y. (2016)[14] reported that it is an alarming call for the government that over 5,000 teachers has left the teaching force itself. Author strongly suggested that administrative loads of the teachers need to be reduced to retain them for long. Findings of the Ministry of Education indicate that annual registration rate of teachers has been only around 3 per cent and total teaching force in the nation has been stable at around 33,000. Author could meet 12 teachers who had left their jobs and 67 per cent of them responded that they left the jobs because of administrative workload. This complaint has been long standing and very necessary to be resolved. Author also reported that in the year 2005, the Ministry hired allied educators who could help teachers in paper work and students' counseling. The government had decided to employ 2,800 allied educators in the span of 10 years.

Study also showed that mainly teachers leave the jobs for three reasons, viz. childcare, other family considerations and a desire for a change of job. Author mentioned about a former chemistry teacher, who left the job in the year 2014 who responded that they had to spend 12 hours at school, half of those hours are spent on organization of school events, and that is why teachers could not get enough time to build the depth in teaching skills. The respondent had to leave the job after 10 years of experience in the profession, as he/she could not focus on teaching.

Author could further found out the reasons which compelled the teachers to leave their jobs, which are Long hours at school, Huge class sizes, and overly demanding parents. Author mentioned about the case of Mr. Bernard Lim, who has experience of teaching in the schools for more than 20 years, who could sense the seriousness about the burden on teachers. Mr. Lim also responded that he left the job as paperwork increased many-fold over time, which put him in two bouts of depression and when he was on the verge of recovery, he could realize that the illness may reoccur and he had no other way than to quit the job.

Study found out that attrition in teaching profession is lower and on the other hand it is the waste of trained teaching talents, when they leave the job. Author mentioned about Head of the Government Parliamentary Committee for Education who said the annual resignation rate for teachers is not overly alarming, compared to other industries, but every excellent educator who leaves the sector is still one too many and that is why the marking load should be reduced. Author quoted about the improvements made by governments in recent years. Government had decided to give 4 to 9 per cent increase in monthly wages to 30,000 teachers to keep pace with market rates. Mr. Clarence Tang, a head of department at Tanjong Katong Secondary School said that the MOE and schools have been looking at ways to assist teachers with the help of allied educators and the schools' administrative team. Educators put their students first and the uniqueness of the profession is that they are ready to sacrifice at their end to fulfill students' lives in better ways.

2.3.2 Attrition of teachers in Developing/ Underdeveloped Countries

2.3.2.1 *Ghana*

Baah *et al.* (2009)[15] undertook a study on teacher attrition in the pre-tertiary educational system in Ghana in the year 2009 to answer the question *Why are teachers leaving the classrooms*? Authors noted that the existing national educational system of Ghana is made up of two components: pre-tertiary and higher education. The pre-tertiary education is sub-divided into: pre-school education (below 6 years); primary education (6–12 years); junior secondary education (13 years and above); and senior secondary/technical/vocational education. For the survey, they distributed a thousand questionnaires to the teachers who are in the teaching profession in ten administrative regions of Ghana, out of which they could get back 890 completed questionnaires. On the basis of survey analysis, they could find out that an average monthly salary of respondents was GH¢405 (or approximately US$ 287 per month in 2009), which lead 98 per cent of the teachers to dissatisfaction with their current pay. The analysis showed that apart from paid study leave and social security, accessibility to other benefits such as medical care, free or subsidized housing, child care services, and free or subsidized transport was not available to teachers. About 64 per cent of teachers who opted for the study leave to further their education intended to come back to the same job, but 36 per cent had plans to opt for other lucrative jobs after the leave. They felt that poor working condition and low pay lead to low morale. As a result of low morale, 72 per cent of the teachers were either 'dissatisfied' or 'very dissatisfied' with their teaching job and 75 per cent told that they would not recommend teaching job to anyone.

Authors recommended that to assist teachers to acquire new skills is not enough but the ultimate focus should be to have them well-trained and motivated. Therefore, 'Study Leave with Pay' system must be complemented by other policies which could motivate teachers to stay in the same profession, rather than going to other developed profession. They also suggested to the Government that they must also work on social amenities particularly in rural and deprived communities and not just the educational infrastructure in all parts of the country to enable 'Education for All'. They strongly concluded that significant improvement in teachers' remuneration would be the most important step towards stemming the high rate of teacher attrition in Ghana. As per their views, the most crucial part of the fight to retain teachers is to change the perception of the public in general about the status of teaching profession. For the same, they suggested help of unions in education to use their network and improve the status of the teaching profession in the society.

2.3.2.2 *Ethiopia*

Getahun *et al.* (2016)[16] did a study to understand the level of organizational commitment and how it gets affected by job satisfaction in 6 primary schools of Ethiopia. They took a sample of 118 teachers (out of total 203 teachers) who were selected by simple random sampling technique and used correlation model. They also tried to find out the correlation of demographic variables (gender, level of education, marital status) with perceived job satisfaction of teachers and organizational commitment. They used two separate methods to fetch information on teachers' perceived job satisfaction and organizational commitment respectively. Author concluded that there is a positive relation between teachers' Job satisfaction and organizational commitment by using mean, standard deviation, t test and correlation matrix. They suggested to improve teachers' commitment to their schools by creating a more conducive and satisfying environment at the work place. As Ethiopian schools have no authority to decide pay and other monetary reward. Authors also suggested to enhance teachers' job satisfaction by creating superior training and development opportunities, improving support system from leaders and management, promoting accountability and involving teachers in decision-making at school. They could find positive relation only between gender, job satisfaction and organizational commitment. The study concluded that other demographic variables are not related to job satisfaction and organizational commitment. So, at the end they emphasized on need to undertake further studies to have better understanding of the nature of the relationship between teachers demographic variables, job satisfaction and organizational commitment in the context of developing countries.

2.3.2.3 *Tanzania*

Boniface (2016)[17] conducted a study to explore teachers' perceived school level challenges and the support of retaining teachers in remote secondary schools in Tanzania. Author was inspired by a supportive management theoretical framework, particularly organizational support, leader-member exchange and coworkers' exchange to conduct a study. Author collected the data in three phases using interviews and survey questionnaires, included 258 secondary schools teachers from 28 remote schools in the Dodoma region in central Tanzania. Author used mixed methods data analysis techniques for interpretation of data. Findings of the study suggested that most of the teachers in the area are male and well-educated as well as with experienced background. Study shows that it is challenging to retain this kind of teachers in remote area as they are not satisfied with the working environment and changes in the working context. Author also considered other demographic factors such as age, number of years in profession and education level. Author found that qualified young teachers having less or more experience in the profession are the most difficult teachers to retain. Therefore properly planned retention programmes to retain critical workforce at remote area is needed. Study clearly shows that housing and other social services are critical determinants to retain teachers in remote areas. Author concluded that supportive working environment, involvement of teachers in changes, relationship at the workplace are the perceived support for the teachers to decide on voice or exit the remote secondary schools.

2.3.2.4 *Kenya*

Manduku *et al.* (2016)[18] conducted a study in 2016 with a purpose to assess stress management strategies used by school management and its influence on teachers' commitment in primary schools in Sabatia district, Kenya. The total sample size was 203 respondents consisting of 25 head teachers, 25 deputy head teachers and 153 teachers by using purposive sampling techniques. Stratified sampling technique was used to select 16 public primary and 9 private primary schools. From selected schools, 153 teachers were selected by random sampling by lottery method. The interview schedules were used as research instruments to collect primary data.

Study found that there are enormous sources of stress amongst primary school teachers in Sabatia district, some of them are school related factors, lack of recognition of efforts by school management and pupil mis-behaviour including indiscipline. Author suggested some stress management strategies to be used at primary schools like employment of PTA teachers to share their workload, use of guidance and counseling to enhance student discipline, teacher motivation, teachers' welfare committee, team work teaching. Self efficacy and role ambiguity are the most effective factors on teachers' job satisfaction, which determines their organizational commitment. Author believed firmly that organizational commitment is the determinant of teachers turn over and recommended to the government to employ more number of teachers at public primary schools to reduce workload of the teachers. Also counseling services for the teachers be arrange to enable them to cope up with the stress.

2.3.2.5 *Pakistan*

Rasheed *et al.* (2016)[19] undertook a study with the purpose to explore/ investigate various issues of teachers' motivation in public sector Higher Educational Institutions of Pakistan in 2016. This research is an exploratory research where surveys have been conducted in the well-known public sector Universities of Pakistan. The questionnaire and in depth face to face interviews was used for primary data collection. Findings showed that compensation packages and financial incentives are important factors for teachers in the competitive market environment of the higher education sector. Study also highlighted some other significant factors like job design and working environment. The performance management system and training and development are equally important to retain teachers for long period in higher education institutes. The research has also explored various issues being faced by teachers in public sector Higher Education Institutes related to the factors discussed before. They undertook a study, which can play a vital role in compelling the higher education authorities to consider the motivational issues of teachers in universities in Pakistan. They also tried to make their research an effectual document for other universities of other countries as well where the same problem is prevalent.

2.3.2.6 *Nigeria*

Oke *et al. (2016)*[20] have done an extensive review of literature available as conference papers, journal articles, internet sources, books, newspapers to find out the factors that determine teachers' attrition and retention in schools particularly in Nigeria. The main objective was to expose the factors that determine teacher's attrition and retention in Nigeria and to suggest to future researchers who may decide to adopt an empirical method to investigate the variables identified in this study for further research. Considering the importance of the profession in the developing countries like Nigeria, they have taken the context of the world as such for detailed study of the problem. They argued that well-trained and knowledge driven education force is required for economic development of any nation.

Authors indicated that effective teachers who are committed and willing to teach to a diverse student population are essential to the success of a school and can make a difference in the lives of each student in any school. These issues are consequential in the Nigerian perspective because losing one's job would result to other adverse external problems due to the fact that the person may not be able to cater to any of his needs and the needs of extended family. The job turnover issue is counter-productive to the attainment of schools' goals and government objective of providing employment to the citizens. Authors tried to find out factors that encourage teachers' attrition, as the persistent labor turnover in schools and high job dissatisfaction among teachers in Nigeria and other parts of the world. Further, they designed the next section with review of relevant studies such as retention of teachers in schools, teacher retention management, attrition of teachers, causes of teacher attrition, factors that help in retaining teachers, impact of attrition to understand the problem in detail.

Authors stated that whether in the developing or developed countries, the challenge for most of the organizations is how best to retain their employees for the long term in the organization (Goswani and Jha, 2012; Long *et al.*, 2012a, b). Study shows that in Nigeria, the turnover rate is above 10 per cent and in Ghana, teacher attrition and retention in the profession has become a matter of great concern. The high rate of teacher attrition impacts negatively on schools improvement efforts as it disrupts the stability and continuity of teaching as a whole. Author included the research finding of Amadi (1983) who argues that irregular payment of the remuneration of teachers is among the most critical challenge of the profession in Nigeria. They suggested that even though adequate remuneration and prompt disbursement of rewards are important encouraging variables, there is evidence that some other variables can weaken obligation to work for teachers. They mentioned that these other variables according to Taylor and Heywood (2008) includes Herzberg's hygiene factors such as working conditions, job security, company policy, relations with colleagues and supervisors.

Author emphasized the truth to understand how to retain the employees for long, which says that majority of employees desire to stay longer on the job and to feel more knowledgeable and more answerable, at any stage on any job. After studying various authors on retention they concluded that attitude of the management inspires innovation and creativity among organizational personnel. They defined the Attrition in a detailed manner, which says that attrition could be the number of employees leaving their jobs which includes both voluntary and involuntary reasons of separation. The problem of attrition is insoluble whether in the education profession or any other profession, some attrition is unavoidable, as some teachers will retire, some will quit for personal reasons, and some will be fired from their jobs whilst some others are encouraged to leave the profession itself. They mentioned the reasons found out by Stockard and Lehman (2004) which summarizes as dissatisfaction of workers with current job, unsatisfactory conditions of work and inadequate remuneration, not enough support from family members, management challenges, colleagues and the public, discipline, challenges of attendance, rising size of classes, inadequate encouragement of students and inadequate opportunities for teachers to contribute.

Author studied causes of attrition, factors that help in retaining teachers, impact of attrition in detail with extensive review of literature of various countries. They concluded that the most important factor for teacher's quitting the profession is inadequate financial reward for teachers. They reported that in the developing country like Nigeria, people who pick up teaching as a profession just expect that the little salary that is due to them should be paid on time. They also concluded that the essential factors that decide the attrition of teachers are the leadership style of school principals and the working condition in schools. Author noted that the job mobility is high in three groups of teachers: One group is of the old teachers who are retiring from their jobs, another group is of the young teachers and the third group is of the new or inexperienced teachers. They suggested that there is not much to be done for the first group, but for the other two following steps can be taken, as follows:

- Public office holders in the educational sector should adopt appropriate strategies to make the teaching profession attractive and to be considered as a noble and financially rewarding profession.
- Providing quality training and development programs for teachers to upgrade their skills of teaching.

- Providing suitable and encouraging work environment for teachers in the schools.
- Ensuring standards are maintained in schools to maintain dignity of the profession.
- Imparting discipline among staffs and students
- Ensuring that the class sizes are minimal and based on the UN recommendations.
- Policy makers should consider the capacity of education system to promote rapid and directed social and economic change as the main agenda.

2.4 Indian Literature

2.4.1 *Studying Student-Staffing Pattern*

Kohli (2015)[21] had visited Molarbund Government Boys Senior Secondary School in South Delhi's Badarpur and reported that there are more students in the corridor than in the classrooms. Author could also get complaints from those who were in the class regarding non-functional Fans, broken desk, teachers' absenteeism, stinking toilets, unavailability of drinking water for students. Senior teachers reported that there are no enough classrooms and there are only 120 teachers for 7,000 students. As per report, government schools are facing various issues, but the most severe is shortage of teachers across the country. India has shortage of 12 lakh teachers and almost 5.23 lakh posts are not filled, as Kapil Sibal, a former Human Resource Development (HRD) Minister told the Rajya Sabha in 2010. As per the Right to Education Act, 2009, one teacher is required for every 30 students, which makes the matter worse. Study revealed that 11 per cent of our schools have only one teacher.

Author stated that in view of Krishna Kumar, (professor of education at Faculty of Education, Delhi University, and former director, NCERT) the scarcity of teachers is not due to lack of qualified professionals, but because of the government's disinclination towards filling up permanent posts and instead hiring cheaper teachers on contractual basis. Kumar also added that the states started downsizing permanent staff in the 1990s when the country was undergoing economic reforms and it was done to manage their fiscal deficit. There are 20,000 contractual teachers in Delhi alone today. Author stated example of the president of the Delhi Government School Teachers' Association, Mr. CP Singh, who addressed the problem of schools in the capital, which are awaiting 18,000 teachers for the last three years, and only 6,000 guest teachers have been appointed to solve the problem of the deficit. These guest teachers are appointed for a year, paid per day, and are also less accountable to education system. The guest teachers have to leave the school before they get acquainted with the needs of students. Study highlighted the fact that salary of contractual teachers is low, which compel them to search of other source of income and on the other hand, when government can hire the teachers with less than half a salary, then why they should hire permanent teachers. Author could also find out from R Govinda, Vice Chancellor, National University of Educational Planning and Administration that faulty recruitment practices are also responsible for non-accountability on part of teachers.

Author noted that only 15 per cent of the candidates cleared the Teachers Eligibility Test and the deficiency of qualified teachers in the country is due to low quality education in numerous private institutes offering B.Ed. degrees, which are mostly self-financed and their distribution among states is also uneven. As per reports of HRD Ministry, numbers of such institutes have grown from less than 2,000, to 14,704 in the year 2011, while only 10 per cent of such institutes are quality ones. The biggest problem here is poor quality of entrants to the profession. Author recommended reforms in the sector like an increase in the duration of B.Ed. and M.Ed. programs from one year to two years, modifications in their course content and an increase in state investment in teachers' training. The report also suggested to introduce four-year integrated programs within the university system at the undergraduate level throughout the nation and to make the course content multi-disciplinary. Author supported inter-disciplinary course within the university campus as it would train teachers in critical thinking, and involve teacher-educators who are specialists in their respective fields. She concluded that the government has limited time to implement reforms as India has to achieve the goal of providing universal elementary education under the Millennium Development Goals by 2015. And she strongly highlighted the fact that nothing can be done without fixing shortage of Teachers.

2.4.2 Teachers' Appointment Pattern

Summiya *et al.* (2008)[22] have done a country wide study on situation of teachers in the country. The study was done to introspect the murder of a teacher at Ujjain by the students. As per their study, in Bangalore, Lucknow and Meerut, teachers have demonstrated as they are very much demoralized. The report also suggested that India has the world's largest child population i.e. 415 million. When discontent of teacher is rising, there is a high time shortage of teachers across the nation. As per their survey, 23,000 teaching posts vacant in Karnataka and 2.3 lakh teaching positions are vacant in Bihar. They also quoted the fact that as per The report of UNESCO Institute of Statistics, *Teachers and Educational Quality: Monitoring Global Needs for 2015* revealed that to meet the Millennium Development Goal of providing elementary education to all children by 2015, "India will be in need of the greatest inflow of new teachers in the world — i.e. more than 2 million teachers".

Authors also came across the fact that now a day one school advertise for 15 to 20 vacancies on the appointments pages of national newspapers and now a days for the first time in the history, jobs are chasing competent teachers, rather than teachers chasing the jobs. Besides, just like government schools, private schools are facing sharp shortage of teachers as a result of high demand of young applicants in IT and BPO sector. As per their research, India needs 800,000 new teachers per annum for the next three consecutive years to meet the shortage and accommodate new student enrollments in private schools. In India, number of private schools have gone up from 50,000 in the year 1996 to 77,140 in the year 2006. The top class five star international schools charge tuition fees of 1 to 6 lakh rupees per annum and provide handsome salaries and healthy working environment to teachers.

As per the study, International schools are facing a problem of motivating and retaining young and competent teachers as they are in need of well talented and committed teachers to maintain international standards in their institutes. The head hunting of competent teachers in internationally acclaimed institutes of the nation has served useful for the improvement of the profession as the most attractive profession with innovative teaching techniques, handsome salary, ongoing training and development, less crowded classes and friendly working environment. They noted that teaching is no longer a second income housewives jobs, now it is considered at par with other respectable professional jobs for knowledgeable and well versed individuals. They concluded that first priority of private schools have been to motivate and retain competent teachers and due to high salary packages, experienced teachers from private schools are moving to international schools with new hope and excitement. They could also conclude that the BPO sector which is growing at the rate of 56 per cent which could pay salary of 10–15 thousands per month can attract teachers from English medium unaided private schools, charging less tuition fees from students.

Study highlighted the fact that schools are spending lakhs of rupees to get their vacancies filled up, but they receive as much as 15 applications against that, which shows that nobody is willing to become a teacher. The pay of public school teachers is 30–50 per cent higher than that of private schools. Though teacher pupil ratio of India is one of the highest in the world, i.e. 1:60, problem is about quality of teachers than the quantity as educators at B.Ed. programs are ill-trained and less motivated to create talented and competent educators, which in turn hampers the quality of teaching at schools. Author stated that higher education and the institutes like IIMs and IITs are also facing the scarcity of competent professional to fill up vacancies. They ended the write up with the worry that the demographic dividend of the country should not turn out to be demographic disaster.

2.4.3 Problems in Attracting Competent Teachers in Private Schools

Varma S. (2014)[23] reported that 43 per cent (i.e. 4.2 million) of school teachers teach in private schools in India, out of that 3.1 million teach in class 1 to 8, and the rest 1.1 million work in secondary and higher secondary schools. The pay of government school teachers is between Rs. 20–40 thousands per month, considering their experience and qualification. As per investigation done by Times of India, teachers at private schools are working with pay of mere Rs. 2,000 per month in many states of India. Author also reported that teachers at many schools get different amount on paper and the actual salary is very low. Author contacted various teachers working for private schools to bring out the fact and found that teachers have to sign blank vouchers and registers to earn maximum salary of just Rs. 3000 per month. In her report, some teachers revealed the truth that in private schools almost everything is flexible. The salary of the teachers also dependent of management's philosophy and their need for money.

As per report, there are 31 lakhs teachers teaching in private schools and 46 lakhs teachers teaching in public schools in primary section from class 1 to 8. There are 11 lakhs teachers teaching in private schools and 9 lakhs teachers teaching in secondary section from class 9 to 12. So, in total 42 lakhs teachers are employed in private schools and 55 lakhs teachers are employed in public schools. Report also showed that the average salary of teachers in government schools is 20–40 thousands per month, the average salary of teachers in big private schools is 20–40 thousands per month and the average salary of teachers in most of the private schools is 5–15 thousands per month, which makes the condition of private teachers worse than ever. She mentioned that the teaching profession is no longer recruiting the most competent teachers.

Author noted that public schools in rural areas face a big problem of absenteeism. Some reports of the states like Uttaranchal and Odisha indicate that jobs are outsourced to proxies and they even split their pay with them. Report prepared by Unified District Information System for Education (UDISE) by NUEPA stated that in private non grantable schools, 25 per cent of the teachers are not even qualified professionally to be teachers, 58 per cent teachers from unrecognized schools are not professionally competent, only 91 per cent of the teachers from grant-in-aid private schools are professionally qualified and 83 per cent of the teachers from public schools are qualified for the profession. Author concluded that as per the expert of the profession, teachers are not trained properly and they are without vision which leads the whole system towards flow of ill prepared teachers for the any type of schools.

2.4.4 Relationship between Different Stakeholders

Kothari and Chavan (2015)[24] studied qualitative and quantitative data to understand the impact of attrition on school administration and psychology of the pupils. They conducted a study at Pimpri Chinchwad in the year 2015 with an objective of understanding the impact of attrition on other stake holders like, management and students. Data were collected from 5 private schools from principal through personal interaction, through group discussion with teachers and parents. Teacher were segregated in to two categories i.e. teachers having experience of more than 5 years of experience in the same school and teachers having experience of more than 5 years of experience in different school. They had selected 5 teachers from each category from each school.

Study results revealed that attrition has been a concern for worry now a days and the main reason for that is teachers are un prepared and not aware of the challenges of the profession and when they realized them, they start comparing their pressure with the financial reward and if it is not up to the expectation they tend to leave the job. The other reasons for the attrition were mushrooming of the schools, under qualified teachers, high or average performance of the teachers, profession demanding and low remuneration. As per principals responses, the impact of attrition as costly and time consuming recruitment and training, difficult implementation of reforms, unequal distribution of work among senior and new staff and ultimately increased pressured on Principal.

Analysis of responses of teachers having experience of more than 5 years of experience in the same school shows that the attrition is mainly due to financial issues, pressure from all different stake holders and less job satisfaction. The study also revealed that the main problems faced by this category of teachers related to attrition are, greater pressure on senior staff, adjustment problems with staff, students inability to adjust and indiscipline students due to attrition among teachers. Authors noted that the main reason for the attrition among the other category of the teachers was due to low pay and working conditions. The teachers who are not qualified change the jobs in search of higher salary. Some of the teachers leave the job due to personal reasons or adjustment problems. Their analysis of parents' responses shows that the major concern of the parents is constantly changing subject and class teacher. The children find it difficult to adjust with the style of teaching and teachers' behavior. The other problems faced by the students are lack of interest in the subject, lack of respect for the teachers, inability to build rapport with the teachers and psychological impact. The study also revealed that parents have no other option than to opt for the alternative of private tuitions which increases economic, physical, mental and emotional cost.

Study concluded that the main problems of attrition are administrative problems for the management, adjustment problems for the teachers, emotional problem for the students and ultimately these all lead to misbehavior of the students and their disrespectful behavior towards teachers, parents and other elderly people. They recommended that for the reforms in education which is mandatory for economic development of the nation would to superficial if the problem of attrition is not dealt with. The retention of the teachers should be the foremost priority for government and administrators; teachers should be appointed and retained on the basis of tenure and reward; teachers, parents and students should be counseled regularly as a part of curriculum; large number of faculty development and faculty exchange programs should be introduced and lastly role of government in the management of private schools should be prominent for proper reward to the teachers for their work.

2.4.5 Reasons and Effects of Attrition

Sindhi S. (2012)[25] presented a conceptual framework on the teachers employed in small scale private schools who are vulnerable to poor job security, low salary and stringent work environment. Author noted that there are so many unreported and silent crimes against the teachers who are employed in a small private schools of the nation and the situation of the teachers is pathetic. The research is a conceptual outline which is based on the grass root observation relating to what issues and challenges are faced by these private teachers on everyday basis. Author stated that private schools have come up rapidly in the country and mentioned about estimates (SRI, 2005; DISE 2006–07) which indicate that 25 per cent of the total enrolment in the primary section is in the private schools. Not only children of non-poor in urban areas but also children of poor families are largely enrolled in private schools. Almost 30 per cent of the Indian villages have availability of private schools within their villages. Private schools run without support of the government and that's why they have to take care of student-teacher ratio, standards for recruitment of principal and teachers, financial arrangements, pay to the teachers, admission procedure, fee structure and so on. Though they grow up like corporate houses, they fail to reward their teachers adequately.

Author suggested that teachers should be rewarded adequately to motivate them to put optimum efforts and also for job satisfaction. The role of principal is very critical in today's scenario, who should handle criticism constructively, praise genuinely and accept teachers' suggestions. Author also suggested for an atmosphere full of trust, confidence and cooperation, where interaction of teachers is possible. She also suggested that efforts should be made to attract competent candidates towards the profession and to retain those who are already in the profession. She also suggested for the similar studies at higher education institutes like colleges and universities. At the end author showed concern towards the teachers who are hardly empathized and whose problems are never understood.

2.4.6 Remedies for the Problem

Ramachandran V. (2005)[26] reviewed the literature available on the elementary school education and stated that the drop our rate from class I to VIII is 52.79 per cent, which is not acceptable at all. Author quoted the article published in *The Hindu*, New Delhi, February 22, 2005 which blamed lack of adequate facilities, large-scale absenteeism of teachers and inadequate supervision by local authorities for the high dropout rate. Author stated that political leaders and administrators have admitted that motivation and accountability among teachers and management is a matter of worry. Though the data of enrolment of students is remarkable, many pupils leave the school without learning how to read and write also. About her own encounter with a bunch of teachers who considered themselves as motivated teachers, author was shocked to know that daily attendance and complying with orders of management and catering to requests for information were rational indicators of motivation for them, on the other hand students and the process of teaching and learning is ignored completely. Author gathered viewpoints of each stakeholders of education, i.e. students, parents, administrators, educationalist and the teachers themselves but the definition of motivation is different for all of them. The main purpose of the teaching and wellbeing of the students is completely overlooked.

Author also studied private schools and the situation is better there and that is the reason of children of teachers of public schools attending private schools. Study brought out the fact that public schools are not a matter of concern for the administrators as poor children are enrolled there and their poor parents do not have a say over any matter. Author studied the matter of motivation in depth and came out with the points to consider. Expansion of the education has been rapid but number of teachers has been in scarcity to match the number of enrolment. Study highlighted the second point as the social distance between the teachers and the pupils is very wide and that is why there are cases of social exploitation and discrimination in the public schools. The fact that teachers in the public schools are not trained to handle diversity in the classrooms where the teachers-students' ratio is very high. The fourth point talks about corruption and the politics entered in to the system, where powerful teachers rarely attend the schools. Fifth point is that the teachers of public schools have to perform various non-teaching duties which deviates them from the main purpose of teaching. Sixth point is about compulsory training programs, which hamper their teaching as they are not planned properly. Seventh point, as per her opinion, the points highlighted above should be handled properly to motivate teachers to focus on their profession.

Venkatesh K. (2016)[27] studied job satisfaction among primary school teachers with respect to age, gender and experience covering 334 primary schools from Medak district of Telangana State. Author defined job satisfaction as the implication of doing a job one enjoys, doing it well and being rewarded for one's efforts. Job satisfaction is different for different people as it may be linked with motivation but it is more an internal state, i.e. one's attitude. When the job enables the material and psychological needs, it is resulted in to job satisfaction. Author supported the logic that a satisfied employee is a happy employee and a happy employee is a successful employee, and that is unavoidable for the success of contemporary companies. Job satisfaction is the combination of feelings and beliefs that people have about their present jobs. Indicators of job satisfaction can range from extreme satisfaction to extreme dissatisfaction.

Author used job satisfaction scale developed by Spector, (1995) as a tool in the study. The findings of his study indicates that the job satisfaction among primary school teachers with an age below 30 years was found to be better than teachers with an age between 31–40 years which was better than teachers with an age of above 40 years, and it was statistically proved significant. The findings also suggested that the job satisfaction was found to be higher in female primary teachers than that of male primary teachers. Author found that primary teachers with an experience of below 10 years was found to be slightly better than teachers with 11 to 20 years of experience in terms of job satisfaction. So, on the basis of statistical analysis and interpretation, all the hypothesis are accepted.

2.5 MOTIVATIONAL THEORIES TO CONTROL ATTRITION

Ingram D. (2009)[28] studies and put together various motivational theories, which can be utilized to control turnover of employees. Author stated that motivational theories attempt to create models to find out what motivates employees to improve their performance. Author also opines that managers try to implement combination of motivational theories as per the situation and type of employees they manage to increase their productivity and commitment. If these theories are not put in place, it might also lead to high rate of employees' attrition. Author summarizes the motivational theories, which can be applied to control employees' turnover in following manner.

(a) *Management by Objectives (MBO) by Peter Drucker*: The theory of Management by Objectives or MBO argues that employees are more motivated by goals and objectives that are set by them. Managers following this theory avoid dictating instructions, quotas and goals from above hierarchy, but they involve employees in strategic decision-making whenever they can, especially in situations that directly affect employees' routines. Ingram feels that if managers fail to put this approach into day to day action, it may cause loss of some of the most competent and self-motivated employees. He opines that the theory does not apply to all employees, but innovative and internally driven employees may leave the jobs if not allowed to participate in strategic decision making.

(b) *Theory X and Theory Y by Douglas McGregor:* This theory combines two different and opposing ends of the motivation spectrum. Theory X puts forth the principle that employees are inherently averse to work and must constantly be motivated externally for better performance. Theory Y puts forth the premise that employees can be internally driven at work place, finding satisfaction in obtaining goals that use their skills, abilities and experience. Ingram opines that none of Theory X or Theory Y is integrally better than the other. He also argues that the successful implementation of the theory depends on the work setting and types of employees one is dealing with. He also says that wrong theory at wrong place may disappoint, confuse and aggravate employees, which leads to increased employee attrition. He quotes an example that if you are dealing with theory Y employees, you need to avoid strict supervision at all times at work place.

(c) *Hierarchy of Needs by Abraham Mashlow:* The theory of hierarchy of needs places employees' needs into five categories in progressive manner, keeping basic physical needs at the base and needs of self-actualization at the top. He states about Mashlow, who claims that needs of the employees should be satisfied at each level to make them committed towards theirs goals at work place. He also opines that if the employer fails to satisfy needs of the employees at any level of hierarchy, it may create a lack of satisfaction in employees' professional front, leading them to fulfill these needs on their own eventually, by finding a new work place, where they would get better opportunities.

(d) *Expectancy Theory by Victor Vroom:* The expectancy theory sets the principle that employees will give an amount of work and commitment equal to what they expect to obtain in return form the employer. Ingram states that commission compensation structures influence this theory by allowing employees to earn as much money as they desire, completely based on their job performance and efforts. He also states that employers should make sure that employees always expect future pay to rise and potential job promotions when due, if they get that they keep working hard to fulfill personal goals. He also states that if employees expect little compensation and no promotional opportunities in return for their efforts and performance, they may give only minimal work performance till they get new employer for new opportunities for career advancement.

Badubi R. (2017)[29] wrote this paper with aim of comparing and contrasting the theories of motivation and how these theories can be used to motivate employees to develop the drive to achieve. She believes that motivation should be priority for organizations to make employees their assets as well as for retention. She conducted the study to help organizations to promote encouraging environment and relationships for employees to work under, and also to make them perform with positive attitude. She considered a qualitative approach and theory based application for the study. She explains the theories of motivation as below:

(a) *Maslow's Hierarchy of Needs:* The way Maslow's theory is explained relies on the reality that people want to get more what they want to achieve in life and according to their importance, their needs are prioritized, according to Smith and Cronje (1992). Mashlow came up with the five level theory, based on the basic physical, biological, social and psychological needs of human beings, tries to place the needs of the individual in five categories and prioritize attainment, viz. (i) Physiological needs (food, shelter, clothing); (ii) Safety and security needs (physical protection, job security); (iii) Social needs (association with others, love and affection); (iv) Esteem needs (receiving acknowledgement of the efforts from others); and (v) Self-actualization needs (the desire for goal accomplishment or to leave behind a legacy).

The theory is useful to explain job satisfaction of the employees at work place. Teachers, like all other professionals, have needs that have to be satisfied. Besides the basic needs for food, shelter and clothing, safety from physical harm and social involvement, they also need the recognition and appreciation of students, colleagues, parents and management.

1. *Herzberg's Two-Factor Theory/Motivator-Hygiene*

Herzberg's Two-factor theory, also known as Motivator-Hygiene, originated from a study conducted among accountants and engineers to understand what makes an individual feel good or bad about their respective jobs (Saif *et al.*, 2012). As per Herzberg, the "Satisfiers" include five features of work such as achievement, recognition, the job itself, responsibility and advancement. At the other end of the spectrum, Herzberg identified factors that may demoralize employees include institutional politics, the management approach, supervision, pay, relationships at work and working conditions. She believes that employees should be promoted after completing certain stages of their career and should receive recognition for special achievements through their efforts. Golshan *et al.* (2011) point out that it fails to distinguish between physical and psychological aspects and to precisely explain what motivators are and how they differ from hygiene factors; it also fails to express the degrees of satisfaction and dissatisfaction as a measure instead of using numbers. Another criticism leveled against it is that it makes assumptions that every individual will react in the same way in the similar situation.

2. *McGregor's X and Y Theories (1960)*

McGregor's theory X and Y models categorize employees as belonging to one of two groups based on two different sets of assumptions. Theory X is based on the assumptions which take a negative perception of people: Employees can have "an inherent dislike for work and they may avoid it if possible; due to this, they must be compelled, controlled, directed and threatened with punishment to make them work to accomplish their goals. As per Saif *et al.* 2012, p. 138. They prefer to be directed, avoid responsibility, have little ambition, and want security". Theory Y is based on positive perception: the mental and physical inputs are consumed at the workplace. External factors or any threats from outside may not be the only influence for applying efforts. Workers can exercise caution and discipline to achieve their objectives, but they are committed to their objectives in accordance with the rewards assigned to achievements of those objectives. When such assumptions are applied to school environment, the two main causes of dissatisfaction among teachers are dealing with problems of students and a strict and inconsiderate management of the school, for example a supportive principal can be a motivational factor for the teachers.

3. *McClelland's Need Achievement Theory*

McClelland's need achievement theory assumes that some people are driven to success through personal achievements rather than rewards themselves. This theory is directly applicable to academic institutions and explains why some teachers achieve higher than others, despite the difficulties faced by them: they set high goals for themselves and by achieving these goals they feel motivated. Alderfer's ERG theory is related to Maslow's hierarchy of needs but reduces five categories of Mashlow's need hierarchy to three; namely, relatedness (esteem/social needs), growth (self-actualization) and existence (security/physiological needs).

4. *The Equity Theory*

He opines that process theories explain 'how' satisfaction comes about, rather than 'what' causes motivation. The theory postulates that employees put their inputs into a job based on the output they receive from it. Regarding this theory, job satisfaction will be experienced by employees who perceive that they receive more output compared to inputs they put in to. Authors have identified five major job characteristics that has impact on the psychology of an employee and affect their motivation, job satisfaction and levels of absenteeism, namely the variety of skills involved in a job task, the identity and significance of the task, autonomy, and feedback. If employees find an inequity in their input-outcome ratio compared to other employees of the organization, they are dissatisfied and demotivated with their jobs.

5. *Value-Percept Theory*

Values of the employees determine their satisfaction with their jobs because they hold different value systems, therefore as per this theory, their satisfaction levels will also differ in accordance with their values. He mentions that in Value - Percept theory, the assumption is that the difference between their expectations and what is actually received can bring dissatisfaction depending on importance of the job to the individual.

6. *Vroom's Expectancy*

He explains Vroom's expectancy theory as employees' behavior is based on the choices available to be prioritized. The idea of the theory is to maximize satisfaction and minimize dissatisfaction among employees. He mentions that the theory also explains that performance, motivation and efforts are within employees themselves and variables such as valence, instrumentality, and expectancy verifies the above mentioned factors. He also feels that higher efforts are directly related to higher performance.

7. *Porter-Lawler Model*

He considers this model as a comprehensive and complete theory of motivation which includes diverse aspects. This model gives details of the relation that exists between job performance and attitudes of managers. The model assumes that individual behavior is influenced by both internal and external factors, employees are rational and make own choices about their behavior, they have different goals, desires and needs. Finally, individuals decide between alternative behaviors based on intrinsic and extrinsic motivators.

He concludes that motivation cannot always be financial rewards, but non-financial rewards can also be used to retain employees. He also believes that although individuals have their own expectations, it is the responsibility of leaders to design and align with theories that are relevant to bring job satisfaction to the employees. He says that there can be a possibility to utilize one or combination of two or more theories of motivation. He believes that to empower workforce, employees should be given a platform to voice out their concerns on how they should be motivated for their competent and sustainable efforts. Employees should be dedicated and aware about the vision and goals of the organization and work together towards those objectives.

2.6 Employees' Retention Models

Kaur R. (2017)[30] conducted a study to understand models of employees' retention and found out three major models of retention to control attrition in any given industry. He conducted the study with objectives to examine the scenario of Employees Retention in Indian IT companies, to identify the major models of Employees' Retention and to find out the major factors affecting the Employees retention in IT companies. He explained the models briefly in the following manner:

1. *Zinger Model*

The model assumes that employee retention is the art and science of engaging people in realistic and recognized connections to strategy, roles, performance, organization, community, relationship, customers, development, energy, and well-being as companies leverage, sustain, and transform their work connections into results.

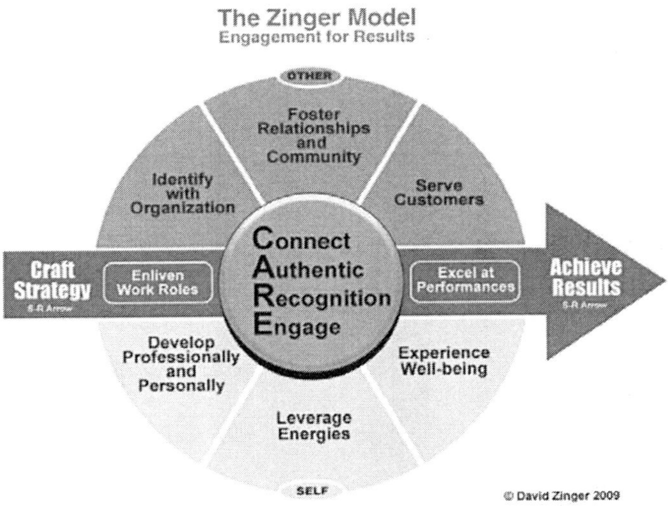

Figure 2.2: Zinger Model

Source: http://www.davidzinger.com/david-zingers-employee-engagement-model-and-video-poland-7398.

According to the Zinger Model, employee retention is driven towards achieving results of the organization that the department, team, or individual desires to achieve. To achieve desired results, companies need to craft an appropriate strategy. Here, the central key is connection for employee retention. In some cases connection is synonymous with engagement, which is not a onetime survey measure or a steady state. Retention of competent employees requires powerful recognitions at work place. He also stated that the model emphasizes that employee retention can contribute to effective performance management and performance demonstrates company's engagement while engagement and retention in turn can help companies excel at performance. He also suggested that good employee retention should foster star performers of the company. The model also comments that employees should experience both personal and professional development at work. The model also suggests that powerful retention involves mastery of physical, mental, emotional, spiritual, and organizational energy to take care of personal and professional well-being of the employees.

2. *ERC's Retention Model*

He stated about Employee Retention Connection's model, which concentrates on applied organizational experience indicating three primary drivers of employee retention at work. He indicated that work can be made stimulating by giving variety of assignments, autonomy to take decisions, resources and support provided to do appropriate work, opportunity to learn, feedback on result and understanding the significance of one's personal contributions towards success of the organization.

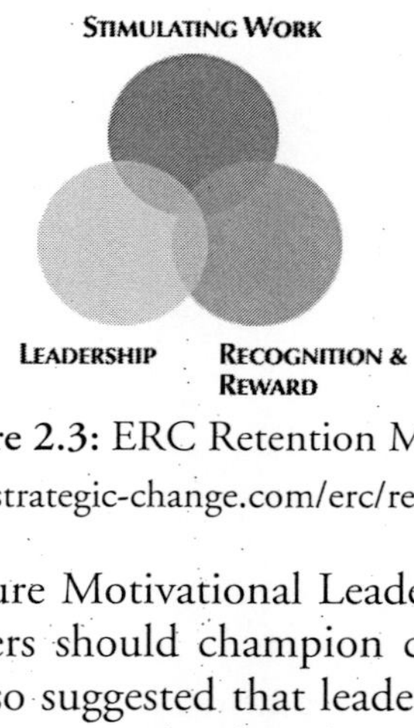

Figure 2.3: ERC Retention Model

Source: http://www.strategic-change.com/erc/retentionsystem.html

As indicated in above figure Motivational Leadership also helps to retain employees therefore leaders should champion change and they must be open to new ideas. He also suggested that leaders should inspire a shared vision of organization direction, develop the competences of employees and become a model for behaviors that reproduces organization morals. He also indicated that companies should recognize and reward a job that is done well and should reinforce anticipated behaviors and create a prominence and focus on recognition to competent employees. The organization should celebrate successes in order to form self-esteem and enhance solidarity and team work.

3. *Integrated System for Retaining Employees*

He has taken care of the fact that Employee Retention Connection transforms the organization culture and improves the competitive edge through the following five-phased approach:

The model has developed further to ERC, which begins by analyzing the organization's motivation and retention culture through surveys and focus groups that is the motivating and demotivating aspects of the culture of the organization. He stated that ERC focuses on planning high-involvement job and work assignments and trains supervisors and managers in recognized methods of motivational leadership at work place.

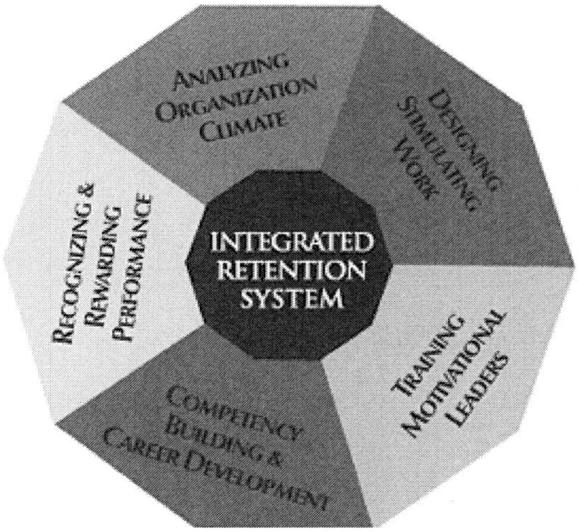

Figure 2.4: Integrated Retention System
Source: http://www.strategic-change.com/erc/retentionsystem.html

In his view, once all other steps are followed, ERC tries to deliver a plan for employee career paths and skill building in employees of various levels. It is done by designing career paths, not necessarily upward in the organizational chart, identifying core competencies for different career paths, planning training and other opportunities to build competencies and mentoring for employee direction for their career advancements. He stated that at the end, ERC builds a personalized reward and recognition system to fit the culture of the organization. To do so, they try to identify activities, attitudes and contributions to be recognized and rewarded. Reward and recognition options are also matched to performance contributions of the employees and specific motivational approaches are also established for retaining employees.

2.7 Summary of the Chapter

After reading and analyzing Indian and international literature on the topic, it can be concluded that attrition of teachers have been one of the biggest concerns for world economies. There is also few literature covering almost all countries to show the impact of turnover of teachers at various levels of education. The problem is understood mostly from the perspectives of teachers or management, but not from students and parents perspectives.

Quality of education decides future of any nation. In various types of literature, many researchers have made attempts to analyze attrition of teachers and its impact on education in a particular part of any country. They tried to cover any state, region or country to understand causes and remedies to control turnover of teachers at school or college level. Some projects have been undertaken to resolve the issue, but results are slow.

On the basis of review of literature, main reasons for the attrition are inadequate salary standards or inappropriate working conditions at school. Most of the reasons are either related to attitude of management or personal. The problem has been analyzed from the point of view of teachers or management, but impact of attrition on students and parents has been completely ignored.

In India, high turnover of teachers has been a very serious issue. The research on the subject has been limited to any region or place. The studies have been conducted with small sample size with the help of schedules or questionnaire. The problem of attrition of teachers is not seen or analyzed from the perspectives of all the stakeholders exclusively. Many articles have been published to analyze the issues of deteriorating standards of education, shortages of teachers and high turnover of teachers. Impact of the problem has never been analyzed in detail from the perspective of all the stakeholders.

Work commitment and Job satisfaction are considered as deciding parameters to control attrition. Almost all countries all over the world whether Developed, Developing or Under developed have researched the problem and found out causes and remedies for the problem, but the problem is still prominent. Retaining qualified, trained and competent teachers for long in any type of school is mandatory to improve quality of education worldwide.

In the first part of the chapter, attempt was made to understand the meaning and scope of Attrition from the books of renowned authors of Human Resource Management to get theoretical framework of the topic.

Then the literature is divided in various categories to get clear picture of impact of Attrition of Teachers in global perspective. In Developed countries, attrition happens mostly due to availability of better prospects. In under developed countries, teachers' turnover is high mostly due to inadequate pay and poor working conditions in the schools. In developing countries, attrition rate is high mostly due to inappropriate attitude of management towards teachers or personal reasons.

Though the reasons for attrition of teachers may be different, the impact is almost the same as ultimately it affects the quality of education. Quality of education has direct linkage with the employability of the students in any country. Teachers are considered as the most important factor in determining the quality of education that children receive as per UNESCO (2006). The issue of teacher motivation is essential to address because of its correlation with the quality of education. The government of any country is responsible to ensure that teachers perform to the best of their competencies. It is very much evident from the above review that teachers are the pioneers in uplifting the level of education in any country. The quality of education should be improved worldwide to resolve the problems of unemployment, low economic growth, issues related to human development and various other important issues for global economic development. Qualified and competent teachers who impart the knowledge to students, should be handled with fair and constant motivational practices. So, Governments of various countries, Management of Schools, Teachers Union should design some policies for the teachers, which can encourage teachers to improve their performance and stay longer in the same school for the improvement in quality of education at school level worldwide. It can also be generalized that the policies, programs and treatment to teachers should be similar in public and private schools in any given nation to handle the issue.

This research will try to provide reference for the further development in the topic in any other part of India or even in abroad. This study also tries to study the problem of attrition of teachers from the perspectives of Permanent teachers, Contractual teachers, Management, Parents and Students. The study covers aided and unaided private schools to analyze the impact of teachers' turnover, where the problem is the most prominent. The study covers Anand district with all its tehsils for in depth understanding of the issue.

CHAPTER 3

Concepts and Methodology

3.1 INTRODUCTION

As discussed earlier, the study is based on primary data collection through field research. The research is carried with the help of four types of schedules designed separately for management, teachers, parents and students. Data is collected personally through interviewing each person under study. This chapter presents the methods used for sampling, designing schedules, data collection, tabulation of data and data analysis. The schedules are prepared in detail considering various parameters under study. To serve the predetermined objectives, research methodology is finalized after considering points noted in review of literature and suggestions received from the experts.

Before discussing the research methodology adopted, the terms used are defined for clear cut understanding of the same and later interpretation and proper formulations.

3.2 DEFINITION OF THE IMPORTANT TERMS

3.2.1 Attrition

Here, "Attrition means Turnover of teachers from one school to other school or elsewhere due to various professional or personal reasons." UNESCO Institute of Statistics, 2018 defined Attrition as "Percentage of teachers at a given level of education leaving the profession in a given school year."

3.2.2 Private, Aided and Self-Financed School

The study is focused on Private Schools of Anand District. Here the definition of Private School is "Any school which is run and managed by Private Trust. Schools, which are managed by Trust but funded by Government as well as Schools, which are managed by Trust and self-financed are covered under the definition of Private Schools". To describe Private Unaided School, they are the schools which are owned, managed and funded privately without any support of the Government. For better recognition, they have to ensure adequate student-teacher ratio, conform to certain qualifications regarding recruitment of permanent teachers and assure their financial sustainability. Most of the administrative decisions are taken by the schools including recruitment procedures for the teachers and pay of the teachers. They have their own admission procedures and fee structure for the students.

The study covered the schools which are Aided Private and Self-Financed Private. Government schools do not face the problem of attrition of teachers due to higher salary, better perquisites and job security given to them. Stability of teachers is there in public schools, but again the quality of education is in doubt. Fully aided private schools also do not face the problem of Attrition due to Job Security and Higher Pay. The problem of Attrition is more prominent at fully self-financed schools, due to various reasons which are not much controllable by any of the stakeholders. These schools are becoming as small and medium scale corporate houses, making additional money, but they do not satisfy the teachers with required payment.

For the purpose of study, English medium schools with Secondary Section were targeted. Teachers, Students, Parents and Management of English Medium Schools were covered under the study for better understanding of the schedules as they were designed in English. Responses of the Students are also valuable, so secondary schools were targeted. Students of secondary section are supposed to be matured enough to understand the subject and give their inputs on that.

3.2.3 Permanent and Contractual Teachers

"Permanent Teachers are those teachers who are confirmed and on the permanent roll of the school, who are entitled to get all the monetary and non-monetary benefits designed by the management, who cannot leave or be laid off without serving the notice period."

"Contractual Teachers are the teachers who are on a contractual employment for few months or years, who are not entitled to any extra benefits other than fixed pay, who can stop coming or be laid off without any notice."

Permanent teachers are of more importance as far as attrition is concerned as cost of hiring and training them is more and they share special psychological bond with the students and parents. Attrition of contractual teachers is supposed to be high as they are always in search of permanent employment in teaching or any other profession. Now a day, private schools are employ contractual teachers mostly to reduce expenses. Contractual teachers may or may not be with required qualifications or skills, which adversely affects the quality of education. Permanent teachers are employed with the help of proper selection tools. Permanent teachers play pivotal role in determining quality of education of any school.

3.3 RESEARCH METHOD

As shown in the previous chapter, rigorous review of literature is done after classification of international and Indian literature in to various categories. The study is focused on four different variables, viz. management, teachers, parents and students. The study is based on quantitative and qualitative data by using descriptive method of the comparative type is used in this study. It attempts to describe and compare the differences in rate of attritions and reasons behind same covering teachers appointed on permanent and contract basis.

3.4 DATA

The study is based on the both secondary and primary level statistics. The secondary data were collected from the published government reports, publications, research papers, newspaper notes, journal papers, edited books and related websites. Secondary data were used for presentation on status of education, teachers, public-private schools and other literacy related parameters in the district, state, country and on the international front. The primary data were collected from the selected stakeholders, viz. management, teachers, parents and students. The Government officials were also interviewed to get idea about the steps taken by them for the issue under study.

3.4.1 Primary Data Collection

The study is mainly based on the primary data collected from the aided and self-financed private schools offering secondary and higher secondary education with medium of instruction as English in seven tehsils of Anand district of Gujarat state. To understand the problem exclusively, data is collected from teachers appointed on permanent as well as contractual basis. The data is collected separately through field survey research from different stake holders, viz. management, teachers, students and parents; through personal interviews with the help of pre-tested schedules. The interview schedules were prepared separately for stakeholders, viz. management, teachers, students and parents.

Survey Schedules

In order to fulfill the objectives of study through report, the four types of survey schedules were developed and canvassed for the collection of primary data.

- **Schedule for School Management 1.0:** for information pertaining to school, student and teachers; demographic information of representatives, pupil-teacher ratio, factors considered for selection of teachers, facilities and incentives provided to teachers, factors to control attrition of teachers, important factors to retain teachers, human resource practices adopted, managerial aspects of schools, information related to students and unique characteristics of the school, etc.
- **Schedule for School Teachers 2.0:** for demographic information of teachers, school and employment information, reasons for attrition, profession related information, pay related information, motivational factors for teachers, professional development of teachers, implications of inappropriate behaviour, reasons for attrition through statements, information related to workload of teachers, opinion of teachers on professional factors for attrition, opinion of teachers on personal factors for attrition, factors which would attract to another job, awareness among teachers about right to education (rte), suggestions/ opinions to handle attrition of teachers, etc.
- **Schedule for Parents 3.0:** for collecting demographic information of parents, factors considered while choosing a school, parents-teachers relationship, effects of attrition, measures to be undertaken by schools to prevent attrition, and ssuggestions and observations of parents about seed production and marketing from the sample beneficiary farmers.
- **Schedule for Students 4.0:** for collecting demographic information of students, student-teacher relation, factors appeal to students while choosing their school, qualities required in a good teacher, and students' comments/view points.

Besides data collected through the above mentioned four types of schedules, the focus-group discussion was conducted among school teachers covering the topic related to present study and personal interview of District Education Officer was conducted to get idea about the plan and actions of the State Government towards the quality education. Also few case studies of teachers and management were recorded in details to understand the aspect of issue under study.

In the schedules, most of the questions were multiple choice questions with few open ended questions based on objectives of the study. Table 3.1 provides the details of total number of descriptive and objective questions in each schedule.

Table 3.1: Details of Number of Questions in Schedules

Schedule	*No. of Objective Questions*	*No. of Descriptive Questions*	*Total No. of Questions*
Management	45	02	47
Teachers	43	05	48
Parents	22	03	25
Students	15	04	19

The schedules were prepared on the basis of the parameters, like demographic characteristics of the stakeholders, motivational factors, job satisfaction, work commitment, personal and professional reasons for turnover of teachers, impact of turnover on management; students and parents, working environment, work involvement, facilities and perquisites provided, job security, pay, work related stress, training and development, Teacher-pupil ratio, selection and recruitment practices adopted, retention factors, performance evaluation, performance recognition, students' performance, retention and promotion practices, characteristics of schools, fee standards, qualities of teachers. The pilot survey was conducted to test the above mentioned four schedules as discussed below.

3.4.1.1 *Pilot Testing of Schedules*

A pilot survey was conducted at selected nearby school in Anand (J.P. Thakkar High School, Sardar Patel Education Trust, Anand) on March 28, 2017 and Principal, Vice-Principal, 10 permanent and 6 contractual teachers, 10 parents and 20 students were interviewed personally for their responses. After evaluating responses, the schedules were modified with necessary changes to serve the objectives in better manner. Also the comments from external experts were invited and considered while finalization of survey schedules.

3.4.1.2 *Survey Research*

The primary survey was conducted during the one month period from March 28, 2017 to April 27, 2017 covering total twenty two schools comprised of three fully aided private schools and nineteen self-financed private schools. The survey covered 22 management personnel, 264 teachers (160 permanent and 104 contractual), 330 students and 111 parents. From each school, 1 management person, 12 teachers, 15 students and 5 parents were contacted and interviewed personally.

Schools were visited only after the prior approval of school management. The management personals, teachers and students were available on the campus, but parents were contacted either on the campus or off the campus through students. Efforts were made to cover the teachers who left the jobs and joined somewhere else in order to capture the real issues behind the attrition of teachers. Total five special cases are identified from various categories and contacted personally to build case studies *(see annexure).*

3.4.1.3 *Survey Methods*

Personal interview method is used to collect data from management personnel with the help of pre-tested schedule. Teachers are also interviewed separately with probing technique, while group discussion technique is also used for some questions. Parents are contacted mostly off the campus for their responses on the questionnaire. Information from students was collected through discussion. Teachers who have already left were also interviewed personally.

Few case studies of some respondents were taken to capture the open ended questions related to the turnover of teachers. Their inputs are considered as valuable to understand the problem thoroughly from different perspectives.

Case 1: A principal who does not allow attrition of teachers in the school.

Case 2: Vice-principal who has come out with ways to control attrition.

Case 3: A teacher who left the job of private school and joined government school.

Case 4: A teacher who is not satisfied with the job, but wants to continue at the same school.

Case 5: A teachers who have changed 4 schools in the teaching career due to various reasons.

Case 6: District Education Officer, Anand to know government's view on attrition of teachers in private schools.

3.4.1.5 *Study Area*

The present study was undertaken in the one of the educationally progressed districts of Gujarat state, i.e. Anand district which is having Vallabh Vidyanagar as educational hub close to it. Anand district is located in Central region of Gujarat where from golden quadrilateral as well as Ntional Expressway 1 passes. Anand is known as one of well developed district of the State. Anand district has eight talukas, viz. Anand, Tarapur, Petlad, Borsad, Sojitra, Umreth, Khambhat and Anklav. The study covers all the eight talukas of the district having more focus on Anand taluka as this taluk has significant number of both granted and non-granted higher secondary schools. The list of the schools in Anand district was obtained from the office of District Education Officer (DEO) of Anand district (Table 3.2).

Map 3.1: Location Map of Anand District (Gujarat)

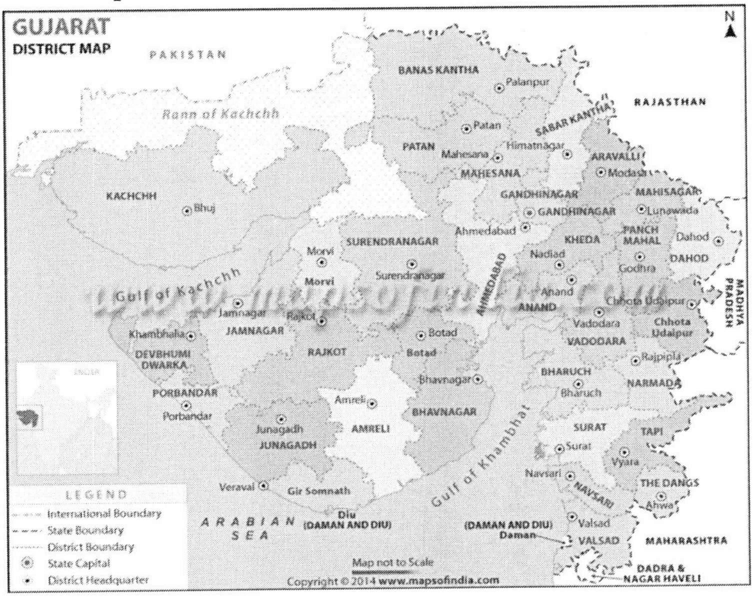

Table 3.2: Tehsil-wise List of Schools in Anand District (2017–18)

Granted/ Non-Granted	*Name of Taluka*	*Medium of Instruction*			*Grand Total*
		English	*Gujarati*	*Gujarati-English*	
Government	Khambhat		1		1
Government Total			**1**		**1**
Granted	Anand	2	53	2	57
	Anklav		14		14
	Borsad		43		43
	Khambhat		25		25
	Petlad	1	42		43
	Sojitra		12		12
	Tarapur		7		7
	Umreth		24		24
Granted Total		**3**	**220**	**2**	**225**
Non-Granted	Anand	17	22	1	40
	Anklav	1	1		2
	Borsad	4	3		7
	Khambhat	3	4		7
	Petlad	4	1		5
	Sojitra	1	3		4
	Tarapur	1	1		2
	Umreth	1	3		4
Non-Granted Total		**32**	**38**	**1**	**71**
Total		**35**	**259**	**3**	**297**

Source: Obtained from the Office of District Education Officer (DEO), Anand.

Map 3.2: Taluka Map of Anand District (Gujarat)

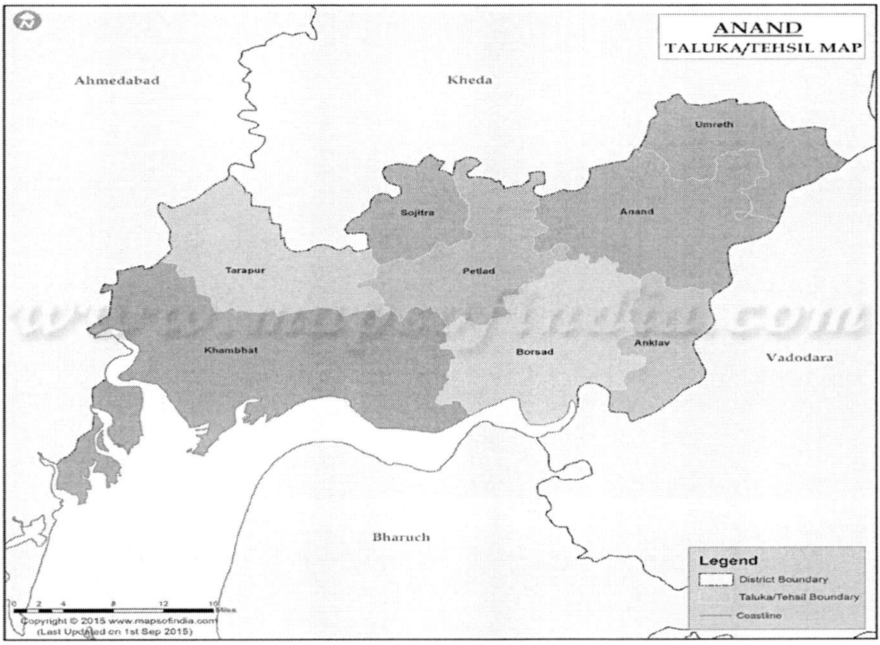

3.4.2 Sampling

3.4.2.1 *Sampling Method*

Stratified random sampling technique was used as sampling method (see, Box 3.1). First strata was made up for classification of aided and unaided private schools. Out of those, fully self-financed schools were more focused on as the problem is more prevalent there.

Another strata is made up of schools having secondary and higher secondary sections only. It is done as students and parents of those sections are more aware of seriousness of the problem.

Last stratification is made up of schools having English as medium of instruction. It is done as every parent wants their child to get enrolled in schools having English medium and there are cases of high turnover of teachers in these schools.

Box 3.1: Stratification Adopted

1st Stratification: Aided and Unaided Private Schools
2nd Stratification: Schools having Secondary and Higher Secondary Sections
3rd Stratification: Schools having English as medium of Instruction

After considering total number of schools in each tehsil of Anand district, number of schools to be undertaken for study from each tehsil was finalized (see, Table 3.3). Data were collected from aided and unaided private schools from each tehsil, as per sampling framework given in Box 3.1 and Table 3.4.

There are total 35 private schools in Anand district comprised of 3 aided and 32 Self-financed private Schools. The survey includes 22 private Schools, out of which 3 are aided private schools and 19 are self-financed Private Schools.

Table 3.3: Number of Schools Covered for the Study

Sr. No.	*Tehsils*	*Schools Covering the Area of Said Taluka*	*Per cent to Total Number of Schools*
1.	Anand	14	73.68
2.	Borsad	01	25.00
3.	Petlad	02	40.00
4.	Umreth	01	100.00
5.	Tarapur	01	100.00
6.	Anklav	01	100.00
7.	Sojitra	01	100.00
8.	Khambhat	01	33.33
Total		22	57.89

3.4.3 Sampling Framework

As discussed earlier, after considering the total number of schools in each tehsil, total 22 schools were selected as sample for study.

- Total 14 schools were selected out of 19 schools from Anand tehsil
- One school was selected out of 4 schools from Borsad tehsil
- Two school were selected out of 5 schools from Petlad tehsil
- One school was selected out of 1 schools from Umreth tehsil
- One school was selected out of 1 schools from Tarapur tehsil

- One school was selected out of 1 schools from Anklav tehsil
- One school was selected out of 1 schools from Sojitra tehsil
- One school was selected out of 3 schools from Khambhat tehsil

Thus, out of total sample, 57.89 per cent of the total schools got selected for the research survey.

3.4.3.1 *Selected Schools*

Table 3.4: List of Selected Schools

Sr. No.	*Name of the School*
1.	V and C Patel English Medium School
2.	Zen School
3.	Bavis Gam Vidhyalaya
4.	J.P. Thakkar High School (Pilot Study)
5.	Charotar English Medium School
6.	Laksh School of Science (Khambat)
7.	V.J. Patel Practicing High School
8.	Adharshila Vidhyalaya (Aaklav)
9.	Shri C.B. Patel English Medium School (Sojitra)
10.	Knowledge High School
11.	Thamna Education Institute (Umreth)
12.	BAPS Swaminarayan Vidyamandir
13.	Swaminarayan Vidyapith
14.	I.B. Patel English School
15.	D.Z. Patel Higher Secondary School
16.	Excellent English Medium School (Borsad)
17.	S.J. Patel English Medium School (Tarapur)
18.	Shree Swaminarayan English Medium School (Petlad)
19.	T.V. Patel Higher Secondary School
20.	Vrajbhoomi International School
21.	Angel English Medium School
22.	H.M. Patel English Medium School (Petlad)

Out of total schools of the tehsils, following schools are selected randomly on the basis of purposive sampling. So sampling within the strata is purposive sampling. All these schools are visited personally to observe the actual picture of the problem other than what is to be mentioned in schedules. The below given list shows the names of the schools which are covered under the study.

3.4.3.2 Composition of Sample

To fulfill the objectives of the topic under study, the survey method was used. The primary data were collected from the selected sample management personals, teachers, parents and students. The data were collected from randomly selected 22 schools and stakeholder therein. Besides, to receive qualitative responses the information (using open ended questionnaire) were collected on selected questions from management, teachers, parents and students using four different schedules developed for same. Total sample size of the study was 726, which includes management, permanent teachers, contractual teachers, parents and students as shown in Box 3.2.

Box 3.2: Sampling Framework

- Total Sample Size: 726
  - Management = 22
  - Teachers = 264 (Permanent & Contractual)
  - Students = 330 (Secondary & Higher Secondary Section)
  - Parents = 110

3.5 STATISTICAL TOOLS FOR DATA ANALYSIS

- Simple tabular analysis was used for data analysis.
- The data was analyzed in terms of frequencies and percentage.
- The data were tabulated and analyzed using Microsoft excel software.
- The data were analyzed and presented in the forms of tables, figures and graphs.
- The statistical tools like arithmetic mean is used for data analysis.

Arithmetic Mean (AM) or Mean of the group:

The arithmetic mean is a mathematical representation of the typical value of a series of numbers, computed as the sum of all the numbers in the series divided by the count of all numbers in the series. The arithmetic mean is sometimes referred to as the average or simply as the mean. The formula for mean is as stated below:

$$\bar{X} = \frac{\sum X}{N}$$

Here,

$\sum$, represents the summation/total

X, represents scores/Values/Observations

N represents number of scores/observations.

3.6 CHAPTER SUMMARY

The chapter shows the steps adopted to collect, tabulate and analyze the data to come out with the results and findings. There is a well-defined path from the step of identifying the variables, parameters and factors necessary to fetch information from management, teachers, parents and students.

Statistical tools are utilized properly to design the whole research methodology of the study. There are different factors considered to design schedules of study for all the stakeholders. Data is collected with minimal errors and with efficiency. All the efforts of the stage of research survey and data collection is photographed and recorded *(see, Annexure).*

None of the rules and regulations of the schools are violated during the phase of data collection. Proper channel of communication is used to contact required personnel without hurting anyone's sentiments. Brochures and documentations related to various aspects are collected and interpreted on the campus. All the schools have given warm hospitality and arranged for campus visit to observe infrastructure and the facilities provided to teachers and students.

CHAPTER 4

Status of Education in Gujarat and Anand

4.1 INTRODUCTION

Before analyzing educational status of Gujarat, education of India is to be seen in global perspective. India has designed certain policies and plans to improve level of education of the nation in comparison with other countries. Education in India is analyzed in terms of public expenditure on education as per cent of Gross Domestic Product (GDP) and gross enrolment rate in global perspective in the following section.

4.2 EDUCATION IN INDIA IN GLOBAL PERSPECTIVE

International comparison on gross enrollment rate and public expenditure on education as a percentage of GDP presented in Table 4.1 indicate that

Table 4.1: International Comparison on Gross Enrollment Rate and Public Expenditure on Education (2014)

Countries	*Public Expenditure on Education as Percent of GDP*	*Gross Enrolment Ratio*			
		Primary (I-V)	*Lower Secondary (VI-VIII)*	*Upper Secondary (IX-XII)*	*Tertiary*
India	4.13	101.4	89.3	62.5	23.0
Bangladesh	1.97	111.9	76.1	44.7	13.4
Nepal	4.71	135.2	90.4	49.7	15.8
Pakistan	2.47	93.6	55.9	31.1	10.4
Sri Lanka	1.62	101.3	99.7	99.1	20.7
China	NA	103.9	100.4	88.8	39.4
Germany	4.93	103.3	101.6	104.6	65.5
Russia	4.15	98.6	98.7	105.1	78.7
South Africa	6.05	99.7	94.9	93.1	19.7
UK	5.68	108.2	112.7	138.2	56.5
USA	5.22	99.5	101.9	93.2	86.7

Source: GOI (2016), Educational Statistics at a Glance, Government of India.

South Africa spends the highest share of its total expenditure (as percentage of GDP) on education followed by United Kingdom (UK), United States of America (USA), Germany, Nepal, Russia and then India. In terms of gross enrolment rate, India does reasonably well. When India is compared on International level, the issues in education are mostly the same, only there is need to work on remedial measures to resolve those issues.

When India is compared to other countries on parameter of Pupil-Teachers Ratio, it is better than that of other developing countries (Table 4.2). But, countries like Germany, USA, China and Russia do exceptionally well by maintaining ratio as below 20:1, which is desirable for all the countries.

Table 4.2: International Comparison on Pupil Teacher Ratio

Countries	***Pupil Teacher Ratio***		
	Primary (I-V)	*Lower Secondary (VI-VIII)*	*Upper Secondary (IX-XII)*
Bangladesh	40.2	36.9	33.2
Brazil	21.2	18.5	15.7
China	16.2	12.6	16.5
Germany	12.3	11.2	14.3
India	25	17	38
Nepal	24	35.4	23
Pakistan	46.5	17.7	21.7
Russia	19.8	NA	NA
South Africa	32.3	NA	NA
Sri Lanka	23.7	17.3	18.2
UK	17.4	15.3	16.2
USA	14.5	14.8	14.8

Source: GOI (2016), Educational Statistics at a Glance, Government of India.

4.3 Status of Education in Gujarat

Before we discuss about the education in Gujarat, let us have a quick outlook of demographic features of Gujarat. As per Gujarat Population Census 2011 data, total population of Gujarat was 6.03 Crores which was approximately 4.99 per cent of total population of our Country *(Gupta A., 2013)*[1]. Table 4.3 presents percentage share of total population by residence indicate that Gujarat is more urbanized in nature having almost three fifth of total population living in urban areas while Anand district has relatively more rural population having share of more than 72 per cent of total population of the district living in rural areas.

Table 4.3: Percentage Share of Total Population by Residence (2001 & 2011)

Sr. No.	*India/Gujarat/ Districts*	*Percentage Share of Total Population, 2001*		*Percentage Share of Total Population, 2011*	
		Rural	*Urban*	*Rural*	*Urban*
1.	India	72.2	27.8	68.9	31.1
2.	Gujarat	62.6	37.4	57.4	42.6
3.	Anand	72.6	27.4	69.7	30.3

Source: GOI (2011), Office of Registrar General and Census Commissioner, GoI.

Gujarat is a hub of a wide variety of industries and is also considered as one among the best industrialized states of India. Gujarat has some of the most prestigious educational institutes of the nation. It is a recognized fact that an education system, which is built on the premises of quality and equity is central to sustainable success in the emerging knowledge economy. Education is the most powerful tool to prepare our citizens in the knowledge society. We need education to amalgamate globalization with localization, to enable our children and youth to become world citizens, with their roots deeply entrenched in Indian culture, values and traditions *(New Education Policy, MHRD, 2016)*[2]. Thus, all states of India are trying to improve quality of education to have all for education and education for all and Gujarat is not an exception.

4.3.1 Education Pattern in Gujarat

In Gujarat, education is provided by both the public and private sector with funding from the federal, state, local level or self-financed institutions. The current education system in Gujarat comprises primary (standard 1–5), upper primary (standard 6–8), secondary (standard 9–10) and higher secondary (standard 11–12) levels of school education. The government of India implemented the *Sarva Shiksha Abhiyan* (SSA) in 2001; Gujarat adopted the flagship program with the aim of universalizing elementary education by working towards universal access and retention, the bridging of gender and social gaps in education, and the enhancement of learning levels in all states of India. Right to Education (RTE) act passed in 2009 mandated free and compulsory education to all children between the ages of 6 and 14, guaranteeing them access to an education of reasonable quality and a teaching-learning process free from fear, stress, and anxiety, which was adopted by schools of Gujarat also. The standards 1 to 8 are covered under SSA and RTE, which are the compulsory grades.

4.3.2 Educational Programs Implemented

Gujarat has successfully implemented and monitored almost all the initiatives of Government of India to improve access and quality of education in the State. Following are some of the programs implemented in the state by the government.

1. ***Sarva Shiksha Abhiyan:*** All the 27 districts and 7 Municipal Corporations in Gujarat are being covered under Sarva Shiksha Abhiyan.
2. *The Kasturba Gandhi Balika Vidyalaya (KGBV):* The Kasturba Gandhi Balika Vidyalaya (KGBV) scheme is merged with Sarva Shiksha Abhiyan from 2007. There are 89 KGBV and 6655 girls are benefitted by the programme in Gujarat till 2014.
3. ***Computer Aided Learning:*** The Computer Aided Learning Program (CAL) was introduced to create a learning environment, where learning and assessment is fun and the opportunities to learn are equal for the rural and urban children. There are 20502 schools providing computer labs in Gujarat.
4. ***National Programme for Education of Girls at Elementary Level (NPEGEL):*** National Programme for Education of Girls at Elementary Level (NPEGEL) in has been implemented in 1584 clusters of 78 rural Educationally Backward Blocks (EBBs) and 39 clusters of 13 urban slums in 21 districts of Gujarat.
5. ***Early Child Care Education (ECCE):*** To provide linkage between pre-primary and primary education, 2450 ECCE Centres are there in Gujarat. Out of that, 1785 ECCE Centers covered under SSA and 665 Centers covered under NPEGEL.
6. ***Pragna—An Activity Based Learning Approach:*** Pragna is an activity based learning approach to convert a classroom to a more holistic place, where children would love to come and learn. Total 3748 schools are covered in Gujarat under this programme in academic year 2012–13.

7. ***Building as Learning Aid (BaLA)/Inclusive – Building as Learning Aid (i-BaLA):*** BaLA (Building as Learning Aid) is an innovative concept originally developed by Vinyas, Centre for Architectural Research and Design with support from UNICEF towards qualitative improvement in education, through developing child-friendly, learning and fun based physical environment in school infrastructure. The program is being implemented in more than 1620 Model Schools in various districts of Gujarat by SSA.
8. ***The Digi School Scheme:*** Under the scheme, 2400 classes of 7th and 8th standards are to be covered in 1200 primary schools of Gujarat to promote ICT based education in the proposed budget of 2018–19.
9. ***Mid-day Meal Scheme:*** Total 1068 crores are allocated to Mid-day Meal scheme in the proposed budget of the financial year 2018–19.
10. ***Free Education to Girl Students:*** Total 7,44,152 girl students of class 9 to class 12 are provided with free education in GIA Schools in the proposed budget of the year 2018–19.
11. ***Gunotsav:*** This is an initiative of Gujarat Government to evaluate primary education scenario and grade primary school teachers. This is mainly to improve quality of education in the state.

4.3.3 Literacy Rate in Gujarat

Literacy is considered as one of the most important indicators of social and economic development of any regions/state/country. Knowledge is linked with literacy and a formal education. Economic growth is related to rate of literacy. Thus, literacy is one of the important needs of life and it is also required for future development of any nation *(Gupta A., 2013)*[3].

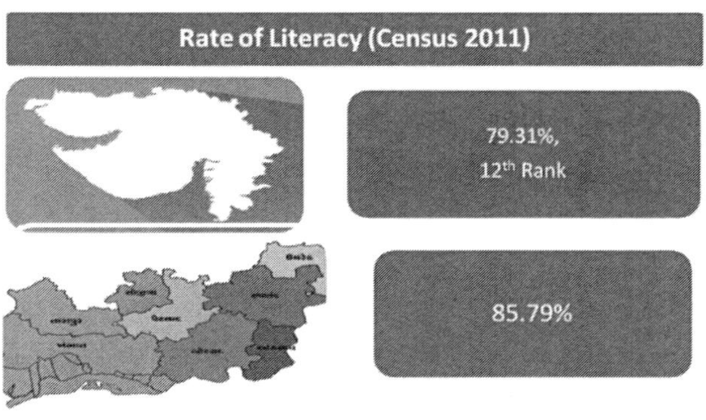

Figure 4.1: Literacy Rate of Gujarat and Anand District

The literacy rate in Gujarat has shown phenomenon improvement and it was 79.31 per cent as per 2011 population census with 12th rank at all India level (Table 4.4). Some of the districts in Gujarat have comparatively higher literacy rate such as Surat with 85.53 per cent, Ahmedabad with 85.31 per cent, Anand with 84.37 per cent, Gandhinagar with 84.16 per cent and Navsari with 83.88 per cent rate of literacy.

Table 4.4: Literacy Rate - Gujarat and India, 1961 to 2011

Particulars	*Literacy Rate (Census-wise) %*					
	1961	*1971*	*1981*	*1991*	*2001*	*2011*
Gujarat	31.5	37.0	44.9	61.3	69.1	79.3
India	28.3	34.5	43.6	52.2	64.8	73.0

Source: GOI (2011), Office of Registrar General and Census Commissioner, GoI.

The trend of literacy rate over the period of last five decades (1961 to 2011) indicates substantial growth in rate of literacy at State as well as at national level. Literacy rate of Gujarat has increased from 31.5 per cent to 79.3 per cent over the period of five decades (1961–2011), which indicates increasing number of students with need of more schools (Table 4.4). It can be seen from the Table 4.5 that rate of literacy rate in rural area in the Census year 2011 was relatively lower than urban areas.

Table 4.5: Literacy Rate by Residence (2011)

Sr. No.	*India/Gujarat/ Districts*	*Literacy Rate*	
		Rural	*Urban*
1.	India	67.8	84.1
2.	Gujarat	71.7	86.3
3.	Anand	82.7	88.2

Source: GOI (2011), Office of Registrar General and Census Commissioner, GoI.

Anand one of the districts of Gujarat having higher rate of literacy, it is deue to the fact that Anand district is an educational hub in the State having education town attached to it, i.e. Vallabh Vidhyanagar. Anand is also considered as a land of Non Resident Indians (NRIs). Most of the population of the district goes abroad on the basis of their educational qualifications. Thus, Anand is an educational centric district, which is also study area of this research.

4.3.4 Educational Institutions, Students & Teachers in Gujarat

Table 4.6 presents the total number of educational institutions, teachers and students (2011–12 to 2015–16) in Gujarat under category of primary, secondary, higher secondary and higher education level. The table also presents number of institutions which only are made for girl students. As per data for the year 2015–16, there were total 44018 primary institutions with 9067 thousand students and 324842 teachers. While total number of secondary and higher secondary institutions was 10940 with 2679 thousand students and 83662 teachers in the state. About 2084 higher institutions covers 1489 thousand students by 59163 teachers. Hardly 3–4 percent school area only for girls in primary to higher secondary school level institutions, while same is around 8 percent in case of higher education institutions.

It is evident from the Table 4.7 that more than major chunk of the schools in Gujarat were primary and upper primary schools. There were 460 new schools established in the State in the year 2015–16. There were total 52283 establishments in education in rural area of Gujarat and total 25764 establishments in education sector in urban area (Table 4.8)

Table 4.6: Educational Institutions, Students & Teachers in Gujarat

Sr. No.	*Item*	*2011–12*	*2012–13*	*2013–14*	*2014–15*	*2015–16*
1.	**Primary**					
(a)	Total Institution (Nos.)	40943	42447	43176	43638	44018
	- Of which only for Girls	1416	1381	1392	1398	1398
(b)	Total Students ('000)	8376	9176	9229	9142	9067
	- Of which Girls	3869	4231	4250	4222	4207
(c)	Total Teachers (Nos.)	273065	302112	309755	319179	324842
	- Of which Women	149329	164398	171039	178068	182065
2.	**Secondary/Higher Secondary**					
(a)	Total Institution (Nos.)	9878	10406	10537	10811	10940
	- Of which only for Girls	666	692	589	573	585

Sr. No.	Item	2011–12	2012–13	2013–14	2014–15	2015–16
	(i) Std. 9 to 10	6045	6127	4572	4424	4349
	- Of which only for Girls	356	343	192	186	173
	(ii) Std. 9 to 12	3833	4279	5965	6387	6591
	- Of which only for Girls	310	349	397	387	412
(b)	Total Students ('000)	2997	2601	2702	2732	2679
	- Of which Girls	1245	1074	1127	1147	1131
	(i) Std. 9 to 10	2161	1695	1719	1746	1732
	- Of which Girls	896	697	704	718	712
	(ii) Std. 11 to 12	836	906	983	986	946
	- Of which Girls	348	377	423	429	419
(c)	Total Teachers (Nos.)	77716	83625	77777	83899	83662
	- Of Which Women	24309	25629	25181	28225	29062
	(i) Std. 9 to 10	40627	47385	17975	17805	16397
	(ii) Std. 9 to 12	37089	36240	59802	66094	67265
3.	**Higher Education***					
(a)	Total Institution (Nos.)	1664	1748	1921	2055	2084
	- Of which only for Girls	144	153	154	161	169
(b)	Total Students ('000)	1175	1307	1391	1442	1489
	- Of which Girls	489	543	579	591	621
(c)	Total Teachers (Nos.)	43831	48219	51261	52675	59163
	- Of which Women	15127	16904	17629	18245	21617

Notes: (1) *Excluding external students; (2) *The data for the year 2014–15 and 2015–16 are provisional.

Source: GOG (2017), Socio-Economic Review, Gujarat State, 2016–17

Table 4.7: Number of Schools by Category in Gujarat (2015–16)

Category	*No. of Schools*	*Percentage*
Primary Only	11840	22.59
Primary with Upper Primary	28827	54.99
Primary with Upper Primary and Secondary and Higher Secondary	1503	2.87
Upper Primary Only	815	1.55
Upper Primary with Secondary and Higher Secondary	220	0.42
Primary with Upper Primary and Secondary	680	1.30
Upper Primary with Secondary	166	0.32
Secondary Only	3504	6.68
Secondary with Higher Secondary	4127	7.87
Higher Secondary Only	742	1.42
All Schools 2015–16	52424	–
All Schools 2014–15	51964	–

Source: GOG (2016), U-DICE, School Education in India, 2015–16.

Table 4.8: Total Number of Education Establishments in Gujarat

Sr. No.	*Particulars*	*Total Number of Establishment*
A.	Rural Area	
	Without hired worker	1746
	With at least one hired worker	40537
	Total	**42283**
B.	**Urban Area**	
	Without hired worker	8330
	With at least one hired worker	17434
	Total	**25764**
C.	State	
	Without hired worker	10076
	With at least one hired worker	57971
	Total	**68047**

Source: Office of the Directorate of Economics and Statistics, Gandhinagar.

It is evident from the Table 4.9 that more than three fifth of total schools in Gujarat are managed by local body while in addition to this about 22.4 per cent of the total schools are private self-financed schools and 11.03 per cent of the schools are private aided schools. The figures indicate that the schools in the state are mostly managed by the private body or trust and thus Government may not have direct control on these schools except few of them fully funded by the Government.

Table 4.9: Schools by Type of Management in Gujarat (2015–16)

Sr. No.	*Type of Management*	*Percentage*
1.	Department of Education	1.67
2.	Tribal/Social Welfare Department	1.83
3.	Local Body	62.73
4.	Private Aided	11.03
5.	Private Unaided	22.40
6.	Other Government	0.15
7.	Central Government	0.18
8.	Unrecognized	0.00
9.	Madarsa Recognized	0.01
10.	Madarsa Unrecognized	0.00
	All Schools	**52424**

Source: GOG (2016), U-DICE, School Education in India, 2015–16.

It can be inferred from the Table 4.10 that about 78 per cent of the total number of schools are located in rural areas and remaining around 22 per cent of the total schools are in urban area of the State. Most of the schools in Gujarat are Co-Educational (Table 4.11).

Table 4.10: Number of Schools as per Location (2015–16)

Particulars	*Rural*	*Urban*	*Total*
No. of Schools	41047 (78.3)	11377 (21.7)	52424 (100)

Note: Figures in parenthesis are percentage to total.

Source: GOG (2016), U-DICE, School Education in India, 2015–16.

Table 4.11: Number of Schools as per Type in Gujarat (2015–16)

Particulars	*Boys*	*Girls*	*Co-Educational*
No. of Schools	1398 (2.67)	1895 (3.61)	49131 (93.72)

Note: Figures in parenthesis are percentage to total.

Source: GOG (2016), U-DICE, School Education in India, 2015–16.

4.3.5 Attributes of Teachers in Gujarat

It can be seen from the Table 4.12 that the highest numbers of teachers were in primary with upper primary section and the lowest numbers of teachers were in upper primary with secondary section in Gujarat during 2015–16.

Table 4.12: No. of Teachers by Category in Gujarat (2015–16)

Sr. No.	*Category*	*No. of Teachers*	*% to Total*
1.	Primary Only	35010	9.01
2.	Primary with Upper Primary	237431	61.12
3.	Primary with Upper Primary and Secondary and Higher Secondary	34474	8.87
4.	Upper Primary Only	4492	1.16
5.	Upper Primary with Secondary and Higher Secondary	3809	0.98
6.	Primary with Upper Primary and Secondary	8823	2.27
7.	Upper Primary with Secondary	992	0.26
8.	Secondary Only	13631	3.51
9.	Secondary with Higher Secondary	45602	11.74
10.	Higher Secondary Only	4200	1.08
	Total Teachers 2015–16	**388464**	**100.00**

Source: GOG (2016), U-DICE, School Education in India, 2015–16.

There were total 210994 employees employed in education sector in rural area, while 171070 employees were employed in education sector in urban area of Gujarat. Thus, in total 382064 employees are employed in education sector in Gujarat during 2015–16.

Table 4.13: Total Number of Persons Employed in Education in Gujarat

Sr. No.	*Particulars*	*Total Number of Persons*
A.	**Rural Area**	
	Without hired worker	2619
	With at least one hired worker	208375
	Total	210994
B.	**Urban Area**	
	Without hired worker	10559
	With at least one hired worker	160511
	Total	171070
C.	**State**	
	Without hired worker	13178
	With at least one hired worker	368886
	Total	**382064**

Source: Office of the Directorate of Economics and Statistics, Gandhinagar.

As we have seen in case of schools, the same picture is observed in case of teachers employed. The highest percentage of teachers are employed in schools run by local body followed by 31.98 per cent of the teachers are employed in private unaided schools and 13.40 per cent are employed in aided private schools in Gujarat (Table 4.14).

Table 4.14: Teachers with Type of Management in Gujarat (2015–16)

Sr. No.	*Type of Management*	*Percentage*
1.	Department of Education	0.84
2.	Tribal/Social Welfare Department	1.13
3.	Local Body	51.90
4.	Private Aided	13.40
5.	Private Unaided	31.98
6.	Other Government	0.14
7.	Central Government	0.59
8.	Unrecognized	–
9.	Madarsa Recognized	0.02
10.	Madarsa Unrecognized	–
	All Schools	**388464**

Source: GOG (2016), U-DICE, School Education in India, 2015–16.

It can be seen from the Table 4.15 that share of female teachers in total teachers were more than that of male teachers in Gujarat. Out of total number of teachers, 91.12 per cent of the total teachers were regular teachers, while 8.88 per cent of the total teachers were on contractual basis.

Table 4.15: Gender-wise Appointment-wise Percentage of Teachers in Gujarat (2015–16)

Sr. No.	*Type of Employment*	*Percentage*
1.	Regular-Male	45.04
2.	Regular-Female	46.08
3.	Regular-Total	91.12
4.	Contractual-Male	3.28
5.	Contractual-Female	5.60
6.	Contractual-Total	8.88
7.	Total Male Teachers	48.32
8.	Total Female Teachers	51.68
	Total Teachers	**388464**

Source: GOG (2016), U-DICE, School Education in India, 2015–16.

The details of teachers with academic qualification in different categories (2015–16) in Gujarat are presented in Table 4.16. It can be seen from the table that in Primary and upper primary level, percentage of teachers qualified to teach is lower than other sections. Total percentage of teachers who are qualified to teach in Gujarat were just 59.06 per cent in 2015–16. Thus, it is vey shocking to note here is that about 41 per cent of the total teachers are not qualified to teach in schools or are a not even graduate which is a matter to great worry.

It can be seen from the Table 4.17 that almost all teachers in various categories are professionally trained to teach at various sections of education in Gujarat. There is decrease in percentage of professionally trained teachers in 2015–16 from previous year by 0.35 per cent. The table also indicates that almost all the teachers in Gujarat have given professional trainings to teach though they are qualified or not.

Table 4.16: Details of Teachers with Academic Qualification in Different Categories (2015–16)

Sr. No.	*Category*	*Percentage of Teachers*
1.	Primary Only	22.56
2.	Primary with Upper Primary	47.39
3.	Primary with Upper Primary and Secondary and Higher Secondary	88.80
4.	Upper Primary Only	73.73
5.	Upper Primary with Secondary and Higher Secondary	93.17
6.	Primary with Upper Primary and Secondary	83.16
7.	Upper Primary with Secondary	90.93
8.	Secondary Only	99.71
9.	Secondary with Higher Secondary	99.81
10.	Higher Secondary Only	99.43
	Total Teachers 2015–16	59.06

Source: GOG (2016), U-DICE, School Education in India, 2015–16.

Table 4.17: Details about Professionally Trained Teachers (2015–16)

Sr. No.	*Category*	*Percentage of Teachers*
1.	Primary Only	99.69
2.	Primary with Upper Primary	99.54
3.	Primary with Upper Primary and Secondary and Higher Secondary	97.94
4.	Upper Primary Only	99.62
5.	Upper Primary with Secondary and Higher Secondary	99.92
6.	Primary with Upper Primary and Secondary	98.37
7.	Upper Primary with Secondary	99.50
8.	Secondary Only	99.77
9.	Secondary with Higher Secondary	99.78
10.	Higher Secondary Only	99.05
11.	Total Teachers 2015–16	99.42
12.	Total Teachers 2014–15	99.77

Source: GOG (2016), U-DICE, School Education in India, 2015–16.

4.3.6 Pupil-Teacher Ratio in Gujarat

The ideal pupil teacher ratio as per Government norms and International standards should be 15 to 20:1. It can be seen from the Table 4.18 that in primary and upper primary level, the ratio is reasonably good, but the situation is very sad in secondary and higher secondary sections (Table 4.18). This is the reason behind mushrooming of private coaching classes for students of secondary and higher secondary sections in the state. That to students finds it difficult to interact with the teachers and vice versa if the ideal ratio is not maintained by the school management or not forced for same by the State Government Education Department.

Table 4.18: Pupil-Teacher Ratio by Level (2015–16)

Sr. No.	*Level*	*Year*	*Percentage*
A.	Primary	2014–15	20
		2015–16	19
B.	Upper Primary	2014–15	13
		2015–16	13
C.	Secondary	2014–15	34
		2015–16	34
D.	Higher Secondary	2014–15	31
		2015–16	29

Source: U-DICE, School Education in India, 2015–16.

4.3.7 Dropout Rate in Gujarat

Table 4.19 shows dropout rate at primary and upper primary level over the period of 1999–00 to 2015–16 in the state of Gujarat. The dropout rate at primary and upper primary level has come down drastically due to efforts of government and awareness among rural area about importance of education for boys and girls both. The dropout rate at primary level has come down from 22.30 to just 1.74 and the same at upper primary level has come down to mere 6.34 from 41.48. This a good sign of social and economic progress of the state. Dropout rate at Secondary level is the highest (Table 4.20). Thus, tables indicate that the dropout rate in primary and upper primary is improved due to Sarva Siksha Abhiyan and Right to Education, but there is need of concrete policy measures to uplift level of education in Gujarat as well as in India.

Table 4.19: Dropout Rate in Primary Education in Gujarat State

Sr. No.	*Year*	*Std. I to V*			*Std. I to VII*		
		Boys	*Girls*	*Total*	*Boys*	*Girls*	*Total*
1.	1999–00	23.77	20.83	22.30	42.76	39.90	41.48
2.	2000–01	21.05	20.81	20.93	40.53	36.90	38.92
3.	2001–02	20.46	20.53	20.50	39.16	35.28	37.22
4.	2002–03	19.08	19.14	19.12	37.80	33.17	35.46
5.	2003–04	17.79	17.84	17.83	36.59	31.49	33.73
6.	2004–05	8.72	11.77	10.16	15.33	22.80	18.79
7.	2005–06	4.53	5.79	5.13	9.97	14.02	11.82
8.	2006–07	2.84	3.68	3.24	9.13	11.64	10.29
9.	2007–08	2.77	3.25	2.98	8.81	11.08	9.87
10.	2008–09	2.28	2.31	2.29	8.58	9.17	8.87
11.	2009–10	2.18	2.23	2.20	8.33	8.97	8.66
12.	2010–11	2.08	2.11	2.09	7.87	8.12	7.95
13.	2011–12	2.05	2.08	2.07	7.35	7.82	7.56
14.	2012–13	2.02	2.06	2.04	6.87	7.37	7.08
15.	2013–14	1.97	2.02	2.00	6.53	7.28	6.91
16.	2014–15	1.94	2.00	1.97	6.19	7.03	6.61
17.	2015–16	1.67	1.81	1.74	5.88	6.79	6.34

Source: Gujarat Council of Elementary Education (S.S.A) Gandhinagar.

Table 4.20: Dropout rate at Elementary, Secondary and Higher Secondary Level (2014–15)

Level	*Boys*	*Girls*	*Total*
Elementary	2.26	3.71	2.93
Secondary	26.29	23.24	25.04
Higher Secondary	8.40	5.26	7.04

Source: U-DICE, School Education in India, 2015–16.

4.3.8 Enrolment Ratio in Gujarat

As per definitions of U-DISE 2015–16, Gross Enrolment Ratio shows total enrolment in primary education, regardless of age, expressed as a percentage of the eligible official primary school-age population in a given school year. Net Enrolment Ratio shows enrolment in primary education of the official primary school-age group expressed as a percentage of the corresponding population. Gross enrolment ratio and net enrolment ratio at primary level in Gujarat has shown significant improvement over the period of time (Table 4.27). Efforts are made by the government to make net enrolment ratio as 100 percentage.

Table 4.21: Details on Enrolment Ratio in Primary Education in Gujarat

Sr. No.	*Year*	*Gross Enrolment Ratio (GER)*			*Net Enrolment Ratio (NER)*		
		Boys	*Girls*	*Total*	*Boys*	*Girls*	*Total*
1.	2004–05	109.68	109.39	109.54	96.06	95.23	95.65
2.	2005–06	110.68	110.39	110.54	96.56	95.73	96.15
3.	2006–07	111.78	111.49	111.64	97.83	96.23	97.03
4.	2007–08	103.11	100.84	101.98	98.17	96.67	97.42
5.	2008–09	104.00	101.72	102.86	98.58	97.07	97.82
6.	2009–10	104.67	104.34	103.51	98.82	98.04	98.29
7.	2010–11	105.03	103.12	104.08	99.06	98.23	98.64
8.	2011–12	105.08	104.20	104.64	99.08	98.53	98.80
9.	2012–13	102.06	100.87	101.47	99.54	98.97	99.25
10.	2013–14	99.74	99.70	99.72	97.12	97.30	97.21
11.	2014–15	102.85	101.96	102.40	98.68	97.90	98.29
12.	2015–16	103.17	102.37	102.63	99.05	98.22	99.11

Source: Gujarat Council of Elementary Education (S.S.A) Gandhinagar.

GER and NER are decreasing with the higher level of education (Table 4.22). That indicates that policies should be incorporated to retain students throughout the level of education. There is slight decrease in GER and NER from the year 2014–15 to 2015–16.

Table 4.22: Details on Level-wise Enrolment Ratio in Gujarat (2015–16)

Sr. No.	*Level*	*Particular*	*GER*	*NER*
A.	Primary	Boys	95.64	81.07
		Girls	99.11	84.09
		Total 2014–15	98.72	83.29
		Total 2015–16	97.24	82.46
B.	Upper Primary	Boys	94.70	72.38
		Girls	96.99	74.55
		Total 2014–15	93.56	71.36
		Total 2015–16	95.73	73.35
C.	Elementary	Boys	95.27	85.60
		Girls	98.31	88.62
		Total 2014–15	96.75	86.89
		Total 2015–16	96.66	86.98
D.	Secondary	Boys	80.26	51.53
		Girls	66.82	42.78
		Total 2014–15	74.34	47.73
		Total 2015–16	74.13	47.54
E	Higher Secondary	Boys	45.17	28.71
		Girls	41.42	26.43
		Total 2014–15	44.93	29.44
		Total 2015–16	43.43	27.65

Source: U-DICE, School Education in India, 2015–16.

4.3.9 Secondary Education Status in Gujarat

As the study is mainly based on schools offering Secondary and Higher Secondary education in Anand district, status of secondary and higher secondary education in Gujarat is analyzed and presented in Table 4.23.

It can be seen from the table that Ahmedabad, Rajkot and Surat are the top most districts having highest number of higher secondary schools, teachers and students. Anand has 328 schools offering higher secondary education with 2918 teachers and 93604 students in those schools in 2015–16.

It is very important note here about the report entitled 'The Annual Status of Education Report' (ASER), the largest annual household survey in rural India focuses on the status of children's schooling and basic learning (the project is facilitated by Pratham, an organization in the field of Education). Their recent Survey covering 779 villages, 15,557 households and 12,923 students in the age group 3–16 from government and private schools shows a sorry state of education in Gujarat *(Makwana V., Member of Pratham)*. The survey revealed that 23.4 per cent students enrolled in class 8 could not correctly read a paragraph in Gujarati, 65.2 per cent class 8 students failed to do division, 62.4 per cent class 8 students can't read English sentence. And this puts a very big question mark on quality of education in the state. Educationalists blame government, teachers and parents for this situation. They blame government due to No Detention Policy, Teachers are blamed as students want to study but teachers are indifferent to their duty and Parents are also responsible for not paying proper attention to children's studies (Rana and Dave, 2017).

Table 4.23: District-wise Secondary Education Status

Sr. No.	*District*	*2015–16*			*2016–17*		
		Schools	*Teachers*	*Students*	*Schools*	*Teachers*	*Students*
	Gujarat	10940	83662	2678648	11478	85856	2692617
1.	Kachchh	360	2217	69107	397	2259	74124
2.	Banas kantha	511	3627	122391	572	3687	125281
3.	Patan	236	1863	58638	254	1874	56752
4.	Mehsana	373	3315	101911	382	3305	101728
5.	Sabar Kantha	334	2360	67395	340	2283	63545
6.	Gandhinagar	355	3057	83632	388	3214	86274
7.	Ahmadabad	1140	9890	309614	1161	9972	309919
8.	Surendranagar	313	1911	60460	332	2011	39693
9.	Rajkot	794	5475	156111	835	5604	158825
10.	Jamnagar	277	1755	55775	293	1802	55341
11.	Porbandar	108	761	25595	120	791	25526
12.	Junagadh	429	2799	87875	436	2811	86832
13.	Amreli	289	2016	62889	300	2046	61138

Sr. No.	District	2015–16			2016–17		
		Schools	Teachers	Students	Schools	Teachers	Students
14.	Bhavnagar	380	2758	107891	416	2966	111759
15.	Anand	329	2930	99330	328	2918	93604
16.	Kheda	327	2568	88583	342	2710	84852
17.	Panch Mahals	299	2001	70473	304	2040	70559
18.	Dohad	374	2601	91030	384	2612	90091
19.	Vadodara	506	4469	132391	517	4575	134117
20.	Narmada	110	621	21485	116	665	20421
21.	Bharuch	299	2106	69773	305	2193	63856
22.	Surat	766	7573	255506	821	8070	278552
23.	The Dangs	53	273	9059	62	319	9446
24.	Navsari	194	2126	65361	204	2197	65775
25.	Valsad	270	2428	79917	289	2518	79580
26.	Tapi	144	937	32765	145	972	31798
27.	Arvali	268	1827	54847	271	1805	53405
28.	Chota Udaipur	142	880	30349	149	881	30756
29.	Mahisagar	241	1621	51099	249	1649	50482
30.	Devbhumi Dwarka	144	744	23334	160	789	24793
31.	Gir Somnath	254	1914	64584	259	1931	61903
32.	Botad	105	693	27624	121	744	28869
33.	Morbi	216	1546	41852	226	1643	43021

Source: (1) Commissionerate of Schools, Gandhinagar; (2) Rastriya Madhyamic Siksha Abhiyan (UDISE).

4.4 NUMBER OF JOB SEEKERS IN GUJARAT

The information on job seekers is given to interpret impact of education on employability. The data shows relation between quality of education and employability of students in Gujarat. Number of job seekers indicates the level of unemployment of educated persons in the state.

Table 4.24: Number of Job Seekers by Level of Education (Register with Employment Exchanges in Gujarat State)

Sr. No.	*Level of Education*	*As on 31st December*				
		1990	*2000*	*2010*	*2015*	*2016**
1.		435429	435996	219480	176435	156131
2.	Inter	81724	230074	267209	186187	173916
3.	Diploma	8766	19319	28341	47722	41569
4.	Graduates	55007	144952	246037	173938	155923
	Arts	16443	59314	103441	70194	61522
	Science	8479	23252	22887	13975	12710
	Commerce	20584	44825	47382	32069	28405
	Others	9501	17561	72327	57700	53286
5.	Engineering Graduates	4085	7579	9876	17119	17365
	Civil	2368	1892	966	1720	2112
	Mechanical	681	1689	2133	5183	5307
	Electrical	370	1589	2326	4179	4549
	Others	666	2409	4451	6037	5397
6.	Post Graduates	8129	17595	50155	38417	33795
	Arts	2355	8561	18599	12518	10722
	Science	2050	3369	7340	6513	5747
	Commerce	1891	3023	7261	5610	4851
	Others	1833	2642	16955	13776	12475
7.	Engineering Post Graduates	15	2	63	466	481
	I Total Educated Unemployed	**593155**	**855517**	**821161**	**640284**	**579180**
	II Total Uneducated Unemployed	**363826**	**212234**	**70488**	**37164**	**31476**
	Grand Total (I + II)	**956981**	**1067751**	**891649**	**677448**	**610656**

Note: *Up to October – 2016.

Source: Directorate of Employment and Training, Gujarat State, Gandhinagar.

The number of educated unemployed is more than uneducated unemployed (Table 4.24). That indicates that the problem of unemployment cannot be resolved with the help of getting more enrolments in schools. But quality of education should be improved with the help of qualified, competent and stable teachers. Higher opportunities should also be created to fight unemployment and educated persons should be motivated to start their own enterprises through lessons of entrepreneurship development.

4.5 EXPENDITURE ON EDUCATION IN GUJARAT

It can be seen from the Table 4.25 that expenditure on education has increased over the period from 2011–12 to 2015–16 on revenue and capital account.

Table 4.25: Expenditure on State Accounts (Rs. in Crore)

Sr. No.	*Item*	*2011–12*	*2012–13*	*2013–14*	*2014–15*	*2015–16 (P)*
I.	**Expenditure on Revenue Account**					
1)	Education, Sports, Art And Culture	11707.97	13078.66	14486.96	16421.11	17976.02
II.	**Expenditure on Capital Account**					
1)	Education, Sports, Art And Culture	801.89	941.82	1180.30	1328.30	1280.66

Source: Finance Department, Government of Gujarat.

The percentage allocation to Education sector has decreased in the current financial year, which questions the intention of Gujarat government to uplift the standard of education in the state.

Table 4.26: Allocation to Education in State Budget

Financial Year	*Total Budget*	*Percentage Allocation to Education*
2017–18	1.72 lakh crores	14.1 per cent
2018–19	1.83 lakh crores	13.9 per cent

Source: Budget Summary, http://financedepartment.gujarat.gov.in

4.6 CHAPTER SUMMARY

In this Chapter, all the information on almost all parameters related to status of education in Gujarat and in selected district is presented and discussed. As per the data on population, it is evident that majority of population in Gujarat and Anand is in rural area. The Annual Status of Education Report' (ASER) shows a sorry state of education in Gujarat. The survey revealed that 23.4 per cent students enrolled in class 8 could not correctly read a paragraph in Gujarati, 65.2 per cent class 8 students failed to do division, 62.4 per cent class 8 students can't read English sentence. And this puts a very big question mark on quality of education in the state. Educationalists blame government, teachers and parents for this situation. They blame government due to No Detention Policy, Teachers are blamed as students want to study but teachers are indifferent to their duty and Parents are also responsible for not paying proper attention to children's studies. State plays critical role in overall development of the nation. But if quality of education and rate of employment is not taken in to consideration adequately, the development cannot be sustainable.

CHAPTER 5

Attrition of Teacher: Management Perspectives

5.1 INTRODUCTION

As mentioned in the earlier Chapter, total 22 schools are covered in the study from Anand District of Gujarat. Out of those 22 schools, 19 schools are un-aided (self-financed) private schools and 3 are aided private schools. For the purpose of survey to know the perspectives of management on retention issue, management perusal or representative of management of the particular school was contacted and interviewed personally.

As required by the land of law, all of the private schools are administered by the Trusts registered under Societies Registration Act. These trusts are pioneered and initiated by educationalists, business people or social groups in Anand district. Management pays keen attention towards functioning of the school. Unfortunately, it was observed that most of the schools management less focus on the quality of education through having adequate and quality teachers and intervenes in the matters pertaining to finance or budget. There is a trend to appoint professional Campus Director in the School premises to monitor functioning of the school. Most of the management personnel of the schools are not from the field of education, so they have to rely on professionally trained campus directors, Chief Executive Officers (CEOs) or even they outsource the management to experts.

Management of the schools are directly involved in issues related to land acquisition, school building, school infrastructure, contracts with agencies, canteen management, fund raising, donation management, promotional practices, recruitment and selection of teaching and non-teaching staff, financial audit and any other prominent problems to be resolved at higher level.

The management personal or their representatives were contacted and interviewed on the following aspects.

5.2 Schools Related Information

The first session in the schedule for management is to fetch some important information on aspects related to schools from the management. The selected school information from management is presented in Table 5.1 and discussed below.

Table 5.1: School Information from Management

<table>
<tr><th colspan="3" rowspan="2">Particulars</th><th colspan="2">Fully Funded</th><th colspan="2">Self-Financed</th></tr>
<tr><th>(n=03)</th><th>%</th><th>(n=19)</th><th>%</th></tr>
<tr><td rowspan="6">Year of Estab-lishment</td><td colspan="2">1960–1970</td><td>1</td><td>33.33</td><td>1</td><td>5.26</td></tr>
<tr><td colspan="2">1970–1980</td><td>2</td><td>66.67</td><td>1</td><td>5.26</td></tr>
<tr><td colspan="2">1980–1990</td><td>–</td><td>–</td><td>2</td><td>10.52</td></tr>
<tr><td colspan="2">1990–2000</td><td>–</td><td>–</td><td>4</td><td>21.05</td></tr>
<tr><td colspan="2">2000–2010</td><td>–</td><td>–</td><td>7</td><td>36.84</td></tr>
<tr><td colspan="2">2010–2020</td><td>–</td><td>–</td><td>4</td><td>21.05</td></tr>
<tr><td rowspan="6">Sections in School</td><td colspan="2">Pre Primary</td><td>2</td><td>66.67</td><td>16</td><td>84.21</td></tr>
<tr><td colspan="2">Primary</td><td>2</td><td>66.67</td><td>17</td><td>89.47</td></tr>
<tr><td colspan="2">Secondary</td><td>2</td><td>66.67</td><td>19</td><td>100</td></tr>
<tr><td rowspan="3">Higher Secondary</td><td>Science</td><td>1</td><td>33.33</td><td>16</td><td>84.21</td></tr>
<tr><td>Commerce</td><td>2</td><td>66.67</td><td>14</td><td>73.68</td></tr>
<tr><td>Arts</td><td>2</td><td>66.67</td><td>0</td><td>0</td></tr>
<tr><td rowspan="4">Boards in School</td><td colspan="2">A. State Board</td><td>3</td><td>100</td><td>14</td><td>73.68</td></tr>
<tr><td colspan="2">B. CBSE</td><td>–</td><td>–</td><td>5</td><td>26.31</td></tr>
<tr><td colspan="2">C. ICSE</td><td>–</td><td>–</td><td>–</td><td>–</td></tr>
<tr><td colspan="2">D. IB</td><td>–</td><td>–</td><td>–</td><td>–</td></tr>
</table>

Source: Field survey data.

5.2.1 Year of Establishment

Out of three aided private schools, one was established before 1970 and the other two were established between 1970 and 1980. While out of 19 self-financed private schools, 11 were established after the year 2000, four of them started between 1990 and 2000; two were initiated during 1980–1990 and two were started before 1980. This indicates that more than 78 per cent of selected self-financed private schools were established after

2000, which may be due to failure of government schools to improve quality of education and ability of parents to afford costly education for their children in the State. Besides, demand for English medium self-financed private schools have increased in urban as well as rural area of the district over the period of time.

5.2.2 Sections of Education

Out of three aided selected private schools of the district, two have all the sections of education, viz. pre-primary, primary, upper primary, secondary and higher secondary. Out of those 2, one has stream of science and commerce in higher secondary and another has streams of commerce and arts in higher secondary section. Out of 3, one school has only higher secondary section of education with stream of Commerce and Arts.

Out of 19 unaided selected private schools, about 84 percent schools have pre-primary section, about 89 percent schools have primary section and all the selected schools have secondary section. Out of 19 unaided private schools, about 84 percent schools have science stream in higher secondary section while about 74 percent of them have commerce stream in higher secondary section. None of self-financed english medium schools have arts stream and that is a reason behind very few students opting for humanities in higher education in the district.

5.2.3 Board Affiliation

All the three aided private schools have affiliation with Gujarat State Education Board (GSEB). While out of 19 self-financed private schools, 74 percent schools are affiliated with Gujarat State Education Board and remaining 26 of them have affiliation with Central Board of Secondary Education. There is no school having affiliation with international boards like, The Indian Certificate of Secondary Education (ICSE), International Baccalaureate (IB) or The International General Certificate of Secondary Education (IGCSE). Thus, most of the schools of the district are governed by state board and few newly started English medium schools are affiliated to CBSE board.

5.3 DEMOGRAPHIC INFORMATION OF REPRESENTATIVES

Characteristics of management representatives can be inferred through their demographic details. Second part of the schedule is designed to understand attributes of school managements in Anand district. As mentioned earlier, managing trustee, member of managing board of the school, campus director or principal were interviewed to find out their views on the problem of attrition of teachers in private schools of the district. The demographic information of management personal/ respondents are presented in Table 5.2.

Table 5.2: Demographic Information of Management

Particulars		*Fully Funded*		*Self-Financed*	
		(n=03)	*Per cent*	*(n=19)*	*Per cent*
Designation	A. Principal	3	100	14	73.68
	B. Director	–	–	4	21.05
	C. Vice-Principal	–	–	–	–
	D. Management Representative	–	–	1	5.26
Average Age (in years)		53	–	46	–
Gender	A. Male	3	100	16	84.21
	B. Female	–	–	3	15.79
Highest Qualification	B.Ed.	2	66.67	12	63.16
	M.Ed.	–	–	2	10.53
	Ph.D.	1	33.33	1	5.26
	Others	–	–	4	21.05
Average Years in Service		28	–	18	94.74
Average Years in the School		9	–	10	52.63

Source: Field survey data.

5.3.1 Designation of the Respondent

All the three respondents of private aided schools are Principals of the schools. While three fourth of respondents from unaided private schools are Principals and two fifth were holding a position of Campus Directors. Only one school management representative from the self-financed schools was interviewed. Thus, table data indicate that the trend of appointing Campus Director is new and emerging in unaided private schools.

5.3.2 Information on Age and Gender

The respondent of self-financed private school was little younger than respondent of aided private school. The average age of the principals responded from aided private schools was 53 years while it was about 46 years in case of management representatives from unaided private schools. This shows that the personnel holding the leading positions in the management of the schools in aided private schools are older than that of unaided private schools. The dominance of male in administration of schools can be seen from the fact that all the respondents in the private aided schools were males. While in case of self-financed private schools, 84 per cent of respondents were male and reaming were female. This indicates that most of the managerial positions are acquired by males in private schools of Anand District.

5.3.3 Highest Qualification and Experience

In case of aided private schools under study, two third of respondents had the highest qualification as B.Ed. while one third possess Ph.D. degree. Around 63 per cent of the respondents from unaided private schools have highest qualification as B.Ed., about 11 percent of them are qualified as M.Ed., about 5 per cent of has highest qualification as Ph.D. and remaining respondents have qualifications as M.B.A., B. Tech. and other professional qualifications.

It can be seen from the table that average years of experience of management representatives of aided private schools in the teaching profession was 28 years, while same was hardly 18 years for management representatives of self-financed private schools. This shows that management personnel at aided private schools are more experienced than that of unaided private schools. However, average years of experience in the school where they are working currently was lower in case of aided private schools (9 years) than management personal of self-financed private schools (10 years). Management representatives of aided private schools have left the previous schools to hold leading positions in the current schools. Most of the leaders in unaided private schools are more stable.

5.4 PUPIL-TEACHER RATIO (PTR)

Pupil-Teacher ratio is one of the most important factors to decide on quality of education in any State or district. As shown in the previous chapter, PTR of Secondary Section was 34 and in Higher Secondary Section, same was 29 in state of Gujarat in the year 2015–16 as per DISE statistics. It can be seen from the table 5.3 that per school average number of students in aided private schools was estimated to be 524 students (combining all the classes of secondary and higher secondary section), while same figure was 343 in case of self-financed private schools. That indicates number of students enrolled in aided private schools were more than that of self-financed private schools may be due high cost of education in self-financed schools.

Table 5.3: Pupil-Teacher Ratio in the School

Particulars	*Fully funded*	*Self-financed*
Avg. No. of Students	524	343
Avg. Male Teachers	13	11
Avg. Female Teachers	6	10
Avg. Total Teachers	19	21
Avg. Pupil/Teacher Ratio	27.57	16.33

Source: Field survey data.

Average number of teachers teaching in secondary and higher secondary section in aided private schools were 19 in three aided private schools covered under study, out of which 68 percent were male and remaining were female teachers. However, in case of unaided private schools, on an average 21 teachers are on board of which almost male and female teachers have equal share in total. The number of male teachers is more in aided private schools because of high pay and job security in aided schools. Males are considered as primary source of income in any household, so they are in search of secured and highly paid jobs. In unaided private schools, they pay less and there is no job security. Female teachers are in the profession to pursue a balanced career as secondary source of income. Female teachers are mostly in the profession to support main earning person of the household. That may be the reason behind more number of female teachers in unaided private schools that in aided private schools.

Further, it can be seen from the table that on an average Pupil-Teacher Ratio of aided private schools covered under study from Anand district as 27.57, which is less than that of Gujarat state average but higher than what is desired as per government norms. While average PTR of unaided private schools covered under study from Anand district was 16.33, which is less than that of Gujarat state and almost equal to desired ratio as per government norms. Unaided private schools can afford to keep more number of teachers at lower pay. Thus, aided private schools are better PTR ratio than self-financed private schools in Anand district.

5.5 Factors Considered for Selection of Teachers

The responses of management personal or his/her representatives on various factors which they consider while selecting any teacher for the school are recorded and presented in Table 5.4. The respondents were asked to rank each factor on the scale of 1 to 8 (1 indicates the most important factor and 8 indicates the least important factor). They were allowed to assign same rate to more than 1 factor if they feel so. The responses from aided and unaided private schools are combined and recorded.

Table 5.4: Factors Considered for Selection of Teachers

	Factors	*Responses (% to total) - Ranked*							
		1	*2*	*3*	*4*	*5*	*6*	*7*	*8*
A.	Friendliness and Congeniality	27.3	36.4	9.1	–	18.2	–	4.6	4.5
B.	A Good Personality	27.3	13.6	31.8	13.6	–	13.6	–	–
C.	Confidence and Perfection	54.6	13.6	4.6	18.2	–	–	4.6	4.5
D.	Deep Knowledge and with a higher qualification	68.2	13.6	9.1	–	4.6	–	4.6	–
E.	A Good Communicator	36.4	36.4	4.6	–	4.6	9.1	4.6	4.5
F.	A Good Listener	36.4	4.6	9.1	13.6	13.6	9.1	9.1	4.5
G.	A Good Sense of Humor	22.7	18.2	9.1	9.1	4.6	9.1	4.6	22.7
H.	Kindness	36.4	9.1	4.6	13.6	9.1	9.1	13.6	4.5
I.	Civic responsibilities	4.6	–	–	–	–	–	–	–
J.	Classroom management	4.6	–	–	–	–	–	–	–
K.	Confidence and perfection	4.6	–	–	–	–	–	–	–
L.	Healthy and fit to teach	4.6	–	–	–	–	–	–	–
M.	Loyalty	4.6	–	–	–	–	–	–	–

Note: 1 indicates the most important factor and 8 indicates the least important factor.

Source: Field Survey Data.

1. ***Friendliness and Congeniality***: The factor is defined as quality of person to be friendly and pleasant with other stakeholders. It was observed that out of 22 schools representatives, 27.3 percent management representatives of private schools ranked it most important while 36.4 per cent have ranked it second most important factor in selecting any teacher.
2. ***Good Personality:*** The factor is defined as good attributes of personality while dealing with others. It is not only outer appearances but also inner attributes of personality. It was observed that 27.3 percent of respondents ranked it as most important factor followed by 31.8 per cent ranked same on third positions. The first four rank together accounts for more than 86 per cent of responses for this factor.
3. ***Confidence and Perfection:*** The factor is defined as confidence level of the candidate while teaching in the class and handling other important work and with how much perfection he/she does the work assigned to him/her. Field survey data shows that out of selected 22 respondents, more than half (54.6 %) respondents noted this factor as the most important while selecting a teacher for the school. Around 18 percent and 13 percent respondents ranked this factor as fourth and second most important factor while selecting teachers.
4. ***Deep Knowledge and with a higher qualification:*** The factor is to understand how deeply a candidate knows his respective subject and the highest qualification he/she has earned in that subject. The 68.2 percent of total respondents have ranked this factor as most important factor while selecting teacher. About 14 percent of respondents ranked it as second important factor.
5. ***A Good Communicator:*** The factors judges verbal and non-verbal communication skills of the candidate while teaching and dealing with other stake holders in English or any other language pertaining to his subject. He/she should be clear and understandable in teaching. Around 36 percent of responses ranked this factor at position one and two as most important factor while selecting a teacher for their schools.
6. ***A Good Listener:*** The factor is defined as a quality of teachers to listen and solve queries of students, how well they can listen to commands of management and complaints of parents. Out of the total respondents, 36.4 per cent of respondents find this factor as the most important while selecting teachers for the school.

7. ***A Good Sense of Humor:*** The factor is defined as candidate's sense of humor while conducting a class in pleasant environment. His ability to convert boring lessons in to fun-filled classes is judged. Out of total respondents, 22.7 per cent responses favor this as important while same number of responses consider this factor as least important factor to select a teacher for the school.
8. ***Kindness***: The factor is defined as how kind a teacher is when dealing with the students, parents and management. Good Teachers are expected to be kind and empathetic while teaching. Out of the respondents, 36.4 respondents find the factor as the most important while selecting a teacher, while last three positions put together about 27 percent respondents does not find this factor important at all.

Other than the factors defined and analyzed above, five other factors are noted to be important as per responses while selecting a teacher for the school. Those five factors are: Civic responsibilities, Classroom management, Confidence and perfection, Healthy and fit to teach and Loyalty.

5.6 FACILITIES AND INCENTIVES PROVIDED TO TEACHERS

In this sections information on facilities, perquisites and monetary/non-monetary incentives provided to teachers were collected and analyzed. The respondents were asked to give their responses on the lists of facilities available and incentives given to teachers at their schools.

It can be seen from the Table 5.5 that aided private schools had provided relative better facilities as compared to its counterpart. The important facilities such as provident fund, gratuity, medical allowances, maternity leaves, counseling center, rest room, personal lockers, separate staff cubicles, festival celebration, staff picnic, health insurance, and sport events were available/provided by the aided private schools to their teachers. However, in case of self-financed private college, not all the teachers have received above mentioned facilities.

Table 5.5: Facilities and Incentives Provided by the School

Sr. No.	Particulars	Fully Funded		Self-Financed	
		(n=03)	%	(n=19)	%
(I)	**Facilities provided by the school**				
	A. Canteen	1	33.33	14	73.68
	B. Information & Communication Technology	1	33.33	17	89.47
	C. Counseling Center	3	100.0	15	78.95
	D. Rest Room	3	100.0	16	84.21
	E. Personal Lockers	3	100.0	17	89.47
	F. Separate Staff cubicles	3	100.0	16	84.21
	G. Transportation	1	33.33	7	36.84
	H. Teachers Resources Center	2	66.67	16	84.21
	I. Medical Facilities	2	66.67	16	84.21
	J. Recreation Center	–	–	9	47.37
	K. Any other				
	50% concession on fees of kids of teachers	–	–	1	5.26
	Free education to kids of teachers	–	–	1	5.26
	Tie up with hospital for medical benefits to Senior teacher	–	–	1	5.26
(II)	**Perquisites/incentives provided by the school**				
	A. Flexi Timing	–	–	5	26.32
	B. Staff Credit Co-op. Society	1	33.33	5	26.32
	C. Provident Fund	3	100.0	14	73.68
	D. Housing	1	33.33	6	31.58
	E. Gratuity	3	100.0	9	47.37
	F. Telephone Allowance	–	–	1	5.26
	G. Medical Allowances	3	100.0	9	47.37
	H. Study Leaves	2	66.67	13	68.42
	I. Festival celebration	3	100.0	17	89.47
	J. Privilege Leaves	1	33.33	8	42.11

Sr. No.	*Particulars*	*Fully Funded*		*Self-Financed*	
		(n=03)	*%*	*(n=19)*	*%*
	K. Gifts	1	33.33	14	73.68
	L. Staff picnic	3	100.0	15	78.95
	M. Health Insurance	3	100.0	3	15.79
	N. Paternity Leaves	1	33.33	9	47.37
	O. Maternity Leaves	3	100.0	15	78.95
	P. Sport Events	3	100.0	15	78.95
	Q. Coupons	1	33.33	–	–
	R. Performance Recognition	2	66.67	15	78.95
	S. Any other				
	50% concession in fees of kids of teachers	–	–	2	10.53
	Casual leaves(1.5 days per month)	–	–	2	10.53
	Conveyance allowance	–	–	1	5.26
	Duty leave, medical leave	–	–	2	10.53
	Encashment of leaves	–	–	2	10.53
	Free education to kids of teachers	–	–	1	5.26
	House Rent Allowance	–	–	1	5.26
	Vacation	–	–	1	5.26

Source: Field Survey Data.

5.6.1 Facilities

A. **Canteen:** About one third of total aided private schools has canteen in the school premises, while three fourth of total unaided private schools have canteens in the school premises. Most of the canteens are run by third party contractors.

B. **ICT (Information and Communication Technology):** About one third of selected aided private schools have ICT facility in campus to help teachers to upgrade their style of teaching. However, about 90% unaided private schools have ICT facilities, like smart classes, laptops, separate computer lab for teachers etc. to enable them to match world standards in teaching.

C. **Counseling Center:** All the selected aided private schools under study have counseling centers for teachers, while about 79 per cent unaided private schools provide counseling services to teachers to resolve their personal or professional stress and it is done mostly by professional counselor, management representatives or principal.

D. **Rest Room:** All the aided private schools have separate rest rooms for teachers for relaxation during working hours. While about 85 per cent of total unaided private schools have separate rest rooms for teachers with pantry and washroom facilities.

E. **Personal Lockers:** All the selected aided private schools provide personal lockers to teachers to store their valuable study materials, documents or personal belongings. Same facility was available in about 90 per cent unaided private schools assign personal lockers to teachers to safeguard important study materials or any other work related documents.

F. **Separate Staff Cubicles:** All the selected aided private schools have provision of separate sitting place to each teacher within the staff room. While about 85 per cent unaided private schools covered under the study have designed the staffroom to provide separate table to each teacher with the staff room/hall.

G. **Transportation Facility:** About one third of total aided private schools provide transportation facility to their teachers. Almost same number of unaided private schools provide to and fro services to the teachers through school buses or separate staff vans. Some of the unaided private schools have made it compulsory for the teachers to commute through school buses only. Some of the unaided private schools reimburse the expenses of transportation.

H. **Teachers Resources Center:** About two third of selected total aided private schools have facility of teachers resource centers within the library or in separate room. In case of unaided private schools, 84.21 per cent schools provide separate place within the school library or separate teachers resource room to upgrade knowledge of teachers in their respective subjects with reading room, computers and internet facilities.

I. **Medical Facilities:** About two third of selected total aided private schools provide medical facilities in the form of on-campus doctor, visiting doctor, medical room and first-aid box to teachers. While about 55 per cent unaided private schools provide medical assistance to the teachers in the premises or by having tie-up with nearby hospital to the teachers.

J. **Recreation Center:** None of the aided private schools provide the facility of recreation Center to their teachers, while 47.37 per cent unaided private schools have recreation Centers for their teachers to pursue their interest in any arts or sports. The center also organizes various events like music concert, sports day, staff picnics, family get-together etc. to refresh their teachers. Such activities of the center improve their productivity and they be more committed to their respective schools.

On being asked about any other facilities provided to teachers in the schools, other than what is discussed above; they mention the following facilities provided by unaided private schools to their teachers:

- Concession on fees of kids of teachers
- Tie up with hospital for medical benefits to Senior teacher.

Thus, except few important facilities, unaided private schools have provided relatively better facilities than that of aided private schools, though the salary may be lower for teachers of unaided private schools.

5.6.2 Incentives

A. **Flexi Timing:** None of the aided private schools provide facility of flexi-time to their teachers, as they are bound by government norms, when it comes to timing of the school. Only 26.32 per cent of unaided private schools allow flexi-time to their teachers, where they have to complete their working hours scheduled as per their own convenience, without any fixed in and out timing. Here, it is assumed that their duty is to complete the syllabus and other assigned duties irrespective of timing of the school.

B. **Staff Credit Co-operative Society:** About one third of aided private schools have Staff credit cooperative society to manage savings of the teachers and provide the required amount to needy staff member at lower interest rates. while 26.32 per cent of unaided private schools have Staff Credit Co-operative society run by and for the teachers to provide financial credits.

C. **Provident Fund:** All the teachers of aided private schools are covered under Provident Fund as they are on the role of government and covered under all government policies for their employees. While

73.68 per cent of unaided private schools provide provident fund to their employees without any government assistant.

D. **Housing:** 33.33 per cent (1 of 3) of aided private schools covered under study proving housing to staff members. The management of the school has built houses for the staff members for the schools covered under the umbrella of Charutar Vidhya Mandal. 31.58 per cent (6 of 19) unaided private schools provide staff quarters to their staff members with nominal rent to motivate them to remain with the school for long.

E. **Gratuity:** Teachers of all of the aided private schools are covered under Gratuity Act of Government. 47.37 per cent (9 of 19) unaided private schools covered under study provide benefit of Gratuity to their teachers.

F. **Telephone Allowance:** None of the aided private schools covered under study give Telephone Allowances to their teachers and only 1 out of 19 unaided private schools give telephone allowances to their teachers. This allowances is given only to the privilege teachers holding or performing special duties for the development of the school.

G. **Medical Allowances:** All the three aided private schools pay medical allowances under the head of incentives to their teachers as per government norms. Only 47.37 per cent of unaided private schools pay medical allowances as a part of salary under the head of special incentives, other schools provide other type of medical benefits, like tie-up with hospitals, annual medical check-ups etc.

H. **Study Leaves:** Two third of aided private schools provides study leaves to their teachers to pursue higher qualifications related to their profession, while about 69 per cent unaided private schools sanction study leaves to teachers who aspire to earn higher qualification to upgrade their knowledge of their respective subjects. Most of the teachers appointed in unaided private schools are not qualified at the time of joining the school, so they are given this benefit to get them qualifications required to continue in teaching profession.

I. **Festival Celebration:** All of the aided schools covered under the study celebrate all important festivals of various religions throughout the year to develop special bond with their teachers. About 90 per cent of the unaided private schools celebrate all important festivals throughout the year with teachers and students both to provide them homely atmosphere in their respective school.

J. **Privilege Leaves:** About one third of aided private schools provide privilege leaves once in a year to their teachers, while about 42 per cent of unaided private schools sanction privilege leaves once in a year for their teachers. This type of leaves can be clubbed with any other type of official leaves given to teachers.

K. **Gifts:** About one third of aided private schools distribute gifts among their teachers on special occasions, like Diwali, New Year, Birthdays, School Foundation day etc. However, in case unaided private schools, 73.68 (16 of 19) schools distribute gifts to their teachers on special occasions throughout the year. In most of the cases, gifts are given in the forms of Yearly Diary, pen, book, box of sweets, chocolate box etc.

L. **Staff Picnic:** Annual picnics are organized in all the aided private schools under study from Anand district, while 78.95 per cent schools organize staff picnics once or twice in a year. Such picnics can be with family or only for staff members. It can be one day, two days or even a long tour. It can be organized by staff members themselves or by third party agent. Such picnics are needed to create family like working environment among the teachers.

M. **Health Insurance:** All the teachers of all the aided private schools are covered under the benefit of Health Insurance. They may opt for various schemes of insurance agency for benefits during illness. Only 15.79 per cent unaided private schools provide benefit of health insurance to their teachers to get reimbursement in case of severe illness. It may be given to all or few competent teachers as a special benefit for their extraordinary performance.

N. **Paternity Leaves:** About one third of selected total aided private schools allow male teachers to take paternity leaves for 15 days after the birth of baby. However, 47.37 unaided private schools sanction paternity leaves of 15 days for male teachers after birth of their baby to take care of baby and mother. This benefit has been a need as families have become nuclear now a days.

O. **Maternity Leaves:** All aided private schools covered under study allow female teachers to take maternity leaves for 26 weeks as per amended law of maternity leaves. While 78.95 per cent of unaided private schools sanction maternity leaves of 26 weeks for female teachers. Number of leaves sanctioned can be different for unaided private schools as it is not statutory for them to grant maternity leaves. Those, who are not granting maternity leaves have to at least allow pregnant female teachers to be at home without pay.

P. **Sport Events:** All the aided private schools covered under study organize sport events for their teachers on sports day along with students or separate sport events. About 79 per cent of unaided private schools organize sport events for their teachers to keep them healthy and fit for the profession.

Q. **Coupons:** About one third of aided private schools provided shopping coupons from their school. None of the schools from the category of unaided private schools give coupons to their teachers. This benefit is common in corporate houses where coupons like Sodexo are given to get them redeemed for any shopping requirements.

R. **Performance Recognition:** About two third of total aided private schools recognize extra ordinary performances of their teachers through monetary and non-monetary incentives, while 78.95 per cent schools from the category of unaided private schools recognize efforts of teachers towards betterment of school. Performance can be recognized through special award, hike in salary, promotion, special gift hamper, bonus, praising in front of colleagues, teacher of the year award at Annual day of the school etc. This is essential to motivate employees to improve their performance and also to control attrition.

Management representatives were asked if they provide any other incentives or perquisites other than mentioned above, some of them mentioned following incentives provided to their teachers other than what are included in the list.

- 50 per cent concession in fees of kids of teachers
- Casual leaves (1.5 days per month)
- Conveyance allowance
- Duty leave and Medical leave
- Encashment of leaves
- Free education to kids of teachers
- House Rent Allowance
- Vacation

5.7 FACTORS TO CONTROL ATTRITION OF TEACHERS

The management representatives were asked to provide their responses to control attrition of teachers in private schools. They were allowed to tick on more than one factor. The responses are analyzed, presented and discussed here (Table 5.6).

5.7.1 DEFINITIONS OF THE FACTORS

A. **Salaries:** Salaries can be defined as total amount received at the end of the month as a reward of their efforts. It includes various components as Basic, Dearness Allowances, House Rent Allowances, PF, Gratuity, Bonus etc.

B. **Incentives:** Incentives are defined as monetary benefits received by teachers other than regular salary based on their performances. It can be monetary as well as non-monetary.

C. **Support System:** Support system can be understood as support of management, principal, colleagues, students and parents in performing duties of teachers and getting desired outcomes at the end.

D. **Timing:** Timing means time at which school starts and time at which school ends. It also means total number of working hours in a school. Timing of the school should be convenient for all types of teachers teaching at the school.

E. **Pleasant Environment:** Pleasant environment is defined as friendly working environment within the school created by management, principal, teachers and students. The working environment of the school should be happy and healthy.

F. **Training:** Trainings means on-the job and off-the job training and development programmes organized by the school for the teachers for their professional development in the field of teaching. Such trainings can be organized by the school or any other consultancy working in the field of training teachers.

Table 5.6: Factors to Control Attrition of Teachers

Characteristics	*Fully Funded*		*Self-Financed*	
	(n=03)	%	*(n=19)*	%
A. Salaries	3	100.00	17	89.47
B. Incentives	1	33.33	15	78.95
C. Support system	2	66.67	16	84.21
D. Timings	3	100.00	14	73.68
E. Pleasant environment	2	66.67	19	100.0
F. Training	3	100.00	16	84.21
G. Attachment with students	3	100.00	15	78.95
H. Any Other	–		–	

Source: Field survey data.

G. **Attachment with Students:** Attachment with students can be understood as how strong the psychological bond shared with students by teachers. Whether teachers are committed to imparting knowledge to their students for their better future or not. Whether teachers are approachable for students in case of problems related to study or personal issues. Whether teachers understand their first priority towards students while at schools. These are the parameters to measure attachment of teachers with students.

5.7.2 Responses on Important Factors

It can be seen from Table 5.6 that the respondents of all three aided private schools covered under study considered salaries, timings, training and attachment with students are the most important factors to control turnover of teachers. Out of three aided private schools, two schools managers feel that support system and pleasant working environment can help reduce attrition of teachers in their schools. Only one school respondent manager finds incentives as important factor to control turnover of teachers. They all feel that stable teacher is prerequisite for long term success of any private schools. They implement various measures to retain qualified, trained and competent teachers for long term.

All of the management representatives of unaided private schools feel that pleasant environment is the most important factor to control attrition. While about 90 per cent managers of unaided private schools feel that salaries play important role to control turnover of teachers. Next important factors are support system and training, incentives and attachment with students. About 74 percent respondents noted that timing of schools is important to retain teachers for long.

5.8 IMPORTANT FACTORS TO RETAIN TEACHERS

In order to retain teachers, managers were asked to give their responses on what are the factors you feel important to control attrition and rate them on a scale of 1 to 9. As mentioned earlier, 1 indicates the most important and 9 indicates the least important factor. Same rating can be given to more than one factor, if they feel they all are equally important to retaining experienced teachers for long. The responses received are presented in Table 5.7 and discussed below:

Table 5.7: Important Factors for Retaining Teachers

	Factors	*Factors for Retaining Teachers (per cent)*								
		1	*2*	*3*	*4*	*5*	*6*	*7*	*8*	*9*
(a)	Working Conditions	68.2	13.6	9.1	–	9.1	–	–	–	–
(b)	Induction and Monitoring Programs	31.8	22.7	18.2	–	4.6	–	9.1	9.1	4.6
(c)	Recruitment Strategies and Policies	50.0	18.2	13.6	4.6	–	4.6	–	4.6	4.6
(d)	Performance Appraisal	45.5	4.6	–	13.6	–	9.1	–	4.6	22.7
(e)	Motivation	50.0	18.2	4.6	13.6	4.6	–	4.6	–	4.6
(f)	Recognition	45.5	27.3	9.1	–	4.6	–	4.6	4.6	4.6
(g)	Decision making involvement	36.4	22.7	9.1	–	13.6	9.1	4.6	–	4.6
(h)	Roles and Responsibilities	59.1	18.2	4.6	4.6	–	9.1	–	4.6	–
(i)	Facilities	36.4	22.7	–	13.6	9.1	4.6	9.1	–	4.6

Source: Field survey data.

A. **Working Conditions:** Working conditions means friendly and convenient working environment in the school for their teachers. About 68.18 per cent respondents mentioned that working environment of the school is the most important factor, while 13.64 per cent of them assign it second rank. Thus, this factor is considered important by all the management representatives.

B. **Induction and Monitoring Programs:** The factor means orientation program for newly appointed teachers to get them acquainted with the school and their monitoring by principal and senior teachers till they become fully involved with functioning of the school. It was observed that 31.72 per cent respondents found this factor as the most important to retain teachers for long. About 23 and 18 percent respondents ranked it second and third position. While 4.55 per cent mentioned that this factor the least important to serve the purpose.

C. **Recruitment strategies and Policies:** The factor defines the steps from advertising the vacancies till getting the candidate on board. Half of the selected respondents felt that this factor as the most important to control teachers' turnover. About 18 and 14 per cent respondents ranked it second and third important factor respectively.

Only 4.55 per cent of the respondents noted that the factor as the least important to retain teachers.

D. **Performance Appraisal:** This factor speaks about steps adopted by the management to evaluate performance of the teachers on predetermined parameters and to reward their performances accordingly. About 46 per cent of the respondents opined that this factor is the most important to solve the problem of attrition of teachers, followed by 4.55 per cent assigned it second rank and 13.64 per cent of them rate it at fourth position as important factor. It was very important to note here is that about 23 per cent of total respondents mentioned that this factor is not at all important in retention of teachers.

E. **Motivation:** Motivation to teachers can be understood as motivational practices adopted by management to make teachers improve their performance and stay with the school for long. Such motivational practices can be monetary or non-monetary. Half of the selected management personals opined that motivation is also one of the most important factors to retain teachers, while 18.18 per cent of the respondents rate the factor with 2nd rating.

F. **Recognition:** Recognition means award or reward for extra ordinary performance of any teachers for betterment of the school or its students. Recognition of special efforts can motivate teachers to perform with best of their capabilities. About 46 per cent of the total respondents mentioned that this factor as the most important factor to retain teachers for a long. Significant number of respondents (27.27 per cent) backed this factor on second rank, while 4.55 per cent of the respondents do not find the factor important at all to control attrition.

G. **Decision making involvement:** The factor speaks about participation of teachers in important decisions related to teachers or any other stakeholders of the school. Whether opinion of teachers is considered while making important decision related school decides commitment of teachers towards school. About 37 per cent of the management representatives opined that this is one of the most important factors to retain teachers followed by 23 per cent of them assign it second positions.

H. **Roles and Responsibilities:** The factor can be understood as roles and responsibilities assign to teachers. Whether roles and responsibilities of teachers are critical or important for smooth functioning of the school decides level of commitment of teachers towards betterment of school. Relatively quite a high number of respondent managers (59.09 per cent) found this factor as the most important factor to retain teachers.

I. **Facilities:** Facilities provided to teachers on campus have direct connection with their performance. If more number of facilities provided at schools, working of those schools become convenient and teachers desire to enjoy those facilities for a long. About 37 per cent of the management representatives found this factor as the most important to control attrition of teachers. 22.73 per cent of them rate the factor with 2nd rating. Only 4.55 per cent of the respondents find the factor as the least important to retain teachers for long in the school.

5.9 HUMAN RESOURCE PRACTICES ADOPTED

In this section what all practices are adopted from recruitment to retirement of the teachers by school management are recorded and evaluated. Human resource strategies and practices for teachers are analyzed and discussed as below. The responses are presented in Tables 5.8 to 5.13 and discussed below.

5.9.1 Recruitment Strategies

All the aided as well as self-financed private schools under study advertised the teaching vacancies through newspapers. One third of aided and almost half of the self-financed schools also consider references of existing teachers while filling up of vacancies. All of the unaided private schools advertise vacancies of teaching positions through Newspapers. The self-financed private schools advertise vacancies also through online job portals and also take help of recruitment consultancies to fill up teaching positions.

5.9.2 Demographic Characteristics (Teachers)

Special demographic characteristics of the teachers such as qualification and past qualifications are considered in the teachers by both kind of schools, while age also taken into consideration while selecting teachers by self-financed schools.

5.9.3 Importance of Salary

About two third of aided private schools covered under study from Anand district felt that salary is important to control attrition by and large, while about 69 per cent of unaided private schools consider salary and related factors important to retain teachers for long in any school. Others do not find salary important to resolve the problem.

5.9.4 Selection Tools for Teachers

Respondents from management category were asked to tick all the selection tools used by them while selecting a teacher for the school. The selection process of aided private schools under study follows only two steps while selecting a teaching candidate for their schools, i.e. organize panel interview and demo lectures. The panel is comprised of management representatives, external subject experts, principal, existing senior teacher of the subject or even government representatives in case of aided private schools. Teachers were asked to give demo lecture to check performance of a probable candidate in the class on various parameters like class management, communication skills, subject knowledge, style of teaching and students feedback on the candidate.

While in case of selection tools used in unaided private schools, besides organization of panel interview to select a teacher., 84.21 per cent of self-financed private schools check references of the candidates to enquire on past employment history and reason for leaving the previous job; 31.58 per cent of them conduct written test for the candidates to check their subject knowledge; 5.26 per cent of them even conduct psychometric test to judge the candidate's inner attributes, attitude, personality and to know if the candidate would be good fit for the school; 5.26 per cent of them have separate Human Resource Department, so they even keep one round with HR experts to evaluate candidate from HR point of view or even to get him acquainted with HR policies of the school; 5.26 per cent of them ask shortlisted candidates to deliver demo lecture to the students and their performance is analyzed on parameters like class management, communication skills, subject knowledge, style of teaching and students feedback on the candidate.

5.9.5 Probation Period

Probation period is a period a newly appointed teachers have to serve before getting confirmed. They are not entitled to any benefits or incentives till they are on probation. Period to be serve under probation may vary for different schools under different categories.

It was observed that two third of aided private schools have rule that teacher should to serve initially on probation for the period up to 5 years as per government norms, while remaining has provision of probation period of 2 years. It is very strange to note different kinds of probation rules adopted by the aided private schools. While in case of self-financed private schools, about 58 percent respondent managers mentioned that teachers need to serve on probation for the period of 2 years, while about 16 per cent of them have no probation period to serve at all. About 5.26 per cent each of unaided private schools have probation period of 6 months and one year as probation period. While some of the self-financed schools have probation period of 1–3 month, some of them is based on performance of candidate.

5.9.6 Training New Teachers

All the aided private schools covered under study from the district provided training to newly appointed teachers with the help of existing senior teachers or sending them to government organized trainings centre. Management of two third of selected schools also organized trainings for new employees through their own training centers or with the help of training consultancies. In case of unaided private schools, 84.21 per cent take help of existing senior teachers to train new employees, 63.16 per cent of them involve external experts to get newly appointed teachers trained as per environment of the school, 10.53 per cent train the teachers through in-house training by principal of the school, 1.05 per cent of them also have on-campus training center run by Director of the school. Remaining schools under the category of private self-financed schools train their teachers through government trainings, CBSE workshops, training by Coordinator, in-house training, doubt-solving sessions, revision sessions, class sessions, trainings of private publishers, training by religious experts, art of living sessions, trainings by CEO of the school, Course trainer, training through learning, teaching workshops and training by teachers of B.Ed. colleges.

5.9.7 Communication with the Management

It was very surprising to note here is that none of the aided schools and hardly 5.26 per cent of unaided private schools communicates with the management through a telephonic call or text messages. None of aided private schools and 10.53 per cent of self-financed private schools communicate with management through suggestion box; 33.33 per cent of aided private schools and 5.26 per cent of unaided private schools allow teachers to communicate with the management by writing letter.

Management of none of aided private schools and 52.63 per cent of unaided private schools allow teachers to meet them through formal or informal meeting. While 33.33 per cent of aided private schools and 57.89 per cent of unaided private schools allow teachers to meet concerned person form management directly.

Table 5.8: Strategies and Parameters Adopted for Recruitment of Teachers

Sr. No.	*Particulars*	*Fully Funded (%)*	*Self-Financed (%)*
1.	**Strategies adopted for recruitment**		
	A. Online Recruitment Practices	–	21.05
	B. Recruitment Consultancies	–	15.79
	C. Referral Programs	33.33	47.37
	D. Newspaper Advertisement	100	100
2.	**Special demographic characteristics of teachers**		
	A. Age	–	42.11
	B. Qualification	66.67	68.42
	C. Past experience	66.67	57.89
3.	**Is salary Important?**		
	A. Yes	66.67	68.42
	B. No	33.33	31.58
4.	**Selection tools for teachers**		
	A. Subject Knowledge Test	–	31.58
	B. Psychometric Test	–	5.26
	C. HR Interview	–	5.26
	D. Panel Interview	100	100
	E. Telephonic Interview	–	–
	F. Demo Lecture	100	5.26
	G. Reference Check	–	84.21

Sr. No.	*Particulars*		*Fully Funded (%)*	*Self-Financed (%)*
5.	**Probation Period?**			
	A. 6 months		–	5.26
	B. 1 year		–	5.26
	C. 2 years		33.33	57.89
	D. No probation		–	15.79
	E. Any other	Based on Performance	–	5.26
		1 month	–	5.26
		3 months	–	5.26
		5 years as per government norms	66.67	

Source: Field survey data.

Table 5.9: Training and Ways for Teachers to Communicate with Management

Sr. No	*Particulars*		*Fully Funded (%)*	*Self-Financed (%)*
1.	Who Trains new teachers			
	A. Existing Senior Teachers		100	84.21
	B. External Experts		–	63.16
	C. Government Trainings		100	5.26
	D. Through CBSE Workshops		–	5.26
	E. Any other way	Training by Coordinator	–	5.26
		In-house training by Principal	–	10.53
		In-house training, doubt solving sessions, revision sessions, class sessions	–	5.26
		Management organized trainings	66.67	–
		On campus training center run by Director	–	10.53
		Private Publishers' training	–	5.26

Sr. No	Particulars		Fully Funded (%)	Self-Financed (%)
		Training by religious experts, art of living	–	5.26
		Training through CEO, Course trainer	–	5.26
		Training through learning	–	5.26
		Workshops, B.Ed college teachers to train	–	5.26
2.	Ways for teachers to communicate with the management			
	A. Through a telephonic call or text messages		–	5.26
	B. Suggestion box		–	10.53
	C. Writing letter at your postal address		33.33	5.26
	D. Through formal or informal meeting		–	52.63
	E. Directly meeting with concern officer/member of management		33.33	57.89

Source: Field survey data.

5.9.8 Recognition to Teachers

None of aided private schools and 42.11 per cent of unaided private schools recognize efforts of teachers through incentives. While 33.33 per cent of aided private schools and 52.63 per cent of unaided private schools recognize teachers' contribution through rewards. All the selected aided private schools and 26.32 per cent of unaided private schools present awards and certificate to best performing teachers. About two third of selected aided private schools and unaided private schools give higher ratings through performance appraisal of high performing teachers.

5.9.9 Bases for Teachers' Performances

- **Quality of the teaching:** All the aided private schools and 78.95 per cent of unaided private schools evaluate the performance of teachers on the basis of quality of teaching.

- **Relation with students:** About two third of aided private schools and unaided private schools evaluate performance of teachers on the basis of their relation with students.
- **Annual Result of Students:** On the basis of Annual result of the students, 66.67 per cent of aided private schools and 57.89 per cent of self-financed private schools appraise teachers' performance.
- **Relation with other Teachers and Management:** Almost two third of selected aided private schools and unaided private schools evaluate teachers' performances on the basis of relation with colleagues and management.
- **Departmental Audit:** On the basis of departmental audit of the section in which they teach, about one third of selected aided private schools and 36.84 per cent of unaided private schools appraise performances of teachers.
- **Performance of School in Inter-School Competition:** About 67 per cent of aided private schools and 52.63 per cent of unaided private schools consider school's performance in inter school competition. When respondents were asked about any other factor considered while evaluating performance of teachers, they mentioned the other factors such as self-appraisal, class control, initiatives taken feedback, 360 degree appraisal, passion towards work, attitude towards the profession, punctuality and review of students' feedback.

5.9.10 Feedback on Facilities

All the selected aided private schools and 73.68 per cent of unaided private schools consider feedback of teachers on facilities provided to them. Such feedback are taken more than twice in a year in case of all the aided private schools, while 21.05 per cent of those unaided private schools which consider feedback take once in a year.

5.9.11 Factors for Promotion

About two third of selected. Aided private schools and 21.05 per cent of unaided private schools promote teachers on the basis of their seniority; 33.33 per cent of aided private schools and 36.84 per cent of unaided private schools consider educational qualification for promotion. None of aided private schools and 94.74 per cent of unaided private schools promote teachers on the basis of performance. This trend shows that self-financed private schools give priority to performance and government aided schools follow rigid structure of promotion based on seniority and qualification. Thus, self-financed schools do better than government schools when it comes to quality of education. About one third of aided private school consider quality of teaching, 5.26 per cent each unaided private schools consider student-teachers relations and accountability of teachers for promotion.

5.9.12 Laying off Teachers

Laying off of any teacher is not allowed in aided private schools as they are governed by government rules and regulations. Management personnel of aided private schools find the matter not applicable to their schools. About 63 per cent of respondents from unaided private schools also do not layoff any teacher in any case. But 36.84 per cent of management personnel lay off their teachers if they are not improving even after giving warnings. Lay off is applicable after notice period to any teacher. When they are asked about the reasons for layoff, 5.26 per cent respondents mentioned the reasons as a:

- If attitude and character is negative.
- Indiscipline, in an extreme condition.
- If not fitting in as a person.
- if they violate code of conduct
- Poor class control.
- When performance is not improving after warnings.

Table 5.10: Recognition and Promotion to Teachers

Sr. No	*Particulars*	*Fully Funded (%)*	*Self-Financed (%)*
1.	**Ways to recognize contributions of teachers**		
	A. Incentives	–	42.11
	B. Rewards and recognition	33.33	52.63
	C. Awards and certificate	100	26.32
	D. Performance appraisal	66.67	63.16
2.	**Bases to evaluate performance of teachers**		
	A. Quality of the teaching	100	78.95

Sr. No	*Particulars*		*Fully Funded (%)*	*Self-Financed (%)*
	B. Relation with student		66.67	68.42
	C. Annual result of student		100	57.89
	D. Relation with other Teachers & management		66.67	63.16
	E. Departmental Audits		33.33	36.84
	F. Performance of school (interschool games)		66.67	52.63
	G. Any other	Self-Appraisal	–	5.26
		Class Control	–	5.26
		Initiatives taken feedback	–	5.26
		360 Degree Appraisal	–	5.26
		Passion towards work	–	5.26
		Attitude towards the profession	–	5.26
		Punctuality	–	5.26
		Review of students' feedback	–	5.26
4.	**Feedback on facilities provided to the teachers**			
	A. Yes		100	73.68
	B. No		–	26.32
5.	**Factor considered for promotion of teachers**			
	A. Seniority		66.67	21.05
	B. Qualification		33.33	36.84
	C. Performance		–	94.74
	D. Any other	Quality of Teaching	33.33	
		Student-teachers Relations	–	5.26
		Accountability	–	5.26

Source: Field survey data.

Table 5.11: Reasons and Strategies to Lay off any Teachers

Sr. No.	*Particulars*		*Fully Funded (%)*	*Self-Financed (%)*
1.	Lay off any teacher?			
	A. Yes		–	36.84
	B. No		–	63.16
	C. NA		100	–
2.	If yes, then why?			
	If Attitude and character is negative		–	5.26
	Indiscipline, in an extreme condition		–	5.26
	If not fitting in as a person		–	5.26
	If they violate code of conduct		–	5.26
	Poor class control		–	5.26
	When performance is not improving after warnings		–	5.26
3.	Who takes decisions related to teachers?			
	A. Management		100	73.68
	B. Principal		100	89.47
	C. Campus Director		–	42.11
	D. Specially appointed Management Representative		–	5.26
	E. Anybody else	Chairman, Founder	–	5.26
		Coordinator	–	5.26
		Faculty heads, Teachers	–	5.26
		HODs	–	5.26
		Senior faculty members	–	5.26

Source: Field survey data.

5.9.13 Decisions Related to Teachers

All the respondents from aided private schools surveyed responded as teachers' related decisions are taken by management and principal both together. Out of total 19, 17 respondents mentioned that respective principal of the school takes decisions related to teachers, while 14 of them respond as management takes decisions related to teachers, 8 of the management personnel of unaided private schools allow campus director to take key decisions related to teachers and specially appointed management representative takes decision in only one self-financed school under study. They are also asked if there is anybody else involved in decision making related to teachers, 5.26 per cent of total respondents mentioned the other personal involved in decision making, those area Chairman, Founder, Coordinator, Faculty heads, Teachers themselves, HODs, Senior Faculty Members.

5.9.14 Reasons to Leave the School

The selected respondents were asked for the reasons, which cause attrition of teachers in their schools. Such causes of the turnover may be specific to any school. Turnover of teachers is not so prominent in aided private schools because of higher pay and job security. Most of the aided private schools surveyed do not face much problem in terms of attrition of teachers and if at all any teachers is leaving that is just to settle down in abroad (33 per cent of total). Almost all management representatives of aided private schools see their teachers leaving the school only after retirement.

While in case of teachers of unaided private schools, turnover of teachers is high. Management personnel of 73.68 per cent of unaided private schools mentioned that the main reason for teachers leaving self-financed schools is to get government job as there is high remuneration with high job security, while 57.89 per cent of them feel that teachers leave the jobs due to transfer of their spouse, as most of the teachers of self-financed schools are female and they work as a secondary source of income for the family. Therefore they have to change the location with transfer to location their husbands' work place. About 47 per cent of respondents feel teachers from unaided private schools leave the job to get married, as many of them are female teachers, while 36.84 per cent of management personnel find turnover in their schools to get better prospects in other school or profession. Out of total respondents, 31.58 per cent find settling down to abroad is a reason for attrition of teachers, as there is a trend among people from Anand district to settle down to abroad. When they are asked about other reasons for teachers from their schools to leave the jobs, 5.26 per cent school managers mentioned other reasons such as: due to remote place of the school, expecting child, commuting problem, getting job nearer to their places, medical issue, and to open personal tuition classes.

5.9.15 Notice Period

If teacher confirmed in the services of aided private schools wish to leave the school, he/she need to give three month notice to schools while for staff on probation need to give 1–3 month notice. While in case of self-financed private schools, almost same kind of procedure is followed.

Table 5.12: Reasons for Teachers Leaving the Job

<table>
<tr><th>Sr. No.</th><th colspan="2">Particulars</th><th>Fully Funded (%)</th><th>Self-Financed (%)</th></tr>
<tr><td>1.</td><td colspan="2">Reasons for teachers leaving the job</td><td></td><td></td></tr>
<tr><td></td><td colspan="2">A. For Government Job</td><td>–</td><td>73.68</td></tr>
<tr><td></td><td colspan="2">B. For Getting Married</td><td>–</td><td>47.37</td></tr>
<tr><td></td><td colspan="2">C. For Settling down to Abroad</td><td>33.33</td><td>31.58</td></tr>
<tr><td></td><td colspan="2">D. For Transfer of Spouse</td><td>–</td><td>57.89</td></tr>
<tr><td></td><td colspan="2">E. For Better Prospects</td><td>–</td><td>36.84</td></tr>
<tr><td></td><td rowspan="7">F. Any Other</td><td>Due to remote place of the school</td><td>–</td><td>5.26</td></tr>
<tr><td></td><td>Expecting child</td><td>–</td><td>5.26</td></tr>
<tr><td></td><td>Commuting problem</td><td>–</td><td>5.26</td></tr>
<tr><td></td><td>Getting job nearer to their places</td><td>–</td><td>5.26</td></tr>
<tr><td></td><td>Medical issue</td><td>–</td><td>5.26</td></tr>
<tr><td></td><td>To open Personal tuition classes</td><td>–</td><td>5.26</td></tr>
<tr><td></td><td>After Retirement</td><td>33.33</td><td>–</td></tr>
<tr><td>2.</td><td colspan="2">Notice Period?</td><td></td><td></td></tr>
<tr><td></td><td rowspan="3">Confirmed Teachers</td><td>3 months</td><td>100</td><td>68.42</td></tr>
<tr><td></td><td>1 month</td><td>–</td><td>10.53</td></tr>
<tr><td></td><td>No formal Notice Period</td><td>–</td><td>21.05</td></tr>
<tr><td></td><td rowspan="3">On probation</td><td>3 months</td><td>66.67</td><td>21.05</td></tr>
<tr><td></td><td>1 month</td><td>33.33</td><td>57.89</td></tr>
<tr><td></td><td>No formal Notice Period</td><td>–</td><td>21.05</td></tr>
</table>

Source: Field survey data.

5.9.16 Effects of Teachers' Turnover

It was observed that two third of aided private schools and 58 per cent of unaided private schools covered under study felt that they face disturbance in the time table due to teachers' turnover. About one third of aided private schools and unaided private schools realized negative impact on annual results of their schools. About one third of selected aided private schools and 42.11 per cent unaided private schools also faced disturbances in the functioning of school due to turnover of teachers. All the aided private schools and about 79 per cent unaided private schools recorded that pressure on other staff members get increased when any teachers leave the school. Management representatives of 66.67 per cent aided and 52.63 per cent unaided private schools feel pressure of hiring a new teacher when any teacher is leaving the school.

5.9.17 Exit Interview

About two third of total aided private schools and 36.84 per cent of self-financed private schools conduct exit interview of teachers leaving the school to understand cause of turnover and how the problem can be resolved to control future attrition. About one third of aided and about two third of unaided private schools do not conduct exit interviews of exiting teachers. About one third aided private schools and 21.05 per cent of unaided private schools have also implemented changes as recommended in exit interview by leaving teacher to control attrition.

Table 5.13: Effects on School Due to Teachers' Turnover and Steps Taken

Sr. No.	*Particulars*	*Fully Funded (%)*	*Self-Financed (%)*
1.	**Effects on School due to teachers' turnover**		
	A. Disturbance in the time table	66.67	57.89
	B. Negative impact on the annual results	33.33	36.84
	C. Disturbance in the functioning of school	66.67	42.11
	D. Increased pressure on other staff members	100	78.95
	E. Pressure of hiring a new teacher	66.67	52.63

Sr. No.	Particulars	Fully Funded (%)	Self-Financed (%)
2.	**Exit interview of the teachers**		
	A. Yes	66.67	36.84
	B. No	33.33	63.16
3.	Any changes implemented based on exit interview? Yes	33.33	21.05
4.	**Ways to deal with turnover of an efficient teachers**		
	A. By evaluating the exit forms	–	10.53
	B. By seeking help from the existing teachers	100	68.42
	C. By hiring volunteers	–	21.05
	D. By arranging extra classes for left outportion	66.67	57.89
5.	**Convincing teachers to stay back?**		
	A. Yes	–	94.74
	B. No	–	5.26
6.	**If yes, then how?**		
	Offering higher salary	–	26.32
	Promotion	–	5.26
	Offering flexi timing	–	5.26
	If decision is in favour of teachers, they are allowed with any solution	–	5.26
	Not applicable	100	–
	Offering any solution to problem (concerned about stability)	–	36.84
	Offers as per norms of trust	–	5.26
	Verbal counseling	–	31.58

Source: Field survey data.

5.9.18 Ways to Deal with Turnover

It was observed that none of the aided private schools and 10.53 per cent of unaided private schools deals with turnover of efficient teachers by evaluating exit interview forms. All selected aided private schools and

68.42 per cent of unaided private schools tried to handle with turnover of an efficient teachers by seeking help from the existing teachers. None of aided private schools and 21.05 per cent of unaided private schools handle turnover of teachers by hiring volunteers to complete the incomplete tasks of left teacher. About two third of aided private schools and 58 per cent of unaided private schools handle with turnover of teachers by arranging extra classes for left out portion.

5.9.19 Convincing Teachers to Stay Back

Management representatives of aided private schools find this issue irrelevant to them as they do not face the problem of attrition of teachers in their schools except some unavoidable turnover. So they feel there is no requirement to convince teachers to stay back. The problem is prominent in unaided private schools of the district. So when management personnel of self-financed schools were asked if they convinced their leaving teachers to stay back, 95 per cent of them respond was positive. They feel consequences of turnover are of long term and it is always better to stop attrition them to appoint new teachers from point of view of costing also. Out of 19, 18 respondents try to convince by resolving their problems in various ways. About 37 per cent of them convince leaving teachers by offering solution to their problems in any probable way as they are concerned about stability of their teachers, while 31.58 per cent of them convince leaving teachers through verbal counseling, 26.32 per cent of them are even ready to offer higher salary to leaving candidate to control attrition. Remaining candidates try to resolve the issue by promoting leaving candidate, offering flexi timing, resolving problem with any stake holder and offering whatever is possible as per norms of the trust under which the school is running.

5.10 MANAGERIAL ASPECTS OF SCHOOLS

In the section how management of any school is done through committees and their meetings is understood. They were asked about annual proceedings undertaken by the management of school for smooth functioning (Table 5.14).

5.10.1 Planning and Year Ending Meeting

Planning meetings are organized at the starting of the year to plan the whole academic year with involvement of teachers. Year ending meetings are conducted at the end of the academic year to evaluate whether the objectives set in planning meetings are achieved throughout the year and yearly time table is followed during the year. All the aided and unaided private schools covered under study from Anand district conduct planning and year ending meeting with teachers.

5.10.2 Local Management Committee

Meeting of local management committee, which is directly involved in routine management of the school.

All the aided private schools covered under study conduct local management committee meetings. About 33 per cent of them conduct local management committee once in a year and 66.67 per cent of them conduct it twice a year, while local management committees are organized by 78.95 per cent of unaided private schools covered under study. About 21 per cent of them do not have Local management committee.

5.10.3 Departmental Audit

Audit of the performance of various section of the school. All the aided private schools covered under study conduct departmental audit, while 33.33 per cent of school conduct departmental audit quarterly and remaining conduct departmental audit annually. In case of self-financed private schools, 84.21 per cent of unaided private schools covered under study conduct departmental audit while remaining 15.79 per cent of them mentioned that they do not conduct any departmental audit to keep check on performance of various sections of the school. About 16 per cent of them conduct departmental audit quarterly, 36.84 per cent of them conduct departmental audit half yearly and 31.58 per cent of them conduct departmental audit annually.

Table 5.14: Information Related to Management of School

Sr. No.	*Particulars*		*Fully Funded*	*Self-Financed*
			(n=03)	*(n=19)*
1.	Planning and Year ending meeting with the teachers?	Yes	100	100
2.	Local Management Committee?	Yes	100	78.95
		No	–	21.05

Sr. No.	Particulars	Fully Funded (n=03)	Self-Financed (n=19)
3.	If yes, then how many times in a year?		
	Once	33.33	21.05
	Twice	66.67	15.79
	Three times	–	5.26
	Once in 2 years	–	5.26
	6–7 times	–	5.26
	Depends on Management	–	5.26
	Every week(Saturday)	–	5.26
	Everyday	–	5.26
	Monthly	–	5.26
	Once in a month or 2 months	–	5.26
4.	Departmental Audit?		
	A. Yes	100	84.21
	B. No	–	15.79
5.	If yes, then how often?		
	A. Quarterly	33.33	15.79
	B. Half yearly	–	36.84
	C. Annually	66.67	31.58

Source: Field survey data.

5.11 Information Related to Students

In the section information related to results of students in the examinations, ways adopted to handle low scoring students and role of students in performance evaluation of teachers is recorded and evaluated as shown below (Table 5.15).

Table 5.15: Students Related Information

Sr. No.	*Particulars*	*Fully Funded*	*Self-Financed*
1.	Average Highest per cent result of the school?	92.33	96.18
2.	Average Lowest per cent result of the school?	39.33	45.36
3.	**Ways to handle low scoring Students**		
	A. Through counseling	100	89.47
	B. By arranging remedial classes	100	100
	C. Supporting students by admitting them in special school for slow learners.		5.26
	D. By taking help of parents for understanding the child's behaviour outside school	100	78.95
	E. Advising parents to admit their kids to other school		26.32
4.	**Students' feedback on performance of teachers?**		
	A. Yes	100	89.47
	B. No	–	10.53

5.11.1 Performance of Students in Exam

Management representatives of schools covered under study were asked about highest and lowest percentages scored by the students of secondary and higher secondary sections of the school. Average highest percentage of the students studying in aided private schools covered under study from Anand district was 92.33 per cent. Average lowest percentage scored by students of aided private schools surveyed was 39.33 per cent. Average highest percentage of the students studying in unaided private schools covered under study from Anand district was 96.18 per cent while average lowest percentage scored by students of self-financed private schools surveyed is 45.36 per cent. Thus, level of scoring of marks of self-financed private schools was higher than that of aided private schools as there is a trend to enroll children in private schools among educated families. Students of self-financed private schools are brighter and more talented. Facilities and assistance provided to self-financed private schools are better than that of aided private schools. Parents of students studying in self-financed private schools are more conscious towards education of their children.

5.11.2 Handling Low-scoring Students

Ways adopted by the schools to handle low scoring students to improve their performance and upgrade their results. Weak students are handled specially in following manner:

- **Through counseling:** All the aided private schools covered under study handle low scoring students through counseling. About 90 per cent of unaided private schools try to counsel low scoring students with the help of teachers or professional counselors.
- **Remedial Classes:** All the aided and unaided private schools covered under study conduct remedial classes for the students of the subjects in which their performance is weak. Such classes can be during school hours or in extra hours.
- **Admitting them in special school:** The practice of supporting low scoring students to get admission in special schools of slow learners is not prominent in the district. None of the aided private schools adopt this way for low scoring students. Only 5.26 per cent of unaided private school adopt this way to get slow learners out of the school.
- **Taking help of parents:** All the aided private schools take help of parents in improving performance of low-scoring students. About 79 per cent of the self-financed schools covered under study opt for this option to understand the problem of low-scoring students with the help of parents.
- **Advising parents to admit their kids to some other school:** The practice of asking parents to take their kids to some other schools is not a common practice in the district. None of the aided private schools opt for this option to handle low-scoring students. About 26 per cent of unaided private schools advise parents to admit their low-scoring kids to some other schools.

5.11.3 Students' Feedback on Teachers

Feedback of students on performance of teachers is necessary while evaluating their performance under 360 degree performance appraisal. Students' say is prominent factor to appraise teaching effectiveness of the teachers. All the aided private schools surveyed involve students in the performance evaluation process of teachers. About 90 per cent of unaided private schools covered under study allow students to give their feedback on performance of their teachers, while 10.53 per cent of unaided private schools do not consider students' feedback while evaluating performance of teachers.

5.12 UNIQUE CHARACTERISTICS OF THE SCHOOL

Management representatives from each school were asked to narrate special characteristics of their respective schools. The special attributes of the school should indicate how the school is different from other schools in the vicinity. What is unique about the school considering infrastructure of the school, teachers of the school, fee structure of the school, timing of the school, facilities to teachers and students, pay to teachers, co-curricular activities, style of teaching, exam pattern, projects given to students, management initiatives, attitude of principal etc. should be mentioned as special features of the school.

5.13 CHAPTER SUMMARY

This chapter presents view of management representatives from selected aided and unaided private schools on various factors covered to understand the problem of attrition and its problems, causes and remedies in Anand district. Views of management personnel are recorded and analyzed rigorously to understand how management of any school sees the problem. Management personnel are interviewed personally with the help of pretested schedules and certain observations are recorded under field survey to check authenticity of their responses.

Management personnel of aided private schools do not find the problem of teachers turnover as prominent as they are covered under government norms so better facilities, higher pay and high job security are enjoyed by their teachers. In most of the cases, teachers of aided private schools of the district do not leave the job before retirement except any extreme personal or professional reason, in view of management.

As it is evident from the findings and discussions of responses of management personnel of unaided private schools of Anand district, the problem of high turnover of teachers affect the schools badly. Management personnel of unaided private schools have adopted various ways with the help of internal or external experts to control attrition. Almost all of the management representatives feel that it is better to control attrition than to resolve its consequences. They are also ready to go to any extent to retain experienced, trained, qualified and competent teachers in the school.

It was observed that education in the district is mostly under control of self-financed schools and the performance of such schools can be affected adversely due to high turnover of teachers. The cost of recruitment, selection and training a teachers as per the requirements of the school is very high. When a teacher leave a school, replacement cost of that teacher is borne by the management. Self-financed schools are entirely run by fees collected from the students. So, with increase in the cost due to turnover of teachers, burden on students goes up.

There is also a rule of government on maximum fees to be collected by the unaided private schools in the district. That brings limit on the income, so to control expenses the problem of attrition should be resolved. Management of unaided private schools are trying to make the jobs more attractive and also at par with aided private schools but unavailability of competent teachers make the problem worse.

It can be concluded from this chapter that management of aided private schools of the district are aware about the problem and its consequences but it is very essential to know views of teachers, parents and students on the matter to get broader picture of the issue.

CHAPTER 6

Attrition of Teacher:

Teachers' Perspectives

6.1 INTRODUCTION

Teachers are responsible to impart knowledge to students, but quality of education goes down if they are not stable. Self-financed schools charge high amount of fees from students, they provide state of the art facilities to the students and the ultimate success of any unaided private school is entirely dependent on quality and stability of teachers. Qualified and experienced teachers are easily available but mushrooming of private schools in the district and trend towards tuition classes makes it difficult to get good teachers in self-financed schools. The study attempts to look into the problem of retention of teachers and it is very important to deeply investigate the issues related to teachers, so this chapter critically investigate the reasons behind retention of teachers and tried to draw any conclusion on the problem. In the chapter, responses of permanent and contractual teachers are recorded, tabulated and analysed to understand their perspectives separately. The reasons for attrition are understood with the help of teachers. Teachers who have already left the school were also contacted and interviewed to get real picture of the problem. In aided private schools, the problem is not prominent as seen in the previous chapter. There were no contractual teachers in aided private schools.

As discussed in earlier chapters, more number of students are enrolled in private schools in urban area of the district. The problem of high turnover of teachers in private schools should be understood from perspectives of permanent teachers and contractual teachers separately as their problems are different from each other. In this chapter, responses of teachers are recorded and analysed for permanent and contractual teachers on various parameters to get in-depth understanding about the causes of heavy turnover of teachers in private schools. In this category, 160 permanent teachers and 104 contractual teachers form 03 aided private schools and 19 unaided private schools from Anand district are covered to understand the problem of Teachers' attrition from teachers' point of view.

6.2 DEMOGRAPHIC INFORMATION OF TEACHERS

This section focuses on demographic characteristics of teachers in private schools. The demographic information of permanent and contractual teachers is presented in the Table 6.1.

6.2.1 Average Age of Teachers

Average age of permanent teachers surveyed was 38 years. Average age of contractual teachers covered under study is 35 years. This indicates that teachers who on permanent positions in private schools are older than that on contractual positions. The situation is such because teachers get permanent jobs after few years of experience in the field of teaching. They are also required to earn necessary qualification to get permanent jobs in any private schools of the district.

6.2.2 Gender of Teachers

Out of total permanent teachers, 57.50 per cent were female teachers and 42.50 per cent were male teachers. Out of total contractual teachers covered under study, 56.73 per cent were female teachers and 43.27 per cent were male teachers. This indicates in both the categories of permanent and contractual, number of female teachers employed in private schools are more than that of male teachers in the district.

6.2.3 Marital Status of Teachers

Out of total permanent teachers, 82.50 per cent were married, 13.13 per cent were single, 1.25 per cent were widow, 0.63 per cent were divorcee and remaining teachers were not covered in the previous four categories of marital status. Out of total contractual teachers, 64.42 per cent were married, 32.69 per cent were single, 1.92 per cent were widow, 0.96 per cent were divorcee and remaining have not defined their marital status. This indicates most of the teachers from both the categories were married. Share of married teachers in permanent category is more as there is tendency among male teachers of the district to get married once they get job security.

6.2.4 No. of Kids of Teachers

Out of total permanent teachers, 34.38 per cent had two kids, 33.75 per cent had one kid, 3.75 per cent had more than two kids and remaining

28.22 per cent of permanent teachers did not have any kids. Out of total contractual teachers, 25.96 per cent had one kid, 10.58 per cent had two kids, 1.92 per cent had more than two kids and remaining 61.54 per cent of contractual teachers did not have kids. Share of teachers not having kids is more in category of contractual teachers than that in category of permanent teachers. This indicates that in Anand district, most of the teachers on contract do not plan for a kid before they get permanent job.

6.2.5 Education of Spouse

Average years of education of spouse of teacher under permanent category was 17 years. That means most of the permanent teachers have spouse with education till post-graduation. While average years of education of spouse under contractual category was 16.66 years. That means most of the contractual teachers have spouse who are post-graduate.

6.2.6 Occupation of Spouse

The percentage of spouses from different categories of occupation is calculated out of total married teachers from permanent and contractual employees. Out of total permanent teachers of aided and unaided private schools, 27.27 per cent were housewives, 26.52 per cent were in the teaching profession, 11.36 per cent had their own businesses and 34.85 per cent of total married permanent teachers had spouses in professions other than mentioned above. Out of total married contractual teachers, 35.82 per cent had their spouses in teaching profession, 11.94 per cent were entrepreneurs, 11.94 per cent were housewives and spouses of 40.30 per cent of them were in other professions. Share of house wives were more in permanent teachers as their pay is secured and high so they may not need secondary source of income for their households.

6.2.7 Type of Family

Out of total permanent teachers covered under survey, 51.25 per cent were from joint family and 48.75 per cent were from nuclear family. Out of total contractual teachers, 68.27 per cent were from joint family and 31.73 per cent were from nuclear family. Share of teachers from nuclear family was more in contractual teachers as most of them were singles, so they stay with their parents and siblings. Share of permanent teachers from nuclear family was more than that in contractual teachers as they are willing to get separated after marriage and after getting permanent jobs.

Table 6.1: Demographic Information of Teachers

Particulars		*Permanent (n=160) per cent*	*Contractual (n=104) per cent*
Average Age (in years)		38	35
Gender	A. Male	42.50	43.27
	B. Female	57.50	56.73
Marital Status	A. Married	82.50	64.42
	B. Single	13.13	32.69
	C. Divorcee	0.63	0.96
	D. Widow	1.25	1.92
No. of Kids	A. One	33.75	25.96
	B. Two	34.38	10.58
	C. More	3.75	1.92
Education of spouse	In average years	17	16.7
Occupation of spouse of married teachers	Teaching	26.52	35.82
	Business	11.36	11.94
	Housewives	27.27	11.94
	Other Profession	34.85	40.30
Type of family	A. Nuclear	48.75	31.73
	B. Joint	51.25	68.27
Education	A. B.Ed.	59.38	53.85
	B. M.Ed.	18.13	11.54
	C. Ph.D.	2.50	1.92
	D. Any other	20.00	32.69
Avg. Distance from School	In Kilometres	7.38	11.37
Mode of Transportation	A. Self –vehicle	77.50	75.00
	B. School transportation	8.75	3.85
	C. Railway	0.00	0.00
	D. Bus	1.88	6.73
	E. Auto Rickshaw	8.75	9.62
	F. Cab	0.00	0.00
	G. Walk	3.13	4.81

Source: Field survey data.

6.2.8 Education of Teachers

Out of total permanent teachers 59.38 per cent possess B.Ed. Degree, 18.13 per cent pursued M.Ed. Degree, 2.50 per cent earned Ph.D. and 20 per cent had qualifications other than mentioned above. Out of total contractual employees, 53.85 per cent have bachelor degree in Education, 11.54 earned M.Ed. degree, 1.92 per cent are Ph.D. holders and 32.69 per cent have qualifications other than mentioned above. The share of teachers having any other degree is more in case of contractual teachers as they have to get qualified before getting permanent.

6.2.9 Average Distance from School

Average distance of their residence to school for permanent teachers was 7.38 kilo meters while same was 11.67 kms for contractual teachers. This indicates that those who are permanent try to settle down nearer to the school. Those who are contractual are ready to commute to longer distances as their appointments are for short term.

6.2.10 Mode of Transportation

Out of total permanent teachers covered under the study, 77.50 per cent teachers use self-vehicles to reach their respective schools, 8.75 per cent take benefit of school transportation facility, 8.75 per cent commute through auto rickshaw, 3.13 per cent live at walk-able distance from school and 1.88 per cent commute to their respective schools through Buses of state transport. Out of total contractual teachers, 75 per cent commute to their respective schools through their own vehicle, 9.62 per cent use auto rickshaw as mode of transportation to reach their schools, 6.73 per cent commute through buses of state transportation, 4.81 per cent reach their schools on their feet and 3.85 per cent get facility of transportation from their schools.

6.3 SCHOOL AND EMPLOYMENT INFORMATION

In this section information related to school, where they are working and their employment related information is gathered and recorded (Table 6.2). The information related to school and employment is recorded separately for aided private schools and self-financed private schools. There are 03 schools covered under the category of aided private schools and 19 schools under the category of unaided private schools.

Information of those schools is recorded separately for permanent and contractual teachers.

6.3.1 No. of Teachers

There were total 31 teachers surveyed from aided private schools. Out of them, 26 were permanent teachers and 5 were contractual teachers. From unaided private schools 233 teachers were covered under study, out of them 134 were permanent and 99 were contractual teachers. On an average there were about 84 percent of permanent teachers in aided private schools and about 58 per cent in self financed school. The remaining teachers were on temporary basis.

Table 6.2: School & Employment Information

Particulars		*Private Fully Aided (n=03) per cent*		*Private Self-financed (n=19) per cent*	
		PT (26)	*CT (5)*	*PT (134)*	*CT (99)*
Av. No. of Teachers		83.87	16.13	57.51	42.49
Education Section	A. Pre Schooling	32.26	0.00	47.64	38.63
	B. Primary	32.26	0.00	51.93	38.63
	C. Secondary	83.87	16.13	57.51	42.06
Medium of Instruction	A. English	58.06	0.00	53.22	37.34
	B. Gujarati	48.39	16.13	18.45	15.88
	C. Hindi	0.00	0.00	2.58	6.01
	D. Other	0.00	0.00	0.00	0.00
Type of Board you teach	A. State Board	83.87	16.13	34.33	38.63
	B. CBSE	0.00	0.00	23.18	3.86
	C. ICSE				
	D. IB				
Type of Board School has	A. State Board	83.87	16.13	34.76	38.63
	B. CBSE	0.00	0.00	22.75	3.86
	C. ICSE				
	D. IB				
Avg. Years of Experience		17.35	4.2	10.61	5.31
Avg. Years in the School		16.09	4.2	7.59	2.94

Source: Field survey data.

6.3.2 Sections of Education in School

All the selected aided private schools have secondary section of education. Only one of them has pre-primary and primary as sections education. Out of total unaided private schools covered under study, 17 have pre-primary, 18 have primary section and 19 of them have secondary section. That indicates that out of 19, 17 have all the section of education, one has all the section except pre-primary and one school has only secondary section.

From aided private schools, 32.26 per cent permanent and none of contractual teachers teach in pre-primary section. Out of them, 32.26 per cent permanent and none from contractual teachers teach in primary section. Out of total teachers from aided private schools, 83.87 per cent permanent and 16.13 per cent from contractual teachers teach in secondary section. From unaided private schools, 47.64 per cent permanent and 38.63 per cent contractual teach in pre-primary section. Out of them, 51.93 per cent permanent and 38.63 per cent contractual teachers teach in primary section and 57.51 per cent permanent and 42.06 per cent contractual teachers teach in secondary section.

6.3.3 Medium of Instruction

Out of total teachers from aided private schools, 58.06 per cent from permanent and none from contractual use English as medium of instruction. Out of total, 48.39 per cent from permanent and 16.13 per cent from contractual use Gujarati as medium of instruction. Out of total teachers covered from unaided private schools, 53.22 per cent permanent and 37.34 per cent contractual teachers use English as medium of instruction. Of them 18.45 per cent permanent and 15.88 per cent contractual teachers use Gujarati as medium of instruction. Out of total, 2.58 per cent permanent and 6.01 per cent contractual teachers use Hindi as medium of instruction. That indicates that English is widely used as medium of instruction in most of the self-financed schools of the district.

6.3.4 Type of Board Teachers Teach

All the permanent and contractual teachers from aided private schools covered under the study from Anand district teach in Gujarat State Education Board. Out of total teachers teach in unaided private schools, 34.33 per cent permanent and 38.63 per cent contractual teachers teach as per Gujarat State Education Board. Out of them, 23.18 per cent permanent and 3.86 per cent contractual teachers teach in Central Board of Secondary Education. There is no aided or unaided private school affiliated to ICSE or IB board in Anand district.

6.3.5 Type of Board

All the aided private schools have affiliation with Gujarat State Education Board. Out of total teachers from unaided schools covered under the study from Anand District, 34.76 per cent permanent and 38.63 per cent contractual teachers teach in the schools having affiliation with Gujarat State Education Board. Out of them, 22.75 per cent permanent and 3.86 per cent contractual teachers teach in the schools having affiliation with Central Board of Secondary Education.

6.3.6 Experience in Teaching

Average years of experience of permanent teachers in the field of education from aided private schools surveyed was of 17.35 years, but same was 4.2 years in case of contractual teachers from aided private schools. While average years of experience of permanent teachers from unaided private schools was of 10.61 years and it is 5.31 years in case of contractual teachers from unaided private schools. That indicates that teachers of aided private schools are of more experience in the field of education. More experience of contractual teachers from unaided private schools show that practice of keeping contractual teachers is prominent in such schools.

6.3.7 Experience in the Same School

Average years spent with the same school was 16.09 years in case of permanent teachers from aided private schools and average years spent by contractual teachers in the same school was 4.2 years. However, average years of experience in the same school was of 7.59 years and 2.94 years respectively in case of permanent and contractual teachers of self-financed schools covered under study. This indicates that teachers at aided schools are stable and teachers of unaided private schools are not stable. Teachers of unaided private schools have left various other jobs and then they are at the current schools.

6.4 REASONS FOR ATTRITION

In the section, a list of probable personal and profession reasons for attrition are given. Teachers were asked if their current job is their first job and if it is not, then they were requested to give reason for leaving the previous job. Out of total, for 34.38 per cent of permanent teachers and 41.35 per cent of contractual teachers this was their first job. While 65.63 per cent of permanent and 58.65 per cent of contractual teachers had left their previous job/s to get their current job. The main focus on the study is on the second type of the teachers.

6.4.1 Professional Reasons for Attrition

The main reason for leaving the previous job by permanent and contractual teachers was less pay. About 24 per cent of permanent teachers and 25 per cent of contractual teachers had left the previous job due to less pay. The least important reason for leaving the previous job was due to Colleagues. Next important reasons for leaving the previous job by permanent teachers was lack of promotional opportunities in previous job, then lack of support from management of previous school, working on contractual basis in previous job and working hours of the previous schools. Other important reasons for attrition among permanent teachers were behaviour policy of previous management, lack of direction from management of previous job, then lack of training and development, then too many responsibilities given in previous job, then inappropriate class size at previous school. Less important factors were inappropriate pupil's behaviour with teachers in previous school, Parental behaviour in previous school, resources at previous school, too few responsibilities and environment of the school.

Next important reasons for leaving the previous job for contractual teachers were working hours of previous schools, working on contractual basis in previous school, behaviour policy of previous management and lack of support of management in previous job. less important reasons for attrition among contractual teachers at private schools are Lack of training and development in previous job, as they experience discrimination/ harassment, lack of direction from previous management, too many responsibilities given in previous job, inappropriate school vicinity, inappropriate class size of previous school, too few responsibilities given in previous job, inappropriate behaviour of pupil in previous school and low reputation of previous school in the society.

Table 6.3: Professional Reasons for Attrition

Sr. No.	*Particulars*	*Permanent (%)*	*Contractual (%)*
1.	Is this your first job?		
	Yes	34.38	41.35
	No	65.63	58.65
2.	**Professional Reasons**		
	A. Working on contractual basis	9.52	11.48
	B. Less Pay	23.81	24.59
	C. Working hours	9.52	19.67
	D. Too many responsibilities	6.67	3.28
	E. Too few responsibilities	0.95	1.64
	F. Lack of promotion opportunity	13.33	6.56
	G. Lack of training/professional development	7.62	4.92
	H. Experience of discrimination/harassment	0.00	4.92
	I. Class size	5.71	3.28
	J. Pupil behaviour	2.86	1.64
	K. Parental behaviour	1.90	0.00
	L. Behaviour Policy of Management	8.57	11.48
	M. School-	0.95	0.00
	i. Environment (e.g. buildings)	0.00	0.00
	ii. Resources	1.90	0.00
	iii. Colleagues	0.00	0.00
	iv. Reputation	0.00	1.64
	v. Vicinity	0.00	3.28
	N. Management—lack of support	10.48	9.84
	O. Management—lack of direction	7.62	4.92

Source: Field survey data.

6.4.2 Personal Reasons for Attrition

The most important personal reasons for permanent teachers of private schools covered under the study from Anand district were getting married, moving to be near partners' job and moving to be near family. The most

Table 6.4: Personal Reasons for Attrition

Sr. No.	*Particulars*	*Permanent (%)*	*Contractual (%)*
3.	Personal Reasons		
	A. Getting married	14.29	18.03
	B. Expecting a child	6.67	3.28
	C. Moving to be near partners job	14.29	6.56
	D. Moving to be near family	14.29	11.48
	E. Poor health	0.95	1.64
	F. Disability	0.00	0.00
	G. Age	0.95	1.64
	H. General dissatisfaction with profession	3.81	1.64
	I. Caring for relatives	1.90	4.92
	J. Education of own kids	3.81	0.00
	K. High Cost of buying accommodation	2.86	3.28
	L. High cost of renting accommodation	0.95	1.64
	M. Commuting -inconvenience	4.76	9.84
	N. Cost of transportation per week	6.67	4.92
	O. Any Other,		
	Adjusting school time with own studies	0.00	1.64
	Better prospects	2.86	0.00
	Due to long distance from school	3.81	0.00
	For Shifting to abroad	0.95	0.00
	For promotion	1.90	0.00
	For the self-development	0.00	1.64
	For further study	2.86	1.64
	To enter in to teaching profession	0.00	1.64
	Due to small kid	0.95	0.00
	Surplus case	1.90	0.00
	As this school is in my own village	0.00	1.64
	Transfer of spouse's job	0.95	0.00
	As was a religious person before	0.00	1.64
	Various other personal reasons	4.76	9.84

Source: Field survey data.

important reasons among contractual teachers were getting married, moving to be near family and Commuting inconvenience time taken in the previous school. Next important reasons of attrition for permanent teachers were expecting a child, cost of transportation, commuting inconvenience/time taken, general dissatisfaction with the profession and for reasons connected with education of own kids. The least important reasons for permanent teachers of private schools were high cost of buying accommodation in previous place, caring for relatives, poor health, age and high cost of renting accommodation. Less important factors among contractual teachers are moving to be near partner's job, caring for relatives, high cost of transportation to previous job, high cost of buying accommodation, poor health, age, dissatisfaction with teaching profession and high cost of renting accommodation in previous location.

Teachers were also asked if there are any additional professional or personal reason for their attrition, other than covered in the table. They gave additional reasons for attrition as: for adjusting school time with own studies, due to long distance from school, for shifting to abroad, for promotion, for the self-development, for further study, to enter in to teaching profession, due to small kid, surplus case, as the school is in the same village, due to transfer of spouse's job and as was a religious person before.

6.5 PROFESSION RELATED INFORMATION

In this section information related to their style of teaching and selection tools used for their selection in the school are recorded in the Table 6.5.

6.5.1 Style of Teaching

In the section, teachers were asked to tick on all the style of teaching adopted by them to impart knowledge in their respective subjects. Out of total teachers from aided and unaided private schools of the district, 64.38 per cent of permanent teachers and 62.50 per cent of contractual teachers used lecture method to deliver knowledge in their respective subjects. Thus, the most popular style of teaching among private schools was a lecture method. Second popular style of teaching among teachers from private schools was group discussion, as 55 per cent of permanent and 50.96 per cent of contractual teachers used the style. Around 40 per cent of permanent and 34.62 per cent of contractual teachers demonstrated necessary concepts in their subjects. Then activities and games were

Table 6.5: Profession Related Information

Particulars		*Permanent (n=160) per cent*	*Contractual (n=104) per cent*
Style of Teaching	A. Lecture	64.38	62.50
	B. Group discussion	55.00	50.96
	C. Role playing	22.50	21.15
	D. Case study	13.75	15.38
	E. Laboratory	30.00	17.31
	F. Demonstration	40.00	34.62
	G. Activities and games	32.50	33.65
	H. Visit	17.50	13.46
	I. Any other: Seminar	0.63	
Tools used for Selection	A. Personal Interview	83.13	85.58
	B. Group discussion	10.00	7.69
	C. Written Test	21.25	8.65
	D. Telephonic Interview	44.38	49.04
	E. Class Demo	26.88	13.46
	F. Panel Interview	5.00	0.96
	G. Any Other		

Source: Field survey data.

utilized to make learning a fun by 32.50 per cent of permanent and 33.65 per cent of contractual teachers, 30 per cent of permanent and 17.31 per cent of contractual teachers used special laboratories assigned to them for practical experiments. Out of them, 22.50 per cent of permanent and 21.15 per cent of contractual teachers opt for role playing to make the process interesting, 13.75 per cent of permanent and 15.38 per cent of contractual teachers used case studies to make the subject more understandable and 17.50 per cent of permanent and 13.46 per cent of contractual teachers take students for field visits to get first hand experiences. Only one permanent teacher used seminar as a style of teaching in the relevant subject.

6.5.2 Selection Tools Used

Teachers were asked about the selection tools used before appointing them to the school and they had to tick on all the steps followed during the selection procedure. Out of total, 83.13 per cent of permanent and 85.58 per cent of the contractual teachers were got selected through personal interview. Thus, personal interview was the most utilized tool for selection of a teacher in any private school. While 44.38 per cent of permanent and 49.04 per cent of contractual teachers were selected through telephonic interview process. This method is popular among private schools to reduce cost of selection. About 27 per cent of permanent and 13.46 per cent of contractual teachers were got selected after class demo; 21.25 per cent of permanent and 8.65 per cent of contractual teachers got shortlisted on the basis of written test. About 10 per cent of permanent and 7.69 per cent of contractual teachers had appeared in group discussion during the selection procedure. About 5 per cent of permanent teachers and less than one percent of contractual teachers had to appear in panel interview. The data is contradictory with responses of management representatives as the tool mostly used for selection is panel interview as per management personnel and it is the least common tool of selection as per teachers' responses.

6.6 PAY RELATED INFORMATION

In this section, teachers were asked to provide information on their pay, facilities and perquisites. They had to choose appropriate option as their response. Again, responses of permanent and temporary teachers were recorded separately and are presented in Table 6.6.

Table 6.6: Pay related Information of Teachers

Particulars		*Permanent per cent*	*Contractual per cent*
Avg. Monthly Pay (in Rupees)	A. Less than 10,000	11.25	49.04
	B. 10,000–20,000	27.50	31.73
	C. 20,000–30,000	17.50	1.92
	D. 30,000–40,000	16.88	1.92
	E. 40,000–50,000	8.75	
	F. 50,000–60,000	6.88	1.92
	G. More than 60,000	1.88	
	H. Not specified	9.38	13.46

Particulars		*Permanent per cent*	*Contractual per cent*
Satisfaction with current pay	A. Yes	60.63	38.46
	B. No	32.50	55.77
	C. Not Applicable	6.88	5.77
	If No, then Why?		
	A. Not matching the Experience	5.77	10.34
	B. Not matching the Workload	9.62	12.07
	C. Not matching the Expectations	9.62	3.45
	D. Not as per government scales	11.54	5.17
	E. Not justified	3.85	
	F. Not sufficient	32.69	32.76
	G. As it is fixed	1.92	3.45
	H. No specific reason	25.00	32.76
Facilities provided by the school	A. Canteen	60.00	52.88
	B. ICT [Information & Communication Facility]	49.38	34.62
	C. Counselling Centre	26.88	14.42
	D. Rest Room	31.25	32.69
	E. Personal Lockers	77.50	74.04
	F. Separate Staff cubicles	30.63	34.62
	G. Transportation	27.50	21.15
	H. Teachers Resources Centre	31.88	15.38
	I. Medical Facilities	31.25	47.12
	J. Recreation Centre	6.88	1.92
	K. Any other		
	Audio Visual Room	0.00	0.96
	Dining Hall	1.25	
	Lunch & Tea,	0.63	

Particulars		*Permanent per cent*	*Contractual per cent*
	Cancer-Krupa Card		
	Special JEE & NEET Sessions	0.63	
	Smart Boards	0.63	
	Wi-fi facility for academic surfing	0.00	0.96
Perquisites/incentives provided by the school	A. Flexi Timing	21.88	24.04
	B. Staff Credit Co-op. Society	13.75	6.73
	C. Provident Fund	70.63	38.46
	D. Housing	20.63	2.88
	E. Gratuity	25.63	2.88
	F. Telephone Allowance	5.63	11.54
	G. Medical Allowances	36.25	12.50
	H. Study Leaves	1.25	0.00
	I. Festival celebration	43.75	61.54
	J. Privilege Leaves	18.13	7.69
	K. Gifts	20.00	40.38
	L. Staff picnic	23.13	32.69
	M. Health Insurance	6.25	5.77
	N. Paternity Leaves	15.63	2.88
	O. Maternity Leaves	40.63	23.08
	P. Sport Events	37.50	56.73
	Q. Coupons	5.00	2.88
	R. Performance Recognition	22.50	28.85
	S. Any other		
	Free education to their children	1.88	
	Extra leave after official maternity leaves	0.63	
	Teacher's counselling	0.63	

Source: Field survey data.

6.6.1 Current Average Monthly Pay

Teachers were asked to write average monthly pay received by them in rupees. Out of total teachers of private schools involved in the study from Anand district, 11.25 per cent of permanent and 49.04 per cent of contractual teachers were paid less than Rs. 10,000 monthly pay. Out of total, 27.50 per cent of permanent and 31.73 per cent of contractual got monthly pay between 10,000 to 20,000 rupees. In the category between 20,000 to 30,000 monthly pay, there were 17.50 per cent of permanent teachers and 1.92 per cent of contractual teachers. About 17 per cent of permanent and 1.92 per cent of contractual teachers got monthly salary between 30,000 to 40,000 rupees, while 8.75 per cent of permanent teachers were paid salary between 40,000 to 50,000 rupees. About 7 per cent of permanent and 2 per cent of contractual teachers were paid between 50,000 to 60,000 rupees. There were 1.88 per cent of permanent teachers who drew salary of more than 60,000 rupees per month. About 10 per cent of permanent and 13.46 per cent of contractual teachers did not specified their monthly pay. Thus, the monthly pay received by most of the contractual teachers was very low compared to permanent teachers or even to other professions so they are ready to leave their current jobs for any other better paid jobs.

6.6.2 Satisfaction with the Current Pay

Permanent and contractual teachers from private schools of Anand district were asked if they are satisfied with the monthly pay they are getting. Out of total teachers involved in the survey, 60.63 per cent of permanent and 38.46 per cent of contractual teachers were satisfied with their monthly pay. About 33 per cent of permanent and 56 per cent of contractual teachers were not satisfied with their current monthly pay. Thus, the latter is vulnerable to the problem of attrition of teachers in private school.

6.6.3 Reasons for Dissatisfaction with Pay

The main reason for dissatisfaction with pay among permanent and contractual teachers was that the pay was not sufficient. Out of total teachers who were not satisfied with their current pay, 32.69 per cent of permanent and 32.76 per cent of contractual did not find their pay sufficient to satisfy their needs as well as need of their families. About one fourth of permanent and one third of contractual teachers were not satisfy while cited no specific reason for their dissatisfaction with their current pay.

About 5 per cent of permanent and 12 per cent of contractual teachers did not find their pay appropriate considering their workload. About 12 per cent of permanent and 5 per cent of contractual teachers found their salary was not as per government scales. About 6 per cent of permanent and 10 per cent of contractual teachers felt that their pay was not matching their experience in the field of teaching. While about 10 cent of permanent and 4 per cent of contractual teachers did not get salary as per their expectations.

6.6.4 Facilities Received

In this section a list of facilities provided to teachers is provided and teachers are asked to tick on all the facilities provided to them by the management.

A. **Canteen:** Out of total teachers involved from private schools of Anand district, 60 per cent of permanent teachers and 52.88 per cent got facility of canteen at nominal charges or even at free of cost. Such canteen can be separate or along with students.

B. **ICT (Information and Communication Technology):** Out of total, 49.38 per cent of permanent and 34.62 per cent of contractual teachers got information and communication facilities from school to help them upgrade their style of teaching. Such ICT facilities include smart classes, laptops, separate computer lab for teachers etc. to enable them to match world standards in the field of teaching.

C. **Counselling Centre:** Out of total, 26.88 per cent of permanent teachers and 14.42 per cent of contractual teachers had counselling centres at their respective schools. Such centres provide counselling services to teachers to resolve their personal or professional issues and it is done mostly by professional counsellor, management representatives or principal.

D. **Rest Room:** Out of total teachers involved in the survey, 31.25 per cent of permanent teachers and 32.69 per cent of contractual teachers had separate rest rooms for teachers in their schools. Separate rest rooms for teachers are provided for relaxation during working hours. Such rest rooms are also with pantry and washroom facilities.

E. **Personal Lockers:** Out of total surveyed teachers, 77.50 per cent of permanent and 74.04 per cent of contractual teachers got personal lockers at their schools. They are provided to teachers to store their valuable study materials, documents or personal belongings.

F. **Separate Staff Cubicles:** Out of total teachers, 30.63 per cent of permanent teachers and 34.62 per cent of contractual teachers were assigned separate sitting place within the staff room.

G. **Transportation Facility:** Facility of transportation to and from school was provided to 27.50 per cent of permanent teachers and 21.15 per cent of contractual teachers. Schools provide to and fro services to the teachers through school buses or separate staff vans. Some of the unaided private schools have made it compulsory for the teachers to commute through school buses only. Some of the unaided private schools reimburse the expenses of transportation.

H. **Teachers Resources Centre:** Out of total teachers, 31.88 per cent of permanent and 15.38 per cent of contractual teachers got facility of teachers resource centres within the library or in separate room. This is provided to upgrade knowledge of teachers in their respective subjects with reading room, computers and internet facilities.

I. **Medical Facilities:** Out of total, 31.25 per cent of permanent teachers and 47.12 per cent of contractual teachers were given medical facilities in the form of on-campus doctor, visiting doctor, medical room and first-aid box. They are provided medical assistance in the premises or by having tie-up with nearby hospital for medical treatments.

J. **Recreation Center:** Out of total teachers 6.88 per cent of permanent and 1.92 per cent of contractual teachers got facility of recreation center within their respective schools. Recreation Centers for the teachers are provided to pursue their interest in any arts or sports. The center also organizes various events like music concert, sports day, staff picnics, family get-together etc. to refresh their teachers. Such activities of the center improve their productivity and they be more committed to their respective schools.

On being asked about any other facilities provided to them by their schools, other than what is discussed above; they mention the following facilities provided to some of the permanent and contractual teachers, viz. audio visual room, dining hall, lunch & tea, cancer-krupa card, special jee & neet sessions, smart boards and wi-fi facility for academic surfing.

All these on-campus facilities are enjoyed by both categories of teachers: Permanent and contractual equally without any discrimination in aided as well as unaided private school of the Anand district.

6.6.5 Perquisites Received

A. **Flexi Timing:** Out of total teachers under study, 21.88 per cent of permanent teachers and 24.04 per cent of contractual teachers enjoy the facility of flexi mining. This is a benefit, where they have to complete their working hours scheduled as per their own convenience, without any fixed in and out timing. Here, it is assumed that they are responsible to complete the syllabus and other assigned duties irrespective of timing of the school.

B. **Staff Credit Co-operative Society:** Out of total teachers covered under the study, 13.75 per cent of permanent and 6.73 per cent of contractual teachers were members of Staff credit cooperative society established by the school to manage savings of the teachers and provide the required amount to needy staff member at lower interest rates. Such Staff Credit Co-operative society run by and for the teachers to provide financial credits.

C. **Provident Fund:** Out of total teachers surveyed, 70.63 per cent of permanent and 38.46 per cent of contractual teachers were covered under Provident Fund act. This benefit is compulsory for teachers of aided private schools, but few of the unaided private schools also provide this benefit to their teachers.

D. **Housing:** Out of total teachers, 20.63 per cent of permanent teachers and 2.88 per cent of contractual teachers got housing from their schools. Housing facilities are provided as staff quarters to their staff members with nominal rent to motivate them to remain with the school for long. Such houses are in the vicinity of the school campus or outside the campus. This benefit is mostly given to confirmed teachers.

E. **Gratuity:** About 26 per cent of permanent teachers and 3 per cent of contractual teachers from aided and unaided private schools of Anand district are covered under Gratuity Act of Government.

F. **Telephone Allowance:** Out of total teachers under study, 5.63 per cent of permanent and 11.54 per cent of contractual teachers got Telephone Allowances. This allowances is given only to the privilege teachers holding or performing special duties for the development of the school.

G. **Medical Allowances:** About 36 per cent of permanent teachers and 13 per cent of contractual teachers were paid medical allowances under the head of incentives as per government norms or their own regulations.

H. **Study Leaves:** Only 1.25 per cent of permanent teachers were entitled to get study leaves to pursue higher qualifications related to the profession. Such leaves are sanctioned for the teachers who aspire to earn higher qualification to upgrade their knowledge of their respective subjects.

I. **Festival Celebration:** About 44 per cent of permanent teachers and 62 per cent of contractual teachers celebrated important festivals at their respective schools. Schools celebrate all important festivals of various religions throughout the year to develop special bond with their teachers. Such celebrations are necessary to provide them homely atmosphere in their respective schools.

J. **Privilege Leaves:** Out of total permanent teachers and 18 per cent contractual teachers got privilege leaves once in a year. This type of special leaves can be clubbed with any other type of official leaves given to teachers.

K. **Gifts:** About 20 per cent of permanent teachers and 41 per cent of contractual teachers got gifts on special occasions, like Diwali, New Year, Birthdays, School Foundation day etc. In most of the cases, gifts are given in the forms of Yearly Diary, pen, book, box of sweets, chocolate box etc.

L. **Staff Picnic:** Out of total permanent teachers, 23.13 per cent and out of total contractual teachers, 32.69 per cent work in schools, where Annual picnics were organized once or twice in a year. Such picnics can be with family or only for staff members. It can be one day, two days or even a long tour. It can be organized by staff members themselves or by third party agent. Such picnics are needed to create family like working environment among the teachers.

M. **Health Insurance:** Out of total teachers covered under the study, 6.25 per cent of permanent and 5.77 per cent of contractual teachers are covered under the benefit of Health Insurance. They may opt for various schemes of insurance agency for benefits during illness. It may be given to all or few competent teachers as a special benefit for their extraordinary performance.

N. **Paternity Leaves:** About 16 per cent of permanent teachers and 3 per cent of contractual teachers are entitled to get paternity leaves for 15 days after the birth of a baby. Such leaves are given to male teachers after birth of their baby to take care of baby and mother. This benefit has been a need as families have become nuclear now a days.

O. **Maternity Leaves:** About 41 per cent of permanent teachers and 23 per cent of contractual teachers were entitled for maternity leaves.

Schools allow female teachers to take maternity leaves for 26 weeks as per amended law of maternity leaves. Those, who are not granting maternity leaves have to at least allow pregnant female teachers to be at home without pay.

P. **Sport Events:** Out of total teachers covered under the study, Schools of 37.50 per cent of permanent and 56.73 per cent of contractual teachers organized sport events for their teachers on sports day along with students or separate sport events. Such events are organized to keep them healthy and fit for the profession.

Q. **Coupons:** Out of total teachers, 5 per cent of permanent and 3 per cent of contractual teachers were given shopping coupons from their school. This benefit is common in corporate houses where coupons like Sodexo are given to get them redeemed for any shopping requirements.

R. **Performance Recognition:** About 23 per cent of permanent and 29 per cent of contractual teachers recognized extra ordinary performances of their teachers through monetary and non-monetary incentives. Performance can be recognized through special award, hike in salary, promotion, special gift hamper, bonus, praising in front of colleagues, teacher of the year award at Annual day of the school etc. This is essential to motivate employees to improve their performance and also to control attrition.

6.7 MOTIVATIONAL FACTORS FOR TEACHERS

In this section, list of motivator factors were given to the teachers and they were requested to rank those factors in their views. 1 means the most important factor and 10 means the least important factor. Thus, teachers were expected to rank each motivator accordingly on the scale of 1 to 10 (Table 6.7).

Table 6.7: Motivational Factors to Teachers

Particulars	*Motivational Factors to Teachers (Rank 1 to 10)*									
	1		*2*		*3*		*4*		*5*	
Motivators	*PT*	*CT*	*PT*	*CT*	*PT*	*CT*	*PT*	*CT*	*PT*	*CT*
A. Work environment	40.6	32.7	18.8	17.3	10.0	14.4	5.6	11.5	7.5	6.7
B. Pay	20.6	11.5	16.9	17.3	7.5	12.5	8.8	4.8	12.5	7.7
C. Relation with colleagues	23.8	15.4	22.5	16.4	15.6	12.5	6.3	11.5	11.3	6.7

Particulars	*Motivational Factors to Teachers (Rank 1 to 10)*									
	1		*2*		*3*		*4*		*5*	
Motivators	*PT*	*CT*	*PT*	*CT*	*PT*	*CT*	*PT*	*CT*	*PT*	*CT*
D. Positive attitude of management	37.5	32.7	16.9	23.1	10.0	5.8	9.4	8.7	6.9	6.7
E. Relation with students	28.1	38.5	20.0	23.1	12.5	7.7	13.1	7.7	8.1	4.8
F. Recognition	10.6	5.8	15.0	15.4	10.6	8.7	3.1	3.9	12.5	12.5
G. Decision making involvement	10.6	7.7	9.4	13.5	10.0	11.5	5.6	8.7	9.4	8.7
H. Role and Responsibilities	16.3	19.2	11.3	12.5	10.6	8.7	11.3	6.7	8.8	14.4
I. Facilities	14.4	11.5	10.6	19.2	4.4	9.6	5.6	4.8	10.0	8.7
J. Good Feedback Ranking	12.5	6.7	13.8	17.3	1.9	8.7	10.6	2.9	6.9	8.7

Notes: (1 = the most important, 10 = the least important); PT = Permanent Teachers, CT = Contractual Teachers.

Source: Field survey data.

Table 6.7 continues...........

Particulars	*Motivational Factors to Teachers (Rank 1 to 10)*									
	6		*7*		*8*		*9*		*10*	
Motivators	*PT*	*CT*	*PT*	*CT*	*PT*	*CT*	*PT*	*CT*	*PT*	*CT*
A. Work environment	7.5	1.9	4.4	5.8	1.3	1.9	1.9	2.9	2.5	1.0
B. Pay	5.6	6.7	2.5	3.9	3.8	6.7	2.5	7.7	19.4	17.3
C. Relation with colleagues	5.0	9.6	1.9	4.8	4.4	6.7	6.3	6.7	2.5	5.8
D. Positive attitude of management	5.0	1.9	2.5	4.8	3.8	5.8	4.4	4.8	3.8	1.9
E. Relation with students	5.6	4.8	3.1	1.0	0.6	3.9	3.8	1.0	5.0	3.9
F. Recognition	11.9	8.7	13.1	8.7	8.8	8.7	8.1	9.6	6.3	14.4
G. Decision making involvement	13.1	9.6	12.5	12.5	10.6	5.8	11.3	12.5	7.5	5.8
H. Role and Responsibilities	6.3	8.7	17.5	8.7	8.1	7.7	6.3	5.8	4.4	3.9
I. Facilities	9.4	8.7	13.1	13.5	16.9	8.7	8.8	5.8	6.9	5.8
J. Good Feedback Ranking	8.8	8.7	7.5	5.8	9.4	15.4	10.0	11.5	18.1	10.6

Notes: (1=the most important, 10=the least important); PT=Permanent Teachers, CT=Contractual Teachers

Source: Field survey data.

6.7.1 Motivational Factors for Teachers

A. **Working Conditions:** Working Conditions means friendly and convenient working environment of the school for their teachers. Out of total teachers, 40.63 per cent of permanent and 32.69 per cent of contractual teachers find the factor as the most effective factor. About 19 per cent of Permanent and 17 per cent of contractual teachers rated the factor as second most effective. About 10 per cent of permanent and 14 per cent of contractual teachers rated the factor with 3rd rating. About 2.50 per cent of permanent and 0.96 per cent of contractual teachers find the factor as the least effective to motivate them to give their best to their respective schools.

B. **Pay:** The factor of pay includes basic pay, allowances, benefits, monetary perquisites and non-monetary incentives. The pay scale, Bonus and annual increments also play important role in making the job attractive for the teachers. Out of total teachers, 20.63 per cent of permanent and 11.54 per cent of contractual teachers find the factor as the most effective factor. About 17 per cent of permanent and 17.31 per cent of contractual teachers rated the factor with 2nd rating while 7.50 per cent of permanent and 12.50 per cent of contractual teachers rate the factor with 3rd rating. About 19.38 per cent of permanent and 17.31 per cent of contractual teachers find the factor as the least effective to motivate them to stay for long in the school. Highest percentage of teachers find the factor as the least important to make the job attractive for them.

C. **Relation with Colleagues:** The factor speaks about the emotional bond shared with other teachers and non-teaching staff at the school. If the relation among the peers are good, the working environment becomes healthy and friendly. And it helps to retain teachers for long in their respective schools. Out of total teachers, 23.75 per cent of permanent and 15.38 per cent of contractual teachers find the factor as the most effective factor to motivate teachers. About 23 per cent of permanent and 16 per cent of contractual teachers rated the factor with 2nd rating while 15.63 per cent of permanent and 12.5 0 per cent of contractual teachers rate the factor with 3rd rating. About 2.50 per cent of permanent and 5.77 per cent of contractual teachers find the factor as the least effective to motivate teachers to improve their performance and to stay at the same school for long time. Most of the teachers covered under study find the factor as the most important.

D. **Positive Attitude of Management:** The factor can be understood as attitude of management personnel towards teachers. If the management is supportive and positive towards teachers, higher performances of teachers can be achieved with mutual efforts. Out of total teachers, 37.5 per cent of permanent and 32.7 per cent of contractual teachers find the factor as the most effective factor to motivate teachers. About 17 per cent of permanent and 23 per cent of contractual teachers rated the factor with second rank while 10 per cent of permanent and 5.77 per cent of contractual teachers rated the factor with 3rd rating. About 4 per cent of permanent and 2 per cent of contractual teachers find the factor as the least effective to motivate teachers and also to control turnover of teachers.

E. **Relation with the Students:** The factor indicates the relation of teachers with students of their respective schools. If they share emotional bonding with their students, they do not feel like leaving them in between. So the factor is important to control attrition of teachers. Out of total teachers, 28.13 per cent of permanent and 38.46 per cent of contractual teachers find the factor as the most effective factor to motivate teachers. About 20 per cent of permanent and 23.08 per cent of contractual teachers rated the factor with 2nd rating while 12.5 per cent of permanent and 7.7 per cent of contractual teachers rate the factor with 3rd rating. About 5 per cent of permanent and 4 per cent of contractual teachers find the factor as the least effective to control turnover of teachers.

F. **Recognition:** Recognition means award or reward for extra ordinary performance of any teachers for betterment of the school or its students. Recognition of special efforts can motivate teachers to perform with best of their capabilities. Out of total teachers, 10.63 per cent of permanent and 5.77 per cent of contractual teachers find the factor as the most effective factor to motivate teachers. About 15 per cent of permanent and 15.38 per cent of contractual teachers rate the factor with 2nd rating while 10.63 per cent of permanent and 8.65 per cent of contractual teachers rate the factor with 3rd rating. About 6.25 per cent of permanent and 14.42 per cent of contractual teachers find the factor as the least effective to motivate teachers.

G. **Decision Making Involvement:** The factor speaks about participation of teachers in important decisions related to teachers or any other stakeholders of the school. Whether opinion of teachers is considered while making important decisions related to school decides commitment of teachers towards school. Out of total teachers, 10.63 per cent of permanent and 7.69 per cent of contractual teachers find the factor as the most effective factor to motivate teachers. About 10 per cent of permanent and 14 per cent of contractual teachers rated the factor with 2nd rating. Around 10 per cent of permanent and 12 per cent of contractual teachers rated the factor with 3rd rating. About 7.50 per cent of permanent and 5.77 per cent of contractual teachers find the factor as the least effective to control attrition of teachers.

H. **Roles and Responsibilities:** The factor can be understood as roles and responsibilities assign to teachers. Whether roles and responsebilities of teachers are critical or important for smooth functioning of the school decides level of commitment of teachers towards betterment of school. Out of total teachers, 16.25 per cent of permanent and 19.23 per cent of contractual teachers find the factor as the most effective factor to motivate teachers. About 11.25 per cent of permanent and 12.50 per cent of contractual teachers rate the factor with 2nd rating, while 10.63 per cent of permanent and 8.65 per cent of contractual teachers rate the factor with 3rd rating. About 4.38 per cent of permanent and 3.85 per cent of contractual teachers find the factor as the least effective to retain teachers for long.

I. **Facilities:** Facilities provided to teachers on campus have direct connection with their performance. If more number of facilities provided at schools, working of those schools become convenient and teachers desire to enjoy those facilities for long. Out of total teachers, 14.38 per cent of permanent and 11.54 per cent of contractual teachers find the factor as the most effective factor to motivate teachers. 10.63 per cent of permanent and 19.2 per cent of contractual teachers rate the factor with 2nd rating. About 4 per cent of permanent and 9.62 per cent of contractual teachers rate the factor with 3rd rating. About 6.88 per cent of permanent and 5.77 per cent of contractual teachers find the factor as the least effective to control attrition of teachers.

J. **Good Feedback Ranking:** The ranking given to teachers on the basis of feedback of students, management and other stake holders. If the ranking is high, the bonus amount or promotional opportunities are also higher. A good feedback ranking on their performance motivate teachers to improve their performance day by day. Out of total teachers, 12.50 per cent of permanent and 6.73 per cent of contractual teachers find the factor as the most effective factor to motivate teachers. About 14 per cent of Permanent and 17.31 per cent of contractual teachers rate the factor with 2nd rating, while 1.88 per cent of permanent and 8.65 per cent of contractual teachers rate the factor with 3rd rating. It is interesting to note that 18.13 per cent of permanent and 10.58 per cent of contractual teachers find the factor as the least effective to resolve the problem of attrition of teachers in private schools.

6.7.2 Teachers' Willingness to Stay

In this section, teachers are asked if they are willing to stay in the same school. If their response is yes, then they are asked for how long (the answer is expected to be in terms of years). This is to know chances of future attrition of the teachers who are not willing to stay in the same school.

Table 6.8: Willingness to Stay in the Same School

Willingness to Stay in the Same School	*Permanent (n=160)*	*per cent*	*Contractual (n=104)*	*per cent*
A. Yes	146	91.25	85	81.73
B. No	14	8.75	15	14.42
If yes, then how long? (in Avg. years)	8.91		4.91	
Till retirement	57	39.04	16	18.82

Source: Field survey data.

Out of total teachers involved in the survey from Anand district, 91.25 per cent of permanent and 81.73 per cent of contractual teachers are willing to stay in the same school (Table 6.8). That indicates that they are happy with their current jobs and there were few chances of them leaving the jobs. About 9 per cent of permanent and 14 per cent of contractual teachers were not happy with the current schools and they are ready to leave their current jobs. Those, who are willing to continue with the same school were asked for how many more years. Permanent teachers are willing to continue for 8.91 years on an average and contractual teachers are willing to continue for 4.91 years on an average. About 39 per cent of permanent teachers who are willing to stay in the current job would continue till retirement and the share was 18.82 per cent in case of contractual teachers who are ready to continue till retirement in the same school.

6.8 PROFESSIONAL DEVELOPMENT OF TEACHERS

In the section, information related to training and development programs organised by schools are gathered and presented in Table 6.9.

6.8.1 Ways to Identify Need for Development

In this teachers were asked how they identify that they need professional development in the field of teaching. They were given options and are expected to tick on all the ways adopted by them to identify need for development.

Out of total teachers responded, 62.50 per cent of permanent and 37.50 per cent of contractual teachers attend courses related to teaching to identify the need of development. About 40 per cent of permanent teachers and 3.69 per cent of contractual teachers got their teaching observed and commented upon to identify the gap between actual and expected performance. Around 38 per cent of permanent teachers and 56 per cent of contractual teachers observed teaching of others to identify where they need to improve through development. About 65 per cent of permanent and 64.42 per cent of contractual teachers studied students' feedback on their performance to know their area of improvement. About 43 per cent of permanent and 35 per cent of contractual teachers got mentoring of experienced colleagues to get idea about need for development. About 57 per cent of permanent and 53 per cent of contractual teachers discuss about their performance with the experts to identify where they need to improve. They were also asked to give any other way adopted by them to identify need for development. Other ways adopted by them are as: all which can help to grow professionally; attending workshops; counselling by experienced teachers, experts & director; encouragement to go extra miles; learning more books and magazines; observing latest techniques for teaching; self-analysis and surfing e-resources related to the subject area.

Table 6.9: Professional Development of Teachers

Sr. No.	*Particulars*	*Permanent per cent*	*Contractual per cent*
1.	**Ways to identify need for development**		
	A. Attending courses on teaching	62.50	37.50
	B. Having your own teaching observed and commented upon	40.00	32.69
	C. Observing others' teaching (Learning by example)	38.13	55.77
	D. Studying students' feedback	65.00	64.42
	E. Mentoring by experienced colleagues	43.13	34.62
	F. Discussion about the performance with the experts	56.88	52.88
	G. Any other		
	All which can help to grow professionally	0.63	
	Attending workshops	0.63	
	Counselling by experienced teachers, experts & director	0.63	
	Encouragement to go extra miles	0.63	
	Learning more books and magazines		0.96
	Observing latest techniques for teaching	0.63	
	Self-Analysis	0.63	
	Surfing e-resources related to subject area		0.96
2.	**Ways to develop yourself**		
	A. Attending Seminars	61.25	42.31
	B. Attending Conferences	41.25	30.77
	C. Attending subject related workshops	68.75	55.77
	D. Attending Refresher Courses	47.50	30.77
	E. Reading books/magazines	79.38	75.96

Sr. No.	Particulars	Permanent per cent	Contractual per cent
	F. Surfing e-resources on the subject	61.88	56.73
	G. Updating through news	60.63	45.19
	H. Interacting with subject experts	61.25	65.38
	I. Regular visit to Library and books reading	68.75	50.00
	J. Any other		
	Interacting and juxtapose with others' method of teaching		0.96
	Making example		0.96
	self-reading		0.96
	sport competition & other sports' activities	0.63	
	Updating subject content	0.63	
	Video lectures of experts		1.92
3	**Frequency of trainings organized by School in a year**		
	A. Not at all	18.75	30.77
	B. 1–5	72.50	57.69
	C. 6–10	3.75	4.81
	D. >10	5.00	6.73
4	**No. of training programs attended by teacher per year**		
	A. Not at all	14.38	35.58
	B. 1–5	76.25	54.81
	C. 6–10	3.75	3.85
	D. >10	5.63	5.77

Source: Field survey data.

6.8.2 Ways for Teachers' Development:

Out of total teachers surveyed from aided and unaided private schools of Anand district, 61.25 per cent of permanent and 42.31 per cent of contractual teachers attended seminars to upgrade their subject knowledge.

About 41 per cent of permanent and 31 per cent of contractual teachers attended national/international conferences to update their knowledge of the subject taught by them. Around 69 per cent of permanent and 56 per cent of contractual attended workshops related to their subject. About 48 per cent of permanent and 31 per cent of contractual teachers attended refresher courses of their respective subjects organized by government or any other educational body. About 80 per cent of permanent and 76 per cent of contractual teachers upgraded their knowledge in their subjects by reading books or magazines related to their subjects. Such books are available through national or international publishers. Highest percentage of the teachers use this to develop themselves in the teaching profession. About 62 per cent of permanent and 57 per cent of contractual teachers opted for e-resources related to their subjects. While 60.63 per cent of permanent and 45.19 per cent of contractual teachers updated themselves through current progress in their subjects, which are available through news. About 61 per cent of permanent and 65 per cent of contractual teachers interacted with their subject experts to learn from their expertise. While 68.75 per cent of permanent and 50 per cent of contractual teachers visited libraries of their schools regularly to get updated knowledge from books. They were also asked about any other ways if they adopt to develop themselves, they gave the other ways as: interacting and juxtapose with others' method of teaching; making example; self-reading; sport competition & other sports' activities; updating subject content and video lectures of experts

6.8.3 Trainings organized by Schools:

In this section, teachers were asked about number of training programs organized by schools. They had tick on appropriate option by considering number of training programs organized in the school premises or outside the campus for teachers.

It was observed that management of Schools organize 1 to 5 training programs for teachers in a year for 72.50 per cent of permanent and 57.69 per cent of contractual teachers. Out of total teachers involved in the study from private schools of Anand district, 5 per cent of permanent and 6.73 per cent of contractual teachers mentioned that their schools organize more than 10 training programs in a year. About 3.75 per cent of permanent teachers and 4.81 per cent of contractual teachers got benefit of 6 to 10 training programs organized by their schools, while 18.75 per cent of permanent and 30.77 per cent of contractual teachers noted that their schools do not organize any training programs throughout the year.

6.8.4 Trainings Attended by Teachers

In this section, teachers were asked about number of training programs attended by them per year. About 77 per cent of permanent and 55 per cent of contractual teachers attend 1–5 training programs per year, while 14.38 per cent of permanent and 35.58 per cent of contractual teachers did not attend any training program throughout the year. The 5.63 per cent of permanent and 5.77 per cent of contractual teachers attended more than 10 training programs throughout the year. The 3.75 per cent of permanent and 3.85 per cent of contractual teachers attend 6 to 10 training programs in a year to upgrade themselves in the field of teaching. They were given trainings related to subject matter or soft skills.

6.9 IMPLICATIONS OF INAPPROPRIATE BEHAVIOUR

In this section, teachers were given a list of inappropriate behaviour and they were asked to give their responses on whether there is any negative

Table 6.10: Behaviour & its Negative Implications

Behaviour	*Always*		*Sometimes*		*Never*	
	PT (%)	*CT (%)*	*PT (%)*	*CT (%)*	*PT (%)*	*CT (%)*
A. For not being on time to school	41.3	32.7	27.5	28.9	35.7	39.4
B. For violating important rules & regulations	47.5	40.4	19.4	21.2	37.9	38.5
C. For conflicting behaviour with peers	35.0	34.6	27.5	23.1	42.9	42.3
D. For misbehaviour with students	39.4	37.5	25.0	20.2	40.7	42.3
E. For not meeting the deadlines	37.5	36.5	32.5	26.9	34.3	36.5
F. For utilizing school hours for personal work	41.3	35.6	17.5	14.4	47.1	50.0
G. For using school property for personal task	41.9	34.6	11.9	18.3	52.9	48.1

Source: Field survey data.

implications on such behaviour. They had to respond in terms of if there negative implications from the management is always, sometimes or never on such behaviour. This is done to get idea about how inappropriate behaviour is handled by the school management. Such negative implications can be memo, warning, punishment, transfer, demotion, termination or even lay off. Some of the management personnel are very strict and some are lenient in handling teachers if they commit mistakes. Table 6.10 presents the behaviour and its negative implications.

A. *For Not Being on Time to School*

Out of total teachers surveyed from the aided and unaided private schools of the Anand district, 41.25 per cent of permanent and 32.69 per cent of contractual teachers were always given punishment for not being on time to school. The 27.50 per cent of permanent and 28.85 per cent of contractual teachers got punishment sometimes from the management while 35.71 per cent of permanent and 39.42 per cent of contractual teachers never faced any negative implication even after being late to the school.

B. *For Violating Important Rules & Regulations*

Out of total teachers surveyed from the aided and unaided private schools of the Anand district, 47.50 per cent of permanent and 40.38 per cent of contractual teachers always face negative implications if they violate important rules and regulations of the school. About 20 per cent of permanent and 21 per cent of contractual teachers got punishment sometimes from the management for doing so, while 37.86 per cent of permanent and 38.46 per cent of contractual teachers were never given any punishment though they violate rules of the school.

C. *For Conflicting Behaviour with Peers*

Out of total teachers surveyed from the aided and unaided private schools of the Anand district, 35 per cent each of permanent and contractual teachers mentioned that they were always punished for conflicting behaviour with their colleagues. About 28 per cent of permanent and 23 per cent of contractual teachers got punishment sometimes from the management for conflicts with other teachers, while 42.86 per cent of permanent and 42.31 per cent of contractual teachers never face any negative implications for conflicts with their peers.

D. *For Misbehaviour with Students*

Out of total teachers surveyed from the aided and unaided private schools of the Anand district, 39.38 per cent of permanent and 37.5 per cent of contractual teachers always got negative implications for misbehaviour with students. While 25 per cent of permanent and 20.2 per cent of contractual teachers got punishment sometimes from the management for misbehaviour with their students. On other side, 41 per cent of permanent and 42 per cent of contractual teachers never got any punishment for misbehaviour with their students.

E. *For Not Meeting the Deadlines*

Out of total teachers surveyed from the aided and unaided private schools of the Anand district, 37.5 per cent of permanent and 36.5 per cent of contractual teachers always got negative implications for not meeting work related deadlines. While 32.5 per cent of permanent and 27 per cent of contractual teachers sometimes got punishment from the management for not meeting the deadlines. The 34.29 per cent of permanent and 36.54 per cent of contractual teachers never got any punishment for not meeting the deadlines.

F. *For Utilizing School Hours for Personal Work*

Out of total teachers surveyed from the aided and unaided private schools of the Anand district, 41.25 per cent of permanent and 35.58 per cent of contractual teachers always got negative implications for personal work during official working hours. About 18 per cent of permanent and 15 per cent of contractual teachers sometimes got punishment from the management for using school hours for personal work. The 47.14 per cent of permanent and 50 per cent of contractual teachers are never given any punishment for doing personal work during working hours.

G. *For Using School Property for Personal Task*

Out of total teachers surveyed from the aided and unaided private schools of the Anand district, 41.88 per cent of permanent and 34.62 per cent of contractual teachers always get punished to use school property for personal task. About 12 per cent of permanent and 18 per cent of contractual teacher sometimes face negative implications from the management for using school properties for personal work. Around half of the permanent and contractual teachers were used school properties for personal work without any negative implications.

6.10 REASONS FOR ATTRITION THROUGH STATEMENTS

In this section, statements related to problem of attrition and its causes are given. Teachers were expected to read each statement and tick on the scale. The Likert's scale used here indicates completely disagree as 1, partially disagree as 2, neutral as 3, partially agree as 4 and completely agree as 5. They had to tick on any of the five scales to give their opinion on each statement. This is to understand their views on various parameters related to the problem of attrition of teachers. There are 10 statements given to be ranked on the scale of 1 to 5. Table 6.11 presents responses on statements.

6.10.1 Involvement in Work Related Decisions May Lead to High Morale

The statement means that if teachers are involved in decisions pertaining to their work, they perform with high morale and commitment towards their respective schools. Out of total teachers of aided and unaided private schools from Anand district, half of the permanent and three fifth of contractual teachers completely agree with the statement followed by 25.63 per cent of permanent and 15.38 per cent of contractual teachers agree with the statement partially. The 6.25 per cent of permanent and 9.62 per cent of contractual teachers disagree with the statement completely. The 14.38 per cent of permanent and 9.62 per cent of contractual teachers neither disagree nor agree with the statement.

6.10.2 Colleague's Supportive Behaviour Leads to Positive Work Environment

The statement means if colleagues are supportive with one another, the working environment of the school becomes positive and friendly. Such working environment is a need of all types of teachers. Out of total teachers of aided and unaided private schools from Anand district, 81.25 per cent of permanent and 78.85 per cent of contractual teachers completely agree with the statement. This is the statement with highest agreement from the teachers. However, 5.63 per cent of permanent and

Table 6.11: Statements to Understand Reasons for Attrition

Sr. No.	*Statements*	*Completely Disagree 1*		*Partially Disagree 2*		*Neutral 3*		*Partially Agree 4*		*Completely Agree 5*	
		PT (%)	*CT (%)*	*PT (%)*	*CT (%)*	*PT (%)*	*CT (%)*	*PT (%)*	*CT (%)*	*PT (%)*	*CT (%)*
1.	Involvement in work related decisions may lead to high morale.	6.3	9.6	3.8	1.0	14.4	9.6	25.6	15.4	50.0	64.4
2.	Colleague's supportive behaviour leads to positive work environment.	5.6	2.9	1.3	0.0	2.5	4.8	9.4	13.5	81.3	78.9
3.	Working environment affects work commitment.	6.3	7.7	0.6	2.9	3.8	9.6	15.0	20.2	74.4	59.6
4.	Job satisfaction may reduce attrition.	13.1	11.5	3.1	4.8	16.9	13.5	20.0	23.1	46.9	47.1
5.	Teaching at the same place for a longer period gets monotonous.	31.9	31.7	18.1	17.3	15.6	13.5	18.1	20.2	16.3	17.3
6.	Jump in early career is necessary for career growth.	17.5	16.4	12.5	7.7	17.5	13.5	23.8	24.0	28.8	38.5
7.	Lack of acknowledgement may cause inefficiency in work.	17.5	8.7	3.1	8.7	11.9	12.5	31.3	18.3	36.3	51.9
8.	Long term job security is a key to retaining teachers.	11.3	12.5	1.3	4.8	8.8	10.6	19.4	16.4	59.4	55.8
9.	Image of teaching profession is lower than other professions in the job market.	41.9	47.1	11.3	12.5	10.0	9.6	21.9	15.4	15.0	15.4
10.	Personal family issues do play a vital role in the performance of teachers.	21.9	26.0	13.8	11.5	12.5	14.4	29.4	25.0	22.5	23.1

Source: Field survey data.

2.88 per cent of contractual teachers disagree with the statement completely. About 3 per cent of permanent and 5 per cent of contractual teachers neither disagree nor agree with the statement.

6.10.3 Working Environment Affects Work Commitment

The statement means that teachers are more committed to their work if they get positive working environment. The statement identifies the link between working environment of school and teachers' work commitment. Out of total teachers of aided and unaided private schools from Anand district, 74.38 per cent of permanent and 59.62 per cent of contractual teachers completely agree with the statement while 6.25 per cent of permanent and 7.69 per cent of contractual teachers disagree with the statement completely. About 4 per cent of permanent and 9.62 per cent of contractual teachers neither disagree nor agree with the statement.

6.10.4 Job Satisfaction May Reduce Attrition

The statement highlights the need of job satisfaction to reduce attrition of teachers. If teachers are satisfied with their job, they are less likely to leave their respective schools. Out of total teachers of aided and unaided private schools from Anand district, hardly 7 per cent of permanent and huge 47 per cent of contractual teachers completely agree with the statement. While 13.13 per cent of permanent and 11.54 per cent of contractual teachers disagree with the statement completely. It was surprising to note that about 17 per cent of permanent and 14 per cent of contractual teachers neither disagree nor agree with the statement.

6.10.5 Teaching at the Same Place for a Longer Period Gets Monotonous

The statement means that if teachers teach at the same place school for long period, they find their jobs boring and monotonous. The statement identifies the need of change and something new after some years in the same job. Out of total teachers of aided and unaided private schools from Anand district, 16.25 per cent of permanent and 17.31 per cent of contractual teachers completely agree with the statement while 31.88 per cent of permanent and 31.73 per cent of contractual teachers disagree with the statement completely. This is the statement with second highest disagreement from the teachers.

6.10.6 Jump in Early Career is Necessary for Career Growth

The statement highlights the recent trend where young candidates feel that they need to change work places in the starting of the career to get better prospects throughout the career. Out of total teachers of aided and unaided private schools from Anand district, 28.75 per cent of permanent and 38.46 per cent of contractual teachers completely agree with the statement while 17.5 per cent of permanent and 16.35 per cent of contractual teachers disagree with the statement completely. The 17.50 per cent of permanent and 13.46 per cent of contractual teachers neither disagree nor agree with the statement.

6.10.7 Lack of Acknowledgement May Cause Inefficiency in Work

The statement means that if efforts of teachers are not recognized, they are de-motivated to improve their performance. That indicates that extraordinary contributions of the teachers should be acknowledged to get efficient work from teachers. Out of total teachers of aided and unaided private schools from Anand district, 36.25 per cent of permanent and 51.92 per cent of contractual teachers completely agree with the statement while 17.50 per cent of permanent and 8.65 per cent of contractual teachers disagree with the statement completely. About12 per cent of permanent and 13 per cent of contractual teachers neither disagree nor agree with the statement.

6.10.8 Long Term Job Security is a Key to Retaining Teachers

The statement identifies the need of long term job security to retain teachers for long. To control attrition, teachers should be given long term job security in their respective schools. Out of total teachers of aided and unaided private schools from Anand district, more than half of the permanent and contractual teachers completely agree with the statement while 11.25 per cent of permanent and 12.5 per cent of contractual teachers disagree with the statement completely. The 8.75 per cent of permanent and 10.58 per cent of contractual teachers neither disagree nor agree with the statement. 19.38 per cent of permanent and 16.35 per cent of contractual teachers agree with the statement partially.

6.10.9 Image of Teaching Profession is Lower Than Other Professions in the Job Market

The statement means that the teaching profession holds lower image in the job market compared to other professions. Now a days the trend is such that candidates opt for teaching positions till they get jobs in other professions as the reputation of the profession is going down. Out of total teachers of aided and unaided private schools from Anand district, 41.88 per cent of permanent and 47.12 per cent of contractual teachers disagree with the statement completely. The 11.25 per cent of permanent and 12.50 per cent of contractual teachers disagree with the statement partially while 10 per cent of permanent and 9.62 per cent of contractual teachers neither disagree nor agree with the statement. About 22 per cent of permanent and 15 per cent of contractual teachers agree with the statement partially. And 15 per cent of permanent and 15.38 per cent of contractual teachers completely agree with the statement. This is the statement with the highest disagreement from both the categories of the teachers.

6.10.10 Personal Family Issues do Play a Vital Role in the Performance of Teachers

The statement highlights impact of personal family issues on the performance of the teachers. Their performance may hamper due to any personal stress. Out of total teachers of aided and unaided private schools from Anand district, 21.88 per cent of permanent and 25.96 per cent of contractual teachers disagree with the statement completely, while 22.5 per cent of permanent and 23.08 per cent of contractual teachers completely agree with the statement. About 13 per cent of permanent and 14 per cent of contractual teachers neither disagree nor agree with the statement.

6.11 INFORMATION RELATED TO WORKLOAD OF TEACHERS

In the section, information on how teachers interact with students other than regular classes, what type of work pressure they get other than teaching and how they handle stress is collected and recorded. They are expected to go through the options given and tick on all the options related to them. Table 6.12 presents details on work load of teachers.

6.11.1 Interaction with the Students

In this section, teachers were asked whether they interact with the students other than regular classes. Out of total teachers surveyed from aided and unaided private schools of the district, 96.25 per cent of permanent teachers mentioned that they interact with students other than regular classes, while 87.5 per cent of contractual teachers interact with the students other than teaching. Remaining teachers from both the categories do not interact with the students other than regular class.

Those who interact with the students were asked about how they interact with them. Options were given and teachers were allowed to tick on more than one option if it is applicable to them. Out of total teachers who interact with the students other than regular classes, 41.56 per cent of permanent and 23.08 per cent of contractual teachers do mentoring of the students to improve their performance in studies. About 87 per cent of permanent and 31.87 per cent of contractual teachers counsel their students on the problems pertaining to study. While 43.51 per cent of permanent and 60.44 per cent of contractual teachers talk to their students casually to build emotional connect with them, however, 57.79 per cent of permanent and 36.26 per cent of contractual teachers counsel students on their personal problems. The 1.95 per cent of permanent and 2.20 per cent of contractual teachers interacted with the students when they come for problem solving to teachers.

6.11.2 Work Pressure on Teachers

In the section, they were asked about type of work pressure they got other than teaching. Out of total teachers involved in the study from both the categories, 68.13 per cent of permanent and 70.19 per cent of contractual teachers handle pressure of co-curriculum activities like participation in inter school competitions, internal competitions, annual day celebrations or getting students ready to participate in state or national level events. About 19 per cent of permanent and contractual teachers get government assignments like census survey, election or any other documentation. About 36 per cent of permanent and 17 per cent of contractual teachers get work from Parent Teacher Association, where they have to coordinate with parents on several occasions. While 72.5 per cent of permanent and 63.46 per cent of contractual teachers have to perform duties related to internal or board exams such as supervision, invigilation, paper correction, moderation etc. they are also asked if they get any other work pressure other than teaching and what is mentioned above. They listed the following work pressures other than teaching: academic planning, computer related work, formulating policies, coordinating with different departments, marketing of the school, co-ordination of various committees, time table preparation, attending trainings, remedial classes and routine workload.

6.11.3 Handling Work Related Stress

In this section, list of ways to handle work related stress is given. Out of total teachers covered under study from both the categories, 50 per cent of permanent and 59.62 per cent of contractual teachers handle work related stress through breaking down their work into smaller tasks while 58.13 per cent of permanent and 56.73 per cent of contractual teachers manage work related stress through effective time management. About 56 per cent of permanent and 58 per cent of contractual teachers listen to uplifting music to handle stress at work peacefully. Thus, these are the most adopted ways by teachers to work without stress. However, 23.13 per cent of permanent and 15.38 per cent of contractual teachers handle stress by not taking things too seriously at workplace, while 44.38 per cent of permanent and 36.54 per cent of contractual teachers meditate for peaceful mind at work. Around 37 per cent of permanent and 36 per cent of contractual teachers talk about their problems to handle stress. Through physical exercises to be fit and healthy, 31.88 per cent of permanent and 25.96 per cent of contractual teachers handle work related stress.

While 36.88 per cent of permanent and 43.27 per cent of contractual teachers handle stress by indulging in their favourite hobby to feel happy and healthy. About 28 per cent of permanent and 15 per cent of contractual teachers handle stress by taking sleep for adequate hours, while 43.13 per cent of permanent and 48.08 per cent of contractual teachers plan an outing with their family and friends to feel fresh to handle stress and be more productive at work. Only 8.75 per cent of permanent and 8.65 per cent of contractual teachers handle stress by asking for help with the jobs they dislike. Thus, this is the least preferred way of handling the stress by teachers. Teachers were also asked if they adopt any other way to handle work related stress other than mentioned in the list and they mentioned as/: by enjoying their work, doing hard work and getting solution, keeping faith in god & counselling and watching movie or hangouts with friends.

Table 6.12: Details on Work Load of Teachers

Sr. No.	*Particulars*		*Permanent per cent*	*Contractual per cent*
1.	**Interaction with students other than regular class**			
	A. Yes		96.25	87.50
	B. No		3.75	12.50
2.	**If Yes, then how?**			
	A. Mentoring		41.56	23.08
	B. Counselling		56.49	31.87
	C. Casual talks		43.51	60.44
	D. Personal counselling		57.79	36.26
	A. Any other	Problem solving	1.95	2.20
3.	**Work Pressure other than teaching**			
	A. Co-curriculum activities		68.13	70.19
	B. Government assignments		18.75	18.27
	C. PTA		35.00	17.31
	D. Assignment from management		26.88	31.73
	E. Exam duties		72.50	63.46
	F. Any other			
	Academic planning		0.63	0.00
	Computer related work		0.63	
	Formulating policies, coordinating with different departments		1.88	
	Marketing of the school		0.63	
	Co-ordination of various committees			0.96
	Time table preparation			0.96
	Attending trainings on NTSE, Foundation, RM etc.		0.63	
	Remedial classes			0.96
	Routine workload		0.63	1.92

Sr. No.	*Particulars*	*Permanent per cent*	*Contractual per cent*
4.	**Ways to manage work related stress**		
	A. Break down your work into smaller tasks	50.00	59.62
	B. Try not to take things too seriously at workplace	23.13	15.38
	C. Through effective time management	58.13	56.73
	D. Meditation	44.38	36.54
	E. Talking about your problems	36.88	35.58
	F. Through Exercise	31.88	25.96
	G. Indulging in your favourite hobby	36.88	43.27
	H. Ask for help with the jobs you dislike	8.75	8.65
	I. By taking adequate sleep	27.50	15.38
	J. Planning an outing with family and friends	43.13	48.08
	K. Listening to uplifting music	55.63	57.69
	L. Any Other		
	Enjoying work	0.63	
	Doing hard work and getting solution		0.96
	Keeping faith in god & counselling	0.63	
	Watching movie or hangouts with friends		0.96

Source: Field survey data.

6.12 OPINION OF TEACHERS ON PROFESSIONAL FACTORS FOR ATTRITION

In this section, all probable professional factors for attrition are given and they have to rate each of them as Very important, Important and Not important in their own perception. The rating is to be done on the scale of 1 to 3, where 1 = Very Important, 2 = Important and 3 = Not Important. This is to know opinion of each permanent and contractual teachers on professional factors which can be a reason for their attrition. Table 6.13 presents opinion on professional factors for attrition.

A. **Working on contractual basis:** The factor is about working on temporary basis, where they can be laid off at any time and their pay is also fixed without any perquisites. Out of total teachers covered under the study from aided and unaided private schools of Anand district, 45.63 per cent of permanent and 36.54 per cent of contractual teachers find the factor as not important with rank 3, while 35.63 per cent of permanent teachers and 29.81 per cent of contractual teachers find the factor as the most important with rank 1.

Table 6.13: Opinion on Professional Factors for Attrition

Factors	*Very Important*		*Important*		*Not Important*	
	PC (%)	*CT (%)*	*PC (%)*	*CT (%)*	*PC (%)*	*CT (%)*
A. Working on contractual basis	35.63	29.81	18.75	33.65	45.63	36.54
B. Pay	60.63	62.5	22.5	26.92	16.88	10.58
C. Working hours	44.38	25.96	31.88	49.04	23.75	25
D. Too many responsibilities	23.13	17.31	31.88	33.65	45	49.04
E. Too few responsibilities	14.38	15.38	29.38	35.58	56.25	49.04
F. Lack of promotion opportunity	46.88	50	24.38	29.81	28.75	20.19
G. Lack of training/ professional development	30	24.04	41.88	44.23	28.13	31.73
H. Experience of discrimination/ harassment	53.13	37.5	20	31.73	26.88	30.77
I. Class size	21.88	20.19	24.38	26.92	53.75	52.88
J. Pupil behaviour	31.88	22.12	31.88	35.58	36.25	42.31
K. Parental behaviour	23.75	22.12	40.63	32.69	35.63	45.19
L. Behaviour Policy of	48.75	36.54	27.5	41.35	23.75	22.12

Management						
M. School – i. Environment (e.g. buildings)	33.13	37.5	30.63	28.85	36.25	33.65
ii. Resources	32.5	37.5	35.63	39.42	31.88	23.08
iii. Colleagues	31.88	31.73	40.63	40.38	27.5	27.88
iv. Reputation	43.13	37.5	33.13	40.38	23.75	22.12
v. Vicinity	28.13	20.19	41.25	46.15	30.63	33.65
N. Management - lack of support	46.25	43.27	31.25	32.69	22.5	24.04
O. Management - lack of direction	41.25	38.46	30.63	35.58	28.13	25.96

Source: Field survey data.

B. **Pay:** The factor includes basic salary, allowances, incentives, benefits, bonus any other monetary and non-monetary perquisites. Out of total teachers covered under the study from aided and unaided private schools of Anand district, 60.63 per cent of permanent teachers and 62.50 per cent of contractual teachers find the factor as the most important with rank 1, while 22.50 per cent of permanent and 26.92 per cent of contractual teachers rate the factor with 2nd rating as they find it important. Only 16.88 per cent of permanent and 10.58 per cent of contractual teachers find the factor as not important with rank 3. This is the factor which is assigned rank 1 by majority of the permanent and contractual teachers, as they find it as the most important.

C. **Working hours:** The factor is about the timing of commencement of the school and closing of the school. It is about total hours, teachers have to spend at school. Out of total teachers covered under the study from aided and unaided private schools of Anand district, 44.38 per cent of permanent teachers and 25.96 per cent of contractual teachers find the factor as the most important with rank 1, while 31.88 per cent of permanent and 49.04 per cent of contractual teachers rate the factor with 2nd rating as they find it important and remaining 23.75 per cent of permanent and 25 per cent of contractual teachers find the factor as not important.

D. **Too many responsibilities:** The factor is about assigning too many responsibilities to the teachers, which are not possible to manage by a single person. Out of total teachers covered under the study from aided and unaided private schools of Anand district, 23.13 per cent of permanent teachers and 17.31 per cent of contractual teachers find the factor as the most important while 31.88 per cent of permanent and 33.65 per cent of contractual teachers rate the factor with 2 most important, however, 45 per cent of permanent and 49.04 per cent of contractual teachers find the factor as not important. This factor is not important for many of them.

E. **Too few responsibilities:** The factor of too few responsibilities is about not assigning enough responsibilities as per calibre of teachers. Too few responsibilities make teachers feel not important at their workplace. Out of total teachers covered under the study from aided and unaided private schools of Anand district, 14.38 per cent of permanent teachers and 15.38 per cent of contractual teachers find the factor as the most important for which second rank was given by 29.38 per cent of permanent and 35.58 per cent of contractual teachers. About 56 per cent of permanent and 49 per cent of contractual teachers find the factor as not important. This is the factor which is not important for highest percentage of permanent and contractual teachers. This indicates that most of the teachers do not consider factors pertaining to responsibilities as important.

F. **Lack of promotion opportunity:** The factor is about no possibilities of getting promoted at their respective schools. Out of total teachers covered under the study from aided and unaided private schools of Anand district, 46.88 per cent of permanent teachers and 50 per cent of contractual teachers find the factor as the most important followed by 24.38 per cent of permanent and 29.81 per cent of contractual teachers rate the factor with 2nd rating as they find it important. However, 28.75 per cent of permanent and 20.19 per cent of contractual teachers find the factor as not important. This factor is among the factors which are very important for majority of the permanent and contractual teachers.

G. **Lack of training/professional development:** The factor is about no provision of training and development programs for teachers to upgrade their knowledge by their respective schools. Out of total teachers covered under the study from aided and unaided private schools of Anand district, 30 per cent of permanent teachers and 24.04 per cent of contractual teachers find the factor as the most important. About 42 per cent of permanent and 44 per cent of contractual teachers rate the factor with 2nd rating as they find it important. About 28.13 per cent of permanent and 31.73 per cent of contractual teachers find the factor as not important. This factor is important for majority of permanent and contractual teachers for attrition.

H. **Experience of discrimination/harassment:** The factor is about unequal treatment to teachers. The practices of partiality and biasness, physical or mental harassment/abuse lead to dissatisfaction towards work. Out of total teachers covered under the study from aided and unaided private schools of Anand district, 53.13 per cent of permanent teachers and 37.50 per cent of contractual teachers find the factor as the most important while 20 per cent of permanent and 31.73 per cent of contractual teachers rate the factor with 2nd rating as they find it important. However, 26.88 per cent of permanent and 30.77 per cent of contractual teachers find the factor as not important. This is the second most important factor for attrition for majority of permanent and contractual teachers as they are intolerant to any harassment or discrimination at workplace.

I. **Class size:** The factor means number of students in a class. The Class size should be appropriate to make the process of learning effective for each student. Out of total teachers covered under the study from aided and unaided private schools of Anand district, 21.88 per cent of permanent teachers and 20.19 per cent of contractual teachers find the factor as the most important with rank 1. About 25 per cent of permanent and 27 per cent of contractual teachers rate the factor with 2nd rating as they find it important. While 54 per cent of permanent and 53 per cent of contractual teachers find the factor as not important. This is the factor which among not important factor as a reason for attrition for permanent as well as contractual teachers.

J. **Pupil behaviour:** The factor is about behaviour of students towards teachers. Students should behave with respect and honour towards teachers. Out of total teachers covered under the study from aided and unaided private schools of Anand district, 31.88 per cent of permanent teachers and 22.12 per cent of contractual teachers find the factor as the most important with rank 1. 31.88 per cent of permanent and 35.58 per cent of contractual teachers rate the factor with 2nd rating as they find it important. 36.25 per cent of permanent and 42.31 per cent of contractual teachers find the factor as not important with rank 3.

K. **Parental behaviour:** The factor is about how parents of the students behave with the teachers. Parents should treat teachers with dignity and respect. Out of total teachers covered under the study from aided and unaided private schools of Anand district, 23.75 per cent of permanent teachers and 22.12 per cent of contractual teachers find the factor as the most important while 40.63 per cent of permanent and 32.69 per cent of contractual teachers rated this factor with second position as they find it important. While 35.63 per cent of permanent and 45.19 per cent of contractual teachers find the factor as not important.

L. **Behaviour Policy of Management:** The factor is about how management treat their teachers. Management should maintain decorum while behaving with teachers as they play critical role in long term success of the school. Out of total teachers covered under the study from aided and unaided private schools of Anand district, 48.75 per cent of permanent teachers and 36.54 per cent of contractual teachers find the factor as the most important. About 28 per cent of permanent and 41 per cent of contractual teachers rate the factor with 2nd rating as they find it important. 23.75 per cent of permanent and 22.12 per cent of contractual teachers find the factor as not important. This is also a very important factor for many of the permanent and contractual teachers.

M. **School (i) Environment (e.g. buildings):** The factor means infrastructure of the school. Building, open space, sport grounds, landscaping, gardens, designing of interior and exterior of the building. Out of total teachers covered under the study from aided and unaided private schools of Anand district, 33.13 per cent of permanent teachers and 37.5 per cent of contractual teachers find the factor as the most important. About 31 per cent of permanent and 29 per cent of contractual teachers rated the factor with 2nd rating as they find it important. About 36 per cent of permanent and 34 per cent of contractual teachers find the factor as not important.

   (ii) **Resources:** The factor is about resources provided to the teachers at the school. Library, reading room, knowledge resource centre and computer lab with internet facility. Out of total teachers covered under the study from aided and unaided private schools of Anand district, 32.5 per cent of permanent teachers and 37.5 per cent of contractual teachers find the factor as the most important. More than 36 per cent of permanent and contractual teachers rated it second important one. However, 32 per cent of permanent and 23 per cent of contractual teachers find the factor as not important.

(iii) **Colleagues:** The factor is about what type of colleagues are appointed in the school. If they are friendly and supportive, working at the school is comfortable. Out of total teachers covered under the study from aided and unaided private schools of Anand district, 31.88 per cent of permanent teachers and 31.73 per cent of contractual teachers find the factor as the most important, while 40.63 per cent of permanent and 40.38 per cent of contractual teachers rate the factor with 2nd rating as they find it important. However, 27.5 per cent of permanent and 27.88 per cent of contractual teachers find the factor as not important.

(iv) **Reputation:** The factor is about impression of the school in the vicinity. With good reputation, good teachers and good students can be attracted. Out of total teachers covered under the study from aided and unaided private schools of Anand district, 43.13 per cent of permanent teachers and 37.5 per cent of contractual teachers find the factor as the most important, while 33.13 per cent of permanent and 40.38 per cent of contractual teachers rated the factor with second rank. About 24 per cent of permanent and 22 per cent of contractual teachers find the factor as not important.

(v) **Vicinity:** The factor is about surroundings and locality of the school. The area where the school is located should be approachable and education friendly. Out of total teachers covered under the study from aided and unaided private schools of Anand district, 28.13 per cent of permanent teachers and 20.19 per cent of contractual teachers find the factor as the most important, while 41.25 per cent of permanent and 46.15 per cent of contractual teachers rated this as second important one. While 30.63 per cent of permanent and 33.65 per cent of contractual teachers find the factor as not important.

N. **Management—Lack of Support:** The factor means lack of support in day to day functioning of the school from the management or even principal. Out of total teachers covered under the study from aided and unaided private schools of Anand district, 46.25 per cent of permanent teachers and 43.27 per cent of contractual teachers find the factor as the most important while 31.25 per cent of permanent and 32.69 per cent of contractual teachers rate the factor with 2nd rating as they find it important. However, 22.5 per cent of permanent and 24.04 per cent of contractual teachers find the factor as not important. This factor is considered as a very important reason for attrition by many of the permanent as well as contractual teachers.

O. **Management—Lack of Direction:** The factor means lack of direction or guidance in the issues related to teaching or any other personal issues from management personnel or even principal. Out of total teachers covered under the study from aided and unaided private schools of Anand district, 41.25 per cent of permanent teachers and 38.46 per cent of contractual teachers find the factor as the most important with rank 1. However, 30.63 per cent of permanent and 35.58 per cent of contractual teachers rated the factor with 2nd rating as they find it important. While 28.13 per cent of permanent and 25.96 per cent of contractual teachers find the factor as not important and assign rank 3 to it. This is also a preferred factor as a reason for teachers' turnover.

6.13 OPINION OF TEACHERS ON PERSONAL FACTORS FOR ATTRITION

In the section a list of personal factors for attrition are given and teachers are asked to rate each personal factor which may be reason for teachers to leave the job. The factors can be rated on the scale of 1 to 3. 1 = Very Important, 2 = Important and 3 = Not important. This is to know teachers' opinion on how important each of the personal factor is as a reason for attrition for them (Table 6.14).

A. **Getting Married:** The factor is about marriage, many of the female teachers leave their jobs as they are getting married and shifting with their in-laws. Out of total teachers covered under the study from aided and unaided private schools of Anand district, 20.63 per cent of permanent teachers and 25.96 per cent of contractual teachers find the factor as very important personal factor. While 12.5 per cent of permanent and 22.12 per cent of contractual teachers rate the factor with 2nd rating as it is important for them. For 66.88 per cent of permanent and 51.92 per cent of contractual teachers, the factor is not important as a reason for attrition and they assign rank 3 to it. The factor is not important personal factor for majority of the teachers as many of them are already married and the factor is not applicable to them.

Table 6.14: Opinion on Personal Factors for Attrition

Factors	*Very Important*		*Important*		*Not Important*	
	PT (%)	*CT (%)*	*PT (%)*	*CT (%)*	*PT (%)*	*CT (%)*
A. Getting married	20.6	26.0	12.5	22.1	66.9	51.9
B. Expecting a child	18.8	21.2	21.9	37.5	59.4	41.4
C. Moving to be near partners job	30.6	17.3	23.8	37.5	45.6	45.2
D. Moving to be near family	27.5	24.0	24.4	42.3	48.1	33.7
E. Poor health	36.3	30.8	34.4	34.6	29.4	34.6
F. Disability	30.6	22.1	28.1	35.6	41.3	42.3
G. Age	16.3	5.8	25.0	28.9	58.8	65.4
H. General dissatisfaction with teaching profession	21.9	20.2	35.0	37.5	43.1	42.3
I. Caring for relatives	18.1	19.2	38.1	25.0	43.8	55.8
J. For reasons connected with education of own kids	31.3	19.2	33.1	36.5	35.6	44.2
K. High cost of renting accommodation	16.9	19.2	33.1	43.3	50.0	37.5
L. High Cost of buying accommodation	15.6	19.2	39.4	40.4	45.0	40.4
M. Commuting—inconvenience/time taken	20.6	15.4	38.8	51.0	40.6	33.7
N. Cost of transportation per week	15.6	15.4	33.1	43.3	51.3	41.4

Source: Field survey data.

B. **Expecting a Child:** This factor is also applicable to female teachers. Many of the female teachers leave their jobs when they expect a child to take care of them and then of their kids. Out of total teachers covered under the study from aided and unaided private schools of Anand district, 20.63 per cent of permanent teachers and 25.96 per cent of contractual teachers find the factor as very important personal factor and assign rank 1. About 12.5 per cent of permanent and 22.12 per cent of contractual teachers rate the factor with 2nd rating as it is important for them. For 66.88 per cent of permanent and 51.92 per cent of contractual teachers the factor is not important as a reason for attrition and they assign rank 3 to it. Many of permanent and contractual teachers find the factor as not important as it is not applicable to them.

C. **Moving to be Near Partners' Job:** This is also the factor mostly pertaining to female teachers as they are expected to move with their partners if they get job elsewhere. Out of total teachers covered under the study from aided and unaided private schools of Anand district, 30.63 per cent of permanent teachers and 17.31 per cent of contractual teachers find the factor as very important personal factor and assign rank 1. About 24 per cent of permanent and 38 per cent of contractual teachers rate the factor with 2nd rating as it is important for them. For 45.63 per cent of permanent and 45.19 per cent of contractual teachers, this factor is not important as a reason for attrition.

D. **Moving to be Near Family:** This is the factor where teachers leave their jobs to get the job in the place, where their family lives. Out of total teachers covered under the study from aided and unaided private schools of Anand district, 27.50 per cent of permanent teachers and 24.04 per cent of contractual teachers find the factor as very important personal factor and assign rank 1. About 24.38 per cent of permanent and 42.31 per cent of contractual teachers rate the factor with 2nd rating as it is important for them. For 48.13 per cent of permanent and 33.65 per cent of contractual teachers, the factor is not important as a reason for attrition and they assign rank 3 to it.

E. **Poor Health:** Issues related to heath. If the health is deteriorating and not permitting the teacher to continue with the profession, the teacher has to quit the job. Out of total teachers covered under the study from aided and unaided private schools of Anand district, 36.25 per cent of permanent teachers and 30.77 per cent of contractual teachers find the factor as very important personal factor and assign rank 1. 34.38 per cent of permanent and 34.62 per cent of contractual teachers rate the factor with 2nd rating as it is important for them. For 29.38 per cent of permanent and 34.62 per cent of contractual teachers, the factor is not important as a reason for attrition and they assign rank 3 to it.

F. **Disability:** The factor is about any physical or mental disability to continue with the teaching profession. Out of total teachers covered under the study from aided and unaided private schools of Anand district, 30.63 per cent of permanent teachers and 22.12 per cent of contractual teachers find the factor as very important personal factor and assign rank 1. About 28.13 per cent of permanent and 35.58 per cent of contractual teachers rate the factor with 2nd rating as it is important for them. For 41.25 per cent of permanent and 42.31 per cent of contractual teachers, the factor is not important as a reason for attrition and they assign rank 3 to it.

G. **Age:** In most of the aided and unaided private schools, retirement age is predetermined. But in some self-financed schools, teachers are appointed irrespective of their old age. In such cases, Old age can be a reason for the turnover. Out of total teachers covered under the study from aided and unaided private schools of Anand district, 16.25 per cent of permanent teachers and 5.77 per cent of contractual teachers find the factor as very important personal factor and assign rank 1. One fourth of permanent and 28.85 per cent of contractual teachers rate the factor with 2nd rating as it is important for them. For 58.75 per cent of permanent and 65.38 per cent of contractual teachers, the factor is not important as a reason for attrition and they assign rank 3 to it.

H. **General dissatisfaction with teaching profession:** the factor speaks about dissatisfaction of the teachers with the profession of teaching itself due to adverse experiences. Out of total teachers covered under the study from aided and unaided private schools of Anand district, 21.88 per cent of permanent teachers and 20.19 per cent of contractual teachers find the factor as very important personal factor and assign rank 1. About 35 per cent of permanent and 37.5 per cent of contractual teachers rate the factor with 2nd rating as it is important for them. For 43.13 per cent of permanent and 42.31 per cent of contractual teachers, the factor is not important as a reason for attrition.

I. **Caring for relatives:** The factor means teachers leave their jobs to take care of any near ones, if they are required personal attention and there is no one to take care of the person. Out of total teachers covered under the study from aided and unaided private schools of Anand district, 18.13 per cent of permanent teachers and 19.23 per cent of contractual teachers find the factor as very important personal factor and assign rank 1. About 38.13 per cent of permanent and 25 per cent of contractual teachers rate the factor with 2nd rating as it is important for them. For 43.75 per cent of permanent and 55.77 per cent of contractual teachers, the factor is not important as a reason for attrition.

J. **For reasons connected with education of own kids:** The factor is about taking care of their own kids' education. If their kids required them to teach or they are moving to other place for their education, parents are also expected to move with them. Out of total teachers covered under the study from aided and unaided private schools of Anand district, 16.88 per cent of permanent teachers and 19.23 per cent of contractual teachers find the factor as very important personal factor and assign rank 1. About 33 per cent of permanent and 43 per cent of contractual teachers rated the factor with 2nd rating as it is important for them. For 50 per cent of permanent and 37.5 per cent of contractual teachers, the factor is not important as a reason for attrition and they assign rank 3 to it.

K. **High cost of renting accommodation:** The factor is about high rental charges of accommodation where they are located now. If such cost is high, they would like to move to the place where they can manage with lower cost. Out of total teachers covered under the study from aided and unaided private schools of Anand district, 16.88 per cent of permanent teachers and 19.23 per cent of contractual teachers find the factor as very important personal factor and assign rank 1. While 33.13 per cent of permanent and 43.27 per cent of contractual teachers rate the factor with 2nd rating as it is important for them. For 50 per cent of permanent and 37.50 per cent of contractual teachers, the factor is not important as a reason for attrition and they assign rank 3 to it.

L. **High Cost of buying accommodation:** The factor is about high buying cost of accommodation where they are situated now. If they cannot afford the accommodation where they are, they would move to the place where cheaper accommodation can be bought. Out of total teachers covered under the study from aided and unaided private schools of Anand district, 15.63 per cent of permanent teachers and 19.23 per cent of contractual teachers find the factor as very important personal factor and assign rank 1. About 39 per cent of permanent and 40 per cent of contractual teachers rate the factor with 2nd rating as it is important for them. For 45 per cent of permanent and 40 per cent of contractual teachers, the factor is not important as a reason for attrition and they assign rank 3 to it.

M. **Commuting—inconvenience/time taken:** The factor is about time taken to commute to the place and approachability of the place from where they reside. Out of total teachers covered under the study from aided and unaided private schools of Anand district, 20.63 per cent of permanent teachers and 15.38 per cent of contractual teachers find the factor as very important personal factor and assign rank 1. While 38.75 per cent of permanent and 50.96 per cent of contractual teachers rate the factor with 2nd rating as it is important for them. For 40.63 per cent of permanent and 33.65 per cent of contractual teachers, the factor is not important as a reason for attrition.

N. **Cost of transportation per week:** This factor is about the cost of transportation from their residents to their schools per week. If the cost of transportation is high, they would change the school where transportation is cheaper per week. Out of total teachers covered under the study from aided and unaided private schools of Anand district, 15.63 per cent of permanent teachers and 15.38 per cent of contractual teachers find the factor as very important personal factor and assign rank 1. About 33 per cent of permanent and 43 per cent of contractual teachers rate the factor with 2nd rating as it is important for them. For 51.25 per cent of permanent and 41.35 per cent of contractual teachers, the factor is not important as a reason for attrition and they assign rank 3 to it.

All the personal factors listed above are not important for most of the permanent and contractual teachers. Each personal factor for attrition has got highest percentage of permanent and contractual teachers in rank 3. It indicates that attrition of teachers is mostly due to professional factors as they are more important for teachers than personal factors.

6.14 FACTORS WHICH WOULD ATTRACT TO ANOTHER JOB

In this section, all the probable factors which may attract teachers to another job are given. Teachers are expected to rate each of the factor on the scale of 1 to 3, where 1 = Very Important, 2 = Important and 3 = Not Important. This is done to know their opinion on each such factors which can be a reason for their turnover in their own perception. Table 6.15 presents opinion on factors which would attract another job.

Table 6.15: Opinion on Factors which Would Attract to Another Job

Factors	*Very Important*		*Important*		*Not Important*	
	PT (%)	*CT (%)*	*PT (%)*	*CT (%)*	*PT (%)*	*CT (%)*
A. Higher salary	61.3	55.8	15.6	31.7	23.1	12.5
B. Better prospects	56.3	50.0	21.3	36.5	22.5	13.5
C. Looks more interesting	36.9	31.7	26.3	38.5	36.9	29.8
D. Wanted a change	16.3	24.0	31.3	37.5	52.5	38.5
E. Easier to get to	11.3	12.5	28.8	37.5	60.0	50.0
F. Better benefits	49.4	41.4	26.9	32.7	23.8	26.0
G. Fits better with my family circumstance	43.1	31.7	33.1	35.6	23.8	32.7
H. Better reputation of the School	36.9	33.7	28.1	38.5	35.0	27.9
I. Important job profile	45.0	45.2	26.3	34.6	28.8	20.2

Source: Field survey data.

A. **Higher Salary:** The factor is about pay, allowances and other monetary incentives. Out of total teachers covered under the study from aided and unaided private schools of Anand district, 61.25 per cent of permanent teachers and 55.77 per cent of contractual teachers find the factor as very important factor which would attract to new job. About 15.63 per cent of permanent and 31.73 per cent of contractual teachers rate the factor with 2nd rating as the factor is important for them to get attracted to another job while 23.13 per cent of permanent and 12.5 per cent of contractual teachers find the factor as not important to get them attracted to new job and it is assigned rank 3 by them. Highest percentage of permanent and contractual teachers find the factor as very important to get them attracted to another job.

B. **Better Prospects:** The factor is about better career prospects of any other job. Out of total teachers covered under the study from aided and unaided private schools of Anand district, 56.25 per cent of permanent teachers and 50 per cent of contractual teachers find the factor as very important factor which would attract to new job and assign rank 1. While 21.25 per cent of permanent and 36.54 per cent of contractual teachers rate the factor with 2nd rating as the factor is important for them to get attracted to another job. 22.50 per cent of permanent and 13.46 per cent of contractual teachers find the factor as not important to get them attracted to new job and it is assigned rank 3 by them. This is the factor which is very important to get attracted to new job by second highest percentage of permanent and contractual teachers.

C. **Looks More Interesting:** The factor if about attractiveness of the new job. If the other job looks more interesting, they would opt for it. Out of total teachers covered under the study from aided and unaided private schools of Anand district, 36.88 per cent of permanent teachers and 31.73 per cent of contractual teachers find the factor as very important factor which would attract to new job and assign rank 1. While 26.25 per cent of permanent and 38.46 per cent of contractual teachers rate the factor with 2nd rating as the factor is important for them to get attracted to another job. 36.88 per cent of permanent and 29.81 per cent of contractual teachers find the factor as not important to get them attracted to new job and it is assigned rank 3 by them.

D. **Wanted a Change:** The factor is based on the reality that change is required in the job to get momentum in the career. Positive change in career is required due to any professional or personal reason. Out of total teachers covered under the study from aided and unaided private schools of Anand district, 16.25 per cent of permanent teachers and 24.04 per cent of contractual teachers find the factor as very important factor which would attract to new job. About 31 per cent of permanent and 38 per cent of contractual teachers rate the factor with 2nd rating as the factor is important for them to get attracted to another job. While 52.5 per cent of permanent and 38 per cent of contractual teachers find the factor as not important to get them attracted to new job. This is the factor with second highest percentage of teachers finding it not important to attract them to new job.

E. **Easier to get to:** The factor is about how easy it is to get to the new job. If it is easier, it becomes more attractive. Out of total teachers covered under the study from aided and unaided private schools of Anand district, 11.25 per cent of permanent teachers and 12.5 per cent of contractual teachers find the factor as very important factor which would attract to new job and assign rank 1. While 29 per cent of permanent and 38 per cent of contractual teachers rate the factor with 2nd rating as the factor is important for them to get attracted to another job. However, 60 per cent of permanent and 50 per cent of contractual teachers find the factor as not important to get them attracted to new job and it is assigned rank 3 by them. Majority of permanent and contractual teachers find the factor as not important to attract them to another job.

F. **Better Benefits:** If benefits provided at the new place are better than what is provided in the current school, teachers are likely to opt for the new place. Out of total teachers covered under the study from aided and unaided private schools of Anand district, 39.38 per cent of permanent teachers and 41.35 per cent of contractual teachers find the factor as very important factor which would attract to new job and assign rank 1. While 27 per cent of permanent and 33 per cent of contractual teachers rate the factor with 2nd rating as the factor is important for them to get attracted to another job. About 24 per cent of permanent and 26 per cent of contractual teachers find the factor as not important to get them attracted to new job. This factor is among the factors, which are very important to get teachers attracted new job.

G. **Fits Better with My Family Circumstance:** If the new job is fitting better with family circumstances of the teachers, they would go for new job to balance personal and professional Life. Out of total teachers covered under the study from aided and unaided private schools of Anand district, 43.13 per cent of permanent teachers and 31.73 per cent of contractual teachers find the factor as very important factor which would attract to new job and assign rank 1. About 33.13 per cent of permanent and 35.58 per cent of contractual teachers rate the factor with 2nd rating as the factor is important for them to get attracted to another job. The 23.75 per cent of permanent and 32.69 per cent of contractual teachers find the factor as not important to get them attracted to new job and it is assigned rank 3 by them.

H. **Better Reputation of the School:** If teachers can get a job in the school which has better reputation in the vicinity than the current school, they would definitely move to new job. Out of total teachers covered under the study from aided and unaided private schools of Anand district, 36.88 per cent of permanent teachers and 33.65 per cent of contractual teachers find the factor as very important factor which would attract to new job and assign rank 1. While 28.13 per cent of permanent and 38.46 per cent of contractual teachers rate the factor with 2nd rating as the factor is important for them to get attracted to another job. However, 35 per cent of permanent and 27.88 per cent of contractual teachers find the factor as not important to get them attracted to new job and it is assigned rank 3 by them.

I. **Important Job Profile:** The factor is about rights and responsibilities of the job. If the job profile is important and critical for the success of the school, teachers would like to take up those profiles available at new school. Out of total teachers covered under the study from aided and unaided private schools of Anand district, 45 per cent of permanent teachers and 45.19 per cent of contractual teachers find the factor as very important factor which would attract to new job and assign rank 1. About 26.25 per cent of permanent and 34.62 per cent of contractual teachers rate the factor with 2nd rating as the factor is important for them to get attracted to another job. While 28.75 per cent of permanent and 20.19 per cent of contractual teachers find the factor as not important to get them attracted to new job and it is assigned rank 3 by them. The factor is also considered among the most attractive factors by the permanent and contractual teachers.

6.15 AWARENESS AMONG TEACHERS ABOUT RIGHT TO EDUCATION (RTE)

In this section, permanent as well as contractual teachers were asked about Right to Education. They have to answer if they are aware about RTE and if yes then they have to specify source of information. They were also asked about merits and demerits of Right to Education in their view points (Table 6.16).

Out of total teachers involved in the survey from aided and unaided private schools of Anand district, 60 per cent of permanent and 55.77 per cent of contractual teachers were aware about the act of Right to Education (RTE). This act is applicable to private schools, then also 40 per cent of permanent and 44.23 per cent of contractual teachers have not heard about RTE, that is really disappointing.

Those who are aware about RTE, were asked about their source of information about RTE. Out of total teachers covered under study, 44.79

Table 6.16: Awareness Regarding RTE among Teachers

Particulars		*PT per cent*	*Ct per cent*
Heard of RTE?	A. Yes	60.00	55.77
	B. No	40.00	44.23
If yes, then sources?	A. B.Ed. Course	4.17	
	B. Books/magazines	20.83	32.76
	C. Newspapers/Channels	44.79	48.28
	D. Social Media	14.58	10.34
	E. Friends	9.38	3.44
	F. Government websites	6.25	5.17

Source: Field survey data.

per cent of permanent and 48.28 per cent of contractual teachers have heard about RTE through newspapers and news channels. While 20.83 per cent of permanent and 32.76 per cent of contractual teachers gathered information about RTE from books and magazines related to initiatives of government in the field of education. About 15 per cent of permanent and 10.34 per cent of contractual teachers have read about RTE from social media, while 9.38 per cent of permanent and 3.45 per cent of contractual teachers got to know about RTE from their friends and colleagues, 6.25 per cent of permanent and 5.17 per cent of contractual teachers got information on RTE from government websites. However, B.Ed. course was a source of information on RTE for 4.17 per cent of permanent teachers.

6.16 SUGGESTIONS/OPINIONS TO HANDLE ATTRITION OF TEACHERS

At the end of the survey, teachers were asked to give their suggestions and opinions on how the problem of high attrition of teachers in private schools of Anand district should be handled. It was made mandatory for each of the teachers for aided as well as unaided private schools to write their suggestions and opinions on the issue. Their suggestions/opinions are divided in to three parts: Suggestions/Opinion for Teachers, Suggestions/Opinion for Management and Suggestions/Opinion for Government and presented in Box 6.1, 6.2 and 6.3.

Box 6.1: Suggestions/Opinion for Teachers

- Focus on students and your responsibility as a teacher.
- Meditation to release stress.
- Teaching and learning methods should be improved.
- Somewhat modifications in teaching levels are required.
- Teacher should be happy with pay, school environment and support from management.
- The mental attitude of both management & teaching staff should be positive towards each other.
- Managing balance between personal & professional life plays an important role towards the efforts in teaching profession.
- Teaching is a passion, those who are able to enjoy the work should only join the field.
- There is lot more to improve and empower ourselves with day to day challenges positively.
- Understand student knowledge and then give the information of related topic, give them knowledge of social problems.
- With positive attitude, without expecting others appreciation, work for our satisfaction, not for others.
- Behaviour of colleagues, principal, students and parents is important to build good atmosphere.
- New teaching methodology should be adopted.

Box 6.2: Suggestions/Opinion for Management

- Increase pay scale as per government rule.
- Academic decisions should be taken after a deep discussion with teaching staff.
- Management must motivate their employees and let them be trained by experienced ones.
- Management should be equal with all his staff there.
- Appreciation and job security should be given to teachers.
- Co-operation, adequate salary, proper timing, support and respect should be given from management.
- Create the best environment, where teachers can teach with innovative styles and methods.
- Good package and open working environment can reduce attrition rate.

- Schools should give better facilities like transport, appropriate school time, good amount of salary as per their work.
- Management should support the teacher and try to understand the situation of teachers in some factors like personal and family as well.
- Working environment should be conclusive. They should also take care about teachers along with student.
- Teachers should not be enforced to act as parents' want.
- Work load should be bearable.
- Encourage the teacher and motivate them regularly.

Box 6.3: Suggestions/Opinion for Government

- Improve a content of text book for NEET.
- Trainings should be arranged and salary should not be affected for moving from private to government.
- Scale of salary should be same for Private and Government Schools.
- Government schools should be taken care of and improve the standards of government schools.
- Teachers should never he molested, exploited and under paid.
- Equal benefit must be provided to the private school teachers (equal security of jobs) like Government school teachers.
- No government agency keeps track of teachers appointed in private schools and care for their interest.
- Yoga workshops should be arranged for teachers.
- All private school teachers are going to training or assessment, given all types of facilities like government teachers to private teachers.
- During training and assessment time, give similar importance to government and private Teachers.
- Ask every employee of government to take admission of their kids in government schools only.
- It is necessary to stop the commercialization of education.

6.17 CHAPTER SUMMARY

The chapter is very important from the study point of view, as teachers are the main stake holders to understand causes, problems and remedies of the problem of attrition of teachers in private schools. 160 permanent and 104 contractual teachers from 3 aided private schools and 19 unaided private schools are interviewed to get their responses on the parameters mentioned in the chapter.

A problem of attrition among teachers of private schools is studied in detail from the perception of teachers. The problem of attrition is more prevalent among teachers of unaided private schools than teachers of aided private schools due to less job security and low pay. Mainly teachers seek adequate remuneration, good facilities, better benefits, trainings, development programs, pleasant working environment, supporting management, supportive colleagues, respect from students & parents, Job security and promotional opportunities.

As the number of female teachers covered under the study is more than that of male teachers, the problem is studied from female teachers' point of view. More than anything else, female teachers want flexi timing, leave provisions, counselling, safe environment and appropriate working hours. They have to balance between personal and professional life, so their main reasons for turnover are related to personal factors.

Teachers of private schools feel that they are not given importance from the management. Students and parents are the priorities of the management as they pay fees to finance functioning of the school. In many cases, teachers of private schools feel exploited as they have to work for more hours with less pay compared to teachers of public schools. Many of the teachers from private schools leave private schools to get in to government schools or even in other profession like Business process outsourcing and Knowledge process outsourcing. Many of the teachers from private schools eave their jobs to start their own Coaching classes as there is trend of sending students to private tuitions in Anand district.

Attrition is high among contractual teachers as they are on fixed pay, with no job security and also not entitled to benefits. They leave their jobs to get permanent jobs in teaching profession or any other profession. Most of the private added schools are dependent on contractual employees. There is direct impact of attrition of contractual employees on the functioning of the self-financed private schools.

The chapter explains all parameters related to teachers of private schools exclusively. Teachers play prominent role to build reputation of the school among parents and students. Private schools of Anand district also faces the challenge of getting teachers who are fluent in English, as medium of instruction is English in almost all the schools under study. Suggestions and opinions of teachers are included in the chapter. Their suggestions and opinions should be considered positively to resolve the problem of attrition in private schools. They give their suggestions separately for other teachers, management personnel and government.

Teachers' turnover not only affect quality of education of the school but also adversely affect reputation of the school in vicinity. The cost of the attrition is also high. Thus, retaining competent, qualified and experienced teachers for long is the only key to improve quality of education of the school. Stable teachers are also important for long term success of any school.

CHAPTER 7

Attrition of Teacher:

Parents' Perspectives

7.1 INTRODUCTION

In this chapter, the problem of attrition is understood from the point of view of parents. Impact of attrition is directly on the education of their kids. They would definitely try to choose those schools for their kids, where the attrition of teachers is low. Five parents are contacted and interviewed from each aided and unaided private schools of Anand district. At school level, choice of school is mostly done by parents. The parents are interviewed through a schedule, which includes questions pertaining to schools of their kids, teachers of their schools, how they get affected due to attrition at their schools and how they handle their students in case of high attrition at schools.

They were also asked about how a management of school should handle attrition of teachers at private schools. Self-financed schools are mostly run by the fees paid by the parents, so their say is considered while making decisions regarding functioning of the school. Their responses to factors pertaining to them are recorded and analysed in the following tables.

7.2 DEMOGRAPHIC INFORMATION OF PARENTS

Parents were contacted in the campus or outside the campus with the help of students and management. In total, 111 parents were involved in the study from both the types of schools. The demographic information of parents in presented in Table 7.1.

7.2.1 Age and Gender

Average age of parents surveyed from aided and unaided private schools of the district was 40 years. Out of total parents covered under the study, 72.97 per cent of them were male respondent and 27.03 per cent of them are female respondent

7.2.2 Qualification and Occupation

Average qualification of the parents involved in the study was 15.37 years. To get the average, qualifications of the parents were converted into years and then the average is calculated. Out of total parents, 42.34 per cent were in the field of teaching, 18.02 per cent of them were housewives and 17.12 per cent of them have their own businesses. Out of total parents surveyed, 22.52 per cent were in the occupation other than what is mentioned above.

7.2.3 Standard of Kids and Board of Kids

Out of selected parents involved in the study, 37.84 per cent had their kids in 12th standard, 14.41 per cent of them had their kids in 10th standard, 13.51 per cent of them have their kids studying in 9th standard, kids of 13.51 per cent of them study in 11th standard and 2.70 per cent of them have their kids in 8th standard. Kids of 18.02 per cent of the total parents study in the sections of pre-primary, primary or upper primary. Kids of 74.77 per cent of the parents covered under the survey, study in Gujarat State Education Board and 25.23 per cent of total parents have their kids studying in Central Board of Secondary Education.

7.2.4 Average Distance to School

Average distance from the resident to the school of all the parents covered under the study from aided and unaided private schools was 7 km.

Table 7.1: Demographic Information of Parents

Particulars		*Responses (n=111)*	*Per cent*
Average Age (in years)		40	–
Gender	A. Male	81	72.97
	B. Female	30	27.03
Average Qualification (years)		15.37	–
Occupation of Parents	A. Teachers	47	42.34
	B. Businessmen	19	17.12
	C. Housewives	20	18.02
	D. Others	25	22.52

Particulars		*Responses (n=111)*	*Per cent*
Standard of Kid	A. 8th	3	2.70
	B. 9th	15	13.51
	C. 10th	16	14.41
	D. 11th	15	13.51
	E. 12th	42	37.84
	F. Others	20	18.02
Board of Kid	A. State Board	83	74.77
	B. CBSE	28	25.23
	C. ICSE	–	–
	D. IB	–	–
Avg. Distance from School (in Kms.)		7	

Source: Field survey data.

7.3 Factors Considered while Choosing a School

In the section, list of factors considered by parents while choosing a school for their kids are given. Parents are expected to tick on all the factors taken in to consideration while making a decision on a school for their kids. Table 7.2 presents factors considered by parents while choosing school.

Table 7.2: Factors Considered while Selecting School for Kid/s

Factors	*No. of Parents (n=111)*	*Per cent*
A. Reputation of school	98	88.29
B. Qualified teachers	101	90.99
C. Teacher-pupil ratio	57	51.35
D. Principal of school	54	48.65
E. Management of school	33	29.73
F. Board availability	69	62.16
G. Infrastructure	68	61.26

Factors	*No. of Parents (n=111)*	*Per cent*
H. Facilities provided to students	71	63.96
I. Co-curricular activities	61	54.95
J. Fee structure	62	55.86
K. Location of School	30	27.03
L. Achievements of school	62	55.86
M. Sports activities	58	52.25
N. Style of teaching	31	27.93
O. Timing of school	66	59.46
P. Year of establishment of school	32	28.83
Q. Uniform of school	32	28.83
R. Quality of students	58	52.25
S. Class size	42	37.84
T. Track record of School in Board result	61	54.95
U. Any other		
Children's own choice	1	0.90
Pollution free natural environment	1	0.90
Teaching learning standard	1	0.90
Whether school is preparing students for facing competition/ entrance exams/inter-school events	1	0.90
Word of mouth	1	0.90

Source: Field survey data.

The factor which is considered by most of the parents is qualified teachers, as 90.99 per cent of the total surveyed parents find the factor as the most important. The second most important factor for parents is reputation of school as 88.29 per cent of them find the factor as important followed by 63.96 per cent of them consider facilities provided to students, 62.16 per cent of them consider board of education available in the school and 61.26 per cent of them consider infrastructure of the school. Thus above five mentioned factors are most important factors while deciding the school for kids by the parents. Other factors which are considered by them are timing of the school; fee structure; achievements of school at district level, state level and national level; co-curricular activities organised by the school; track record of school in board result; quality of students enrolled in the school; sports activities organised in the school; teacher pupil ratio of the school. About 49 per cent of selected parents mentioned that they take in to consideration the Principal of the school and about 38 per cent of them consider number of students in a class. The others factors relatively not on top of the list were managing trust under which the school is functioning; uniform of the school for the students; style of teaching adopted by the teachers, which is very disappointing and location of school.

Following are the factors considered by some of the parents other than the factors listed above.

- **Children's own choice:** Considered by 0.90 per cent of the parents.
- **Pollution free natural environment:** Considered by 0.90 per cent of the parents.
- **Teaching learning standard:** Considered by 0.90 per cent of the parents.
- **Whether school is preparing students for facing competition/ entrance exams/inter-school events:** Considered by 0.90 per cent of the parents.
- **Word of mouth:** Considered by 0.90 per cent of the parents.

7.4 PARENTS-TEACHERS RELATIONSHIP

This section present information about interaction between teachers and parents is presented and discussed. Information on how they interact, how many times they interact, what benefits parents get out of such meetings and what factors parents consider in a suitable teachers is gathered, recorded and analyzed in the Table 7.3.

7.4.1 Parents-Teachers Meetings

Out of total parents involved in the study from aided and unaided private schools of Anand district, about 92 per cent parents mentioned that their schools organize parent-teacher meetings in the schools, while remaining schools did not organise parent-teacher meetings at schools.

Table 7.3: Parents-Teachers Relationship

Sr. No.	*Particulars*	*Responses (n=111)*	*per cent*
1.	**Does the school conduct Parent Teacher Meeting?**		
	A. Yes	102	91.89
	B. No	9	8.11
2.	**If yes, how often?**		
	A. Once a year	13	12.75
	B. Twice a year	30	29.41
	C. Thrice a year	4	3.92
	D. Four times a year	31	30.39
	E. More than Four Times	12	11.76
	F. Every Month	21	20.59
3.	**Benefits from such meetings**		
	A. Better understanding of child's performance	89	80.18
	B. Able to know the teacher well	65	58.56
	C. Getting idea about different facilities provided by the school	60	54.05
	D. Involvement in decision making regarding important aspects	57	51.35
	E. Getting to know if everything is as per expectations	41	36.94
	F. Guidance on good parenting from teachers	66	59.46
	G. Report of Grievances no proper teaching	27	24.32
	H. High Teacher turnout and its impact on leaning of subject by student	32	28.83
	I. Any other		
	Get to know the in-house things		0.90
	Will be able to build a rapport as a parent with the teachers		0.90
	Get to learn different aspects of the challenges faced by our child		0.90
	We become aware that whether our child is responsive in class or not		0.90

Sr. No.	*Particulars*	*Responses (n=111)*	*per cent*
4.	**Factors considered in a suitable teacher**		
	A. Years of experience	61	54.95
	B. Interpersonal skills	47	42.34
	C. Good communication	83	74.77
	D. Understanding of the subject	66	59.46
	E. Style of teaching	83	74.77
	F. Discipline of Teacher	54	48.65

Source: Field survey data.

Then those who responded positively were asked about frequency of such meetings. Around 20 per cent of parents mentioned that such meetings are held every month in a year, while 30 percent each of total parents attended such meeting twice and four times in a year. While around 12 per cent each of parents attended the said meeting either once or more than four times in year. Thus there is no fixed criteria for such meeting in the schools, some of them organize it monthly basis, while some on bimonthly basis, quarterly and so on.

Parents were asked about benefits from such meetings in their point of view. Parents were informed to tick on the benefits they realized through such meetings. The highest response of 80.18 per cent of total selected parents was for better understanding of child's performance from such meetings with teachers, while 59.46 per cent of them felt that through such meetings they get guidance from teachers on good parenting. About 59 per cent of the parents mentioned that such meetings are beneficial as they were able to know the teacher well, while 54.05 per cent of the parents got idea about different facilities provided by the school through such meetings. In fact, about 51.35 per cent of them felt that through such meetings they got involved in decision making regarding important aspects. While 36.94 per cent of the parents got to know if everything is as per their expectations or not through such meetings. Surprisingly hardly 29 per cent of parents mentioned that they got idea about high attrition of teachers and its impact on students' learning. Out of total parents, 24.32 per cent can report grievances on improper learning of the students while interacting with the teachers. Parents also gave other benefits of such meetings.

7.4.2 Factors Consider in Suitable Teachers

Parents were asked about the factors they considered in a suitable teacher for their kids. They were expected to tick on the factors considered by them. Out of total parents covered under study, about three fourth of them considered the style of teaching adopted by teachers to make the subject understandable for the students is important one. While same number of parents considered communication skills of the teachers is also important aspect. Understanding of the teachers of the subjects they teach was felt important one by 59.46 per cent parents, while about 55 per cent of parents considered that long experience of the teachers in the field of teaching is a suitable teacher. About 49 per cent of them considered discipline maintained by the teachers as an important factor, while 42.34 per cent of them considered interpersonal skills of the teachers important to make teachers suitable for their kids.

7.5 EFFECTS OF ATTRITION

In this section, parents were asked about how they and their kids got affected due to exit of any teacher. They were also asked about how they and their kids got adjusted with the new teachers.

7.5.1 Effects of Attrition on Parents

Out of total parents under study from aided and unaided private schools from Anand district, 64.86 per cent of parents mentioned that they got affected with the exit of any of their kids' teachers, while 13.51 per cent of them were highly affected and 10.81 per cent were least affected. Surprisingly, 10.81 per cent of the parents mentioned that they were not affected at all with the changing teachers.

7.5.2 Effects of Attrition on Students

In this section, parents were asked if their kids got affected with exit of any of their teachers and if yes then how they were got affected due to attrition of their teachers. Out of total parents involved in the study, 83.78 per cent parents noted that their kids were got affected due to exit of any teacher in between the academic year, while remaining of 16.22 per cent of them do not find any impact on their kids due to exit of any teacher in between.

Table 7.4: Effects of Attrition

Sr. No.	*Particulars*	*Responses (n=111)*	*per cent*
1.	**How are you affected due to exit of any of your child's teachers?**		
	A. Highly affected	15	13.51
	B. Affected	72	64.86
	C. Least affected	12	10.81
	D. Not affected	12	10.81
2.	**Would your child's study be affected due to exit of any teacher in between?**		
	A. Yes	93	83.78
	B. No	18	16.22
3.	**Impact on child due to teacher's attrition**		
	A. Difficulty in learning & understanding	57	61.29
	C. Unable to adjust with the new teacher	40	43.01
	D. Negative impact on child's percentage	15	16.13
	E. Lack of interest in the subject	33	35.48
	F. All of Above	19	20.43
4.	**Difficult to adjust with the new teacher for students**		
	A. Yes	76	68.47
	B. No	35	31.53
5.	**If yes, then how do you help your child?**		
	A. Counselling him/her	66	86.84
	B. Personal Attention	66	86.84
	C. Talking to the new teacher	53	69.74
	D. Taking help of the teacher who left	10	13.16
	E. Taking help of child's friends	9	11.84
	F. Any other way		
	I try to deal with that subject	1.32	1.32
	Started teaching that subject at home	1.32	1.32

Source: Field survey data.

Out of total parents, who feel that their kids were got affected also responded on symptoms of same. About 62 per cent of them felts that their kids were finding difficult in learning and understanding the subject, while 43.01 per cent of them felt that their kids were unable to adjust with the new teacher. However, 35.48 per cent of parents felt that their kids were not at all interested in the subject which was taught by the teacher who left the school. About 16 per cent of parents found negative impact of attrition of teachers on their kids' marks/grade. Overall, about 20.43 per cent of the parents felt that their kids were got affected in all the above mentioned ways due to turnover of teachers in between the academic year.

7.5.3 Adjusting with new Teachers

Parents were asked if their kids found it difficult to adjust with new teachers. In case of positive response, they were requested to answer how they helped their kids to cope up with that situation. Out of total parents covered under study, 68.47 per cent of them mentioned that their kids had faced difficultly in adjusting with the new teachers while remaining kids did not find any difficulty.

Out of total parents whose kids found it difficult, 86.84 per cent had counseled their kids to adjust with new teachers, while 86.84 per cent of those parents paid personal attention to their kids while they were facing the difficulty with new teachers. About 70 per cent of those parents talked to new teachers regarding difficulty their kids faced, while 13.16 per cent of them took help of those teachers who left to handle the situation. However, 11.84 per cent of affected kids' parents took help of child's friends to minimise the impact of attrition on their kids. Very few parents had dealt with the subject by themselves and started teaching that subject to their kids at home.

7.6 MEASURES TO BE UNDERTAKEN BY SCHOOLS TO PREVENT ATTRITION

In this section, parents were given a list of measures a school should adopt to deal with attrition and they have to tick on the measures which they feel important to handle attrition of teachers. They may have ticked on more than one measure.

Out of total parents covered under study, 56.76 per cent of parents opined that attrition can be prevented by providing better facilities; 54.95 per cent of them consider evaluation of students' feedback as important measure to handle attrition if it is done effectively, while 52.25 per cent of them felt timely pay to the teachers is effective measure to control attrition. About 51 per cent of them consider on-the-job observation and coaching in the classroom is important to retain teachers, while 50 per cent of them mentioned that structured induction for beginning teachers play important role to control turnover of teachers. About half of the parents opined that attrition can be controlled through mentoring programmes for the teachers, while 33.33 per cent of the total parents feels that it can be controlled through involved believe that attrition can be controlled through counseling, while 32 per cent of the parents support peer assistance and review programs as effective measures to retain teachers for long in any school.

Table 7.5: Measures to be Undertaken by Schools to Prevent Attrition

Measures	*Responses (n=111)*	*per cent*
A. Structured induction for beginning teachers	55	49.55
B. On-the-job observations & coaching in classroom	56	50.45
C. Conducting mentoring programs for the teachers	55	49.55
D. Peer Assistance and Review Programs	35	31.53
E. Timely pay to the teachers	58	52.25
F. Facilities provided to them	63	56.76
G. Effective evaluation of student feedback report	61	54.95
H. Through Counseling	37	33.33

Source: Field survey data.

7.7 RELATED OTHER INFORMATION

In the section, information related to other stakeholders and other parameters pertaining to schools were gathered and evaluated in the following manner.

Table 7.6: Contact with Management and Related Information about School

Sr. No.	*Particulars*	*Responses (n=111)*	*per cent*
1.	**Contacted Management ever?**		
	A. Yes	29	26.13
	B. No	82	73.87
2.	**If Yes, then how many times?**		
	A. Once	11	37.93
	B. Twice	5	17.24
	C. Thrice	2	6.90
	D. Many a times	11	37.93
3.	**Actions taken by management after meeting?**		
	A. Positive Response	5	17.24
	B. Issues resolved	20	68.97
	C. Supportive behaviour	4	13.79
4.	**Any donation at the time of Admission?**		
	A. Yes	12	10.81
	B. No	99	89.19
5.	**If yes, how much amount? (Rs.)**		
	5000	2	16.67
	7000	2	16.67
	10000	3	25.00
	15000	5	41.67
6.	**Amount is fully refundable**	12	100.00
7.	**Facilities from School**		
	A. Books	40	36.04
	B. Notebooks	30	27.03
	C. Uniform	31	27.93
	D. Shoes	17	15.32
8.	**Facilities outside School**		
	A. Books	59	53.15
	B. Notebooks	67	60.36
	C. Uniform	68	61.26
	D. Shoes	78	70.27

Table 7.6 continues....

Sr. No.	*Particulars*	*Responses (n=111)*	*per cent*
9.	**Since when your child is enrolled in the school? (No. of years)**		
	0.25	1	0.90
	1	32	28.83
	2	15	13.51
	3	9	8.11
	4	5	4.50
	5	6	5.41
	6	3	2.70
	7	7	6.31
	8	3	2.70
	9	1	0.90
	10	9	8.11
	11	3	2.70
	12	6	5.41
	13	6	5.41
	14	3	2.70
	15	2	1.80
	From which Standard?		
	Play Group	7	6.31
	Nursery	9	8.11
	KG	11	9.91
	1st	2	1.80
	2nd	4	3.60
	3rd	5	4.50
	4th	1	0.90
	5th	7	6.31
	6th	3	2.70
	7th	1	0.90
	8th	2	1.80
	9th	3	2.70
	10th	2	1.80
	11th	3	2.70

Source: Field survey data.

7.7.1 Meeting the Management

Out of total parents in the study from aided and unaided private schools of Anand district, 26.13 per cent of them have contacted management for any reason, while 73.87 per cent of them have never contacted management for any purpose. Out of those who have contacted the management, 37.93 per cent each of them have contacted management once and many times, while 17.24 per cent of the parents had met the management twice till the date and 6.90 per cent of them came in contact with management for thrice since their kids were admitted in the school. As parents have contacted management to resolve various issues related to school, about 69 per cent of the parents who sought help from management got their issues resolved after the meeting while 17.24 per cent of them had got positive response from the management to address the matter. About 14 per cent of them could experience supportive behaviour of the management during the meeting.

7.7.2 Donations for Admissions

In this, parents were asked about if they had given any donation at the time of admission, how much amount they gave as donation and is it refundable or not. Out of 111 parents involved in the study from aided and unaided private schools, only 10.81 per cent gave donation at the time of admission, while 89.19 per cent of them did not give any donation. Out of the parents who paid donation at the time of admission, 41.67 per cent paid donation of Rs. 15,000. 25 per cent of them paid rupees 10,000 as donation at the time of admission of their kids to private schools. For 16.67 per cent of them, the amount of donation was rupees 7,000 and 16.67 per cent of them paid rupees 5,000 as donation amount at the time of admission of their kids in private schools. Amount of donation is fully refundable for all of the parents who paid donation at the time of admission.

7.7.3 Facilities to Students

In the section, parents were asked if they got books, notebooks, uniform and shoes from the schools or outside the schools for their kids. Around 36 per cent of them had got books from their respective schools while 53.15 per cent of them purchased books from outside, and remaining did not specify the source from where they got books for their kids. About 28 per cent of them get notebooks and uniform from their schools. While

15.32 per cent of the parents got shoes for their kids from the school and remaianing 70.27 per cent of them purchased shoes from outside for their kids and remaining do not specify their sources. Majority of the parents purchased books, notebooks, uniform and shoes from outside sources and not from the schools of their kids.

7.7.4 Their Association with the School

In the section, parents were asked since when their kids were admitted in the school and from which standard. Out of 111 parents involved in the study from aided and unaided private schools, only 28.83 per cent of parents have mentioned that they had admitted their kids to schools since last one year. Majority were since the period of 1–2 years. Out of total parents surveyed, 9.91 per cent of them admitted their kids in the school from KG. The spread of enrolment of kids in schools is scattered.

7.8 SUGGESTIONS AND OBSERVATIONS OF PARENTS

In this, parents were asked for their suggestions and opinions to control attrition of teachers. It was advisable, but not compulsory for parents to give theirs valuable opinions and suggestions. Parents were also asked to write their observations pertaining to turnover of teachers in the private schools.

Box 7.1: Suggestions/Opinions of Parents

- Qualified and trained Teachers should be appointed.
- Government should take care of private schools when they are intervening in the fee Structure.
- Teachers should be counseled effectively, their behaviour is also affected by financial criteria.
- Permanent teachers should be appointed to sustain students for long.
- Competent teachers should be appointed.
- Schools should keep on adding Innovative ways of teaching.
- Required facilities for modern education should be provided.
- Assessment pattern for students should have the provision for Logical thinking and Life skill development, rather than just subject learning.

Box 7.2: Observations of Parents

- Behaviour of teacher in class matters a lot for student, student needs motivation & encouragement from teachers & parents also.
- Good school, good facilities, good teaching style, good progress of students are the most required ingredients for good education.
- Education should be burden free, with great interest (make interesting).
- Satisfied with the present school till 10th std. But needs to coach students for facing entrance exams like JEE, NEET in 11th and 12th science stream.
- School management should take care of teachers based on their experience & popularity.
- Students are highly influenced by the teacher's knowledge, attitude and way of expression. So, the teacher should take utmost care that they should think about the students' study and how they can help to bring the level of the students high.
- Teachers should be given freedom to explore their subject and field.

7.9 CHAPTER SUMMARY

The discussion about the responses of the parents indicate that parents were aware about the problem of attrition among teachers of private schools and its implications. They considered qualified and experienced teachers as a key factor to be considered while selecting a school for their kids. They played active role in functioning of the private schools of the district.

They opted for private schools with English as a medium of instruction for their kids. They wanted world-class quality education for their kids. But they strongly believed that competent and stable teachers are required to improve quality of education in aided and unaided private schools. They were aware about the adverse impact of turnover of teachers on their kids. They were ready to help their kids to get adjusted to high attrition rate of teachers among private schools.

All the parents involved in the survey strongly recommended that teachers can be retained for long by providing better and desired facilities to them. On the other hand, they also recommended teachers not leave their jobs in between the academic year, as it affects studies of their kids adversely. Parents are considered as an important stakeholder in private school. So, their recommendations and observations should also be considered to control turnover of teachers from aided and unaided private schools of all the tehsils of Anand district.

CHAPTER 8

Attrition of Teacher:

Students' Perspectives

8.1 INTRODUCTION

Students of private schools are the main victims of the high rate of attrition among teachers in Anand district. Students of aided and unaided private schools get adversely affected due to turnover of teachers. Students learn the subject from the perception of the teacher teaches it. But when the teacher leaves in between the academic year, students find it difficult to get adjusted to new teacher.

As students share emotional bond with the teachers, when those teachers are not in the school, they start lacking interest in studies. When students lose their favourite teachers, they start feeling bored in the school environment. This is the reason behind trend towards coaching classes after school hours. Students are burdened with school and tuitions, so ultimately their performance in studies goes down.

In the chapter, responses of fifteen students from each aided and unaided private schools were recorded, tabulated and evaluated. For the purpose of study, students of secondary and higher secondary sections are covered. Students involved in the study must know English to get better understanding of the questions. Management of the school must consider suggestions of students as they suffer the most due to changing of teachers now and then. Before taking decision about relieving any teacher, opinions of students should be considered. Feedback of students on performance of teachers should be evaluated to get idea about which teachers are more competent in the field of education. Students' attrition is also an issue to handle along with teachers' attrition.

8.2 DEMOGRAPHIC INFORMATION OF STUDENTS

In this section, information on demographic characteristics of students is presented and discussed (Table 8.2). For the purpose of study, students of secondary and higher secondary sections were targeted. Almost all the students were from the schools where medium of instruction is English. In total 330 students were covered under the study from aided and unaided private schools of Anand district. They were contacted in person as well as in a group and all the questions were explained to them one by one. Students could connect with the study as they face the consequences of attrition of teachers directly. There were also cases where students left their schools when their favorite teachers left their jobs.

Table 8.1: Demographic Information of Students

Particulars		*Students (n=330)*	*per cent*
Average Age (in years)		15.53	–
Gender	A. Male	143	43.33
	B. Female	187	56.67
Standard	A. IX	58	17.58
	B. X	113	34.24
	C. XI	51	15.45
	D. XII	107	32.42
Board	A. State Board	193	58.48
	B. CBSE	137	41.52
	C. ICSE	–	–

Source: Field survey data.

8.2.1 Age and Gender of Students

Average age of the students involved in the study from three aided private schools and nineteen unaided private schools from Anand district was 15.53 years. Out of total students involved in the survey, 56.67 per cent were girl students and 43.33 per cent of them were boys.

8.2.2 Standard and Board of Students

As the study involves students from secondary and higher secondary sections of education, 34.24 per cent of the students respondents were from standard X, while 32.42 per cent of them were from standard XII, 17.58 per cent of the students are from standard IX, 15.45 per cent of the total students covered under the study were from standard XI. Out of total students surveyed, 58.48 per cent were studying in the schools affiliated with Gujarat State Education Board, while 41.52 per cent of the students were enrolled in the schools affiliated with Central Board of Secondary Education.

8.3 STUDENT-TEACHER RELATION

In the section, information regarding their favourite teachers, exit of their teachers and impact on their studies, farewell given to teachers, problems faced by them due to exit of the teacher, feedback given to their teachers, complaints about teachers and if they want any of their left teachers to come back were gathered and tabulated. Table 8.2 presents the same.

Table 8.2: Details on Student-Teacher Relation

Sr. No.	*Particulars*	*Responses (n=330)*	*per cent*
1.	**Favourite Teacher (No.)**		
	A. 1 teacher	184	55.76
	B. 2 teachers	117	35.45
	C. None	29	8.79
2.	**Subject taught by favourite teacher (max Response)**		
	Accounts	7	2.33
	All	1	0.33
	Biology	31	10.30
	Business studies	11	3.65
	Chemistry	31	10.30
	Computer	13	4.32
	Economics	7	2.33
	English	44	14.62
	Gujarati	11	3.65
	Hindi	9	2.99
	History	4	1.33
	Maths	64	21.26
	Music	2	0.66
	None	27	8.97
	Physics	12	3.99
	Science	23	7.64

Sr. No.	*Particulars*	*Responses (n=330)*	*per cent*
	Social Science	26	8.64
	Sports	2	0.66
	Statistics	5	1.66
3.	**Any teacher left whom you recall?**		
	A. Yes	234	70.91
	B. No	96	29.09
4.	**Want any of the teachers to come back?**		
	A. Yes	202	86.32
	B. No	32	13.68
5.	**If yes, then why?**		
	A. In depth knowledge of the subject	107	32.42
	B. Innovative methods and style of teaching	154	46.67
	C. Good human attributes	49	14.85
	D. Any other	20	6.06

Table 8.2 continues..............

Sr. No.	*Particulars*	*Responses (n=330)*	*per cent*
6.	Way of bidding farewell to teachers		
	A. By presenting a gift individually to the teacher	54	16.36
	B. By offering a gift on behalf of the class as a token of love	142	43.03
	C. By organizing a party	82	24.85
	D. Giving away an Admiration Speech	119	36.06
7.	**In contact with left teachers?**		
	A. Yes	155	46.97
	B. No	159	48.18
8.	**Feedback on teachers' performance?**		
	A. Yes	243	73.64
	B. No	87	26.36

Sr. No.	*Particulars*	*Responses (n=330)*	*per cent*
9.	**Complain, if unhappy with any teacher?**		
	A. Yes	193	58.48
	B. No	137	41.52
	If yes, to whom?		
	A. Class Representative	11	5.70
	B. Class Teacher	66	34.20
	C. Supervisor	42	21.76
	D. Principal	83	43.01
	E. Management	23	11.92
10.	**Any impact on your performance due to exit of any teacher?**		
	A. Yes	263	79.70
	B. No	67	20.30
11.	**Problems/difficulties you are likely to encounter with the exit of any teacher?**		
	A. Poor concentration	104	31.52
	B. Interest limited to specific topics	130	39.39
	C. Boredom	74	22.42
	D. Difficulty in learning and understanding	208	63.03
	E. Feel unprepared for the class	85	25.76
	F. Absenteeism	45	13.64
	G. Difficulty to cope up with the subject	105	45.45

Source: Field survey data.

8.3.1 Information on Favourite Teachers

In this section, students were asked about how many their favourite teachers from their school were. Out of total students involved in the study, 55.76 per cent students mentioned that they have one teacher as their favourite teacher, while 35.45 per cent of them have two teachers. While remaining 8.79 per cent of the total students do not find any teacher, who can be considered as their favourite teacher. Students were also asked about subject taught by favourite teacher. Almost all the subject teachers were their favourite teachers.

Students of private schools were asked if they recall any of their teachers who have left. About 71 per cent of them mentioned that they recall their teachers, while strangely about 29 per cent of them did not recall any of their teachers after their exit from their schools. Students who recall their teachers who left the school, out of them about 86 per cent of the students want their teachers to come back to school.

Students were asked about the reasons for which they want their teachers to come back. Out of total students responded, about 47 per cent wanted same because of innovative methods and style of teaching adopted by them. About 33 per cent of them wanted their teachers back due to their in depth knowledge of the subject, while 14.85 per cent of them wanted their teachers to come back because of their admirable human attributes.

8.3.2 Bidding Farewell to Teachers

Students were asked about bidding farewell to the teachers when they were leaving the school. Students generally develop emotional bond with their teachers, so they want to make their teachers' farewell memorable. Out of total students involved in the study, 43.03 per cent bid farewell to exiting teachers by offering a gift on behalf of the class as a token of love, 36.06 per cent of the students gave admiration speech on their teachers' farewell, 24.85 per cent of the students organised party on occasion of teachers' farewell and 16.36 per cent of the students presented a gift individually to the exiting teachers. Students were also asked if they are in contact with any of their teachers who have left their schools. About 47 per cent of the total students were in contact with left teachers.

8.3.3 Feedback on Teachers' Performance

Students were asked if they were involved in evaluating performance of their teachers by giving their feedback. Students were also asked if they complained about the teachers if they had any issues with them. They were also expected to answer about whom they complained about their teachers' inappropriate behavior.

Out of total students surveyed from aided and unaided private schools of Anand district, 73.64 per cent students played active role in evaluation of teachers' performance by giving their feedback, while 26.36 per cent of them did not give their feedback on performance of teachers. Out of total students involved in the study, 58.48 per cent complained if they were unhappy with their teachers due to any reason. About 42 per cent of them did not complain about their teachers to any one though they were unhappy with them on certain matter. Out of those complaints, 43.01 per cent student complained to principal of the school, 34.2 per cent of them submitted complaint to their class teacher; 21.76 per cent of them complained to supervisor; 11.92 per cent of the students complained to management about inappropriate behavior of teachers with them. While 5.70 per cent of the total students took help of student class representative to complain about any teacher.

8.3.4 Impact of Attrition on Performance:

In this section, students were asked if they got affected due to exit of any of their teachers. They were also asked about what difficulties they had faced due to exit of any of their teachers. Out of total students involved in the study, 79.70 per cent of the students mentioned that they faced negative impact on their performance in studies due to exit of any of their teachers, while 20.3 per cent of them did not get any impact on their performance in studies due to turnover of teachers in their schools. All the students were expected to tick on the type of difficulties they encounter due to exit of any of their teachers. About 63 per cent of total students found it difficult to learn and understand the subject due to exit of any teacher, while 45.45 per cent of them faced difficulties to cope up with the subject, which was taught by the teacher who left. Around 40 per cent of them felts that their interest got limited to specific topics when teachers leave. However, 31.52 per cent of them found it difficult to concentrate and 25.76 per cent of them felt unprepared for the class due to exit of their subject teachers. About 22.42 per cent of them face problem of boredom in the subject which is taught by new teacher, while 13.64 per cent of them remained absent in the class of the subject which is taught by the new teacher.

8.4 Factors Appeal to Students while Choosing Their School

In the section, students were asked about factors which were considered while choosing a school for them at the time of admission. The list of factors were given to the students and they were expected to tick on the factors considered at the time of their admission in their respective schools. Table 8.3 presents the factors that appeal to students while choosing their school. Out of total students under study from aided and unaided private schools of the district, 83.64 per cent students considered qualified teachers of the school at the time of admission. This is the factor which is ticked by the highest percentage of students. While 75.45 per cent of the students considered style of teaching adopted by their teachers at the time of admission. Thus, these are the factors considered by most of the students and both of them are pertaining to teachers. The other factors which were considered (of course with support of their parents and review from their friends and student friends already studying in that school) were management of school, facilities provided, reputation of the school, the board with which the school is affiliated, sports activities,

Table 8.3: Factors Appeal to Students While Choosing Their School

Factors	*Students (n=330)*	*per cent*
A. Reputation of school	219	66.36
B. Qualified teachers	276	83.64
C. Teacher-pupil ratio	86	26.06
D. Principal of school	126	38.18
E. Management of school	223	67.58
F. Board availability	196	59.39
G. Infrastructure	130	39.39
H. Facilities provided to students	221	66.97
I. Co-curricular activities	175	53.03
J. Fee structure	147	44.55
K. Location of School	164	49.70
L. Achievements of school	184	55.76
M. Sports activities	186	56.36
N. Style of teaching	249	75.45
O. Timing of school	171	51.82
P. Year of establishment of school	72	21.82
Q. Uniform of school	112	33.94
R. Quality of students	169	51.21
S. Class size	128	38.79

Source: Field survey data.

achievements of school at state and national level, co-curricular activities organised in the school, timing of the school at the time of admission, quality of other students who are already enrolled in the school, location of the school, fee structure, infrastructure of school, number of students in a class, principal of the school, uniform for students in a school, number of teachers per students and lastly year of establishment of school.

8.5 QUALITIES REQUIRED IN A GOOD TEACHER

In this the list of qualities of a good teacher is given and students have to rate each of the quality on the scale of 1 to 5. Here, 1 = the most important and 2 = the least important. Thus, if students consider the factor as the most important quality, they have to assign rank 1 to the quality. If the quality if not important for a good teacher in their perception, they assign rank 5 and accordingly rank 2,3 and 4 are assigned to each of the qualities required in a good teacher.

Table 8.4: Qualities to be Required in a Good Teacher

Qualities of a Good Teacher	*Ratings*				
	1 (%)	*2 (%)*	*3 (%)*	*4 (%)*	*5 (%)*
A. Good Personality	59.70	19.39	7.88	3.33	9.70
B. Innovative and Effective style of Teaching	72.42	14.85	5.45	1.21	6.06
C. Clear Objectives for Lessons	63.94	18.79	5.15	4.24	7.88
D. Excellent Discipline Skills	46.06	26.97	13.94	3.33	9.70
E. Good Classroom Management Skills	40.00	28.18	14.55	6.67	10.61
F. Good Communication skills	56.97	24.24	6.97	3.64	8.18
G. Strong Rapport with Students	37.88	27.88	16.06	6.67	11.52
H. Calm and Patient towards students	55.45	19.39	10.30	2.73	12.12
I. Leniency	22.12	29.39	22.12	9.70	16.67
J. Knowledge of Subject Matter	73.64	11.82	2.73	3.33	8.48
K. Approachability	47.58	25.76	10.30	2.73	13.64
L. No Biasness	57.27	14.85	11.21	3.33	13.33

Source: Field survey data.

A. **Good Personality:** This factor is about outer appearance of a teacher. Personality is a combination of inner attributes which are reflected in outer appearance of a teacher. Out of total students involved in the study from Anand district, 59.70 per cent found the factor as the most important and rank first, while 9.70 per cent of the students involved in the study considered the factor as the least important as a quality of a good teacher.

B. **Innovative and Effective style of Teaching:** The factor is about creative and innovative ways adopted to teach students effectively. Out of total students involved in the study from Anand district, 72.42 per cent found that this factor as the most important one.

C. **Clear Objectives for Lessons:** The factor is about setting objectives of each lesson clearly before start teaching it. Out of total students involved in the study from Anand district, 63.94 per cent found the factor as the most important and rank first, while 18.79 per cent of them assign rank second. However, 7.88 per cent of the students involved in the study consider the factor as the least important as a quality of a good teacher.

D. **Excellent Discipline Skills:** The factor is about management of students with disciplinary actions implemented while teaching. Out of total students involved in the study from Anand district, 46.06 per cent found the factor as the most important one while 26.97 per cent of them assign rank second 2 as a quality of a good teacher.

E. **Good Classroom Management Skills:** The factor is about how teachers manage a class while teaching to get every student involved in the process. Out of total students involved in the study from Anand district, 40 per cent student mentioned this factor as one of the most important factors while 28.18 per cent of them assign rank second as the least important as a quality of a good teacher.

F. **Good Communication skills:** The factor is about verbal and non-verbal communication practices adopted to make the subject understandable for students. Out of total students involved in the study from Anand district, 56.97 per cent found the factor as the most important as a quality of a good teacher.

G. **Strong Rapport with Students:** The factor is about strong emotional bonding with their students to accomplish the objectives. Out of total students involved in the study from Anand district, 37.88 per cent found the factor as the most important and rank followed by

16.06 per cent of the total students who ranked it second while 11.52 per cent of the students involved in the study considered the factor as the least important as a quality of a good teacher.

H. **Calm and Patient towards students:** The factor is about handling students calmly with patience and without being hyper. Out of total students involved in the study from Anand district, 55.45 per cent noted this factor as the most important as a quality of a good teacher.

I. **Leniency:** The factor is about not being strict and being lenient in while dealing with students and their performance. Out of total students involved in the study from Anand district, 22.12 per cent students recorded this factor as the most important followed by 29.39 per cent of them ranked it second as a quality of a good teacher.

J. **Knowledge of Subject Matter:** The factor is about expertise of teachers in their respective subjects. They should know their subject thoroughly. Out of total students involved in the study from Anand district, 73.64 per cent student mentioned that this factor as the most important as a quality of a good teacher.

K. **Approachability:** The factor is about availability of teachers to resolve problems of students. Teachers should be approachable whenever their students need them. Out of total students involved in the study from Anand district, 47.58 per cent found the factor as the most important while 13.64 per cent of the students involved in the study consider the factor as the least important as a quality of a good teacher.

L. **No Biasness:** The factor is about handling the students without any discrimination. Teachers should treat all the students equally without any partiality. Out of total students involved in the study from Anand district, 57.27 per cent find the factor as the most important and rank the factor as 1.

8.6 STUDENTS' COMMENTS/VIEW POINTS

In this section, students were asked to give their comments on the problem of attrition of teachers in their schools. They had to consider the impact of teachers' turnover on their performances. To understand problem of attrition from students' point of view, they were asked to give their opinion on how teachers should be handled to retain them for long. Their suggestions for management and teachers were recorded separately and presented in Box 8.1 to 8.2.

Box 8.1: Student's/comments on Teachers

- Teachers themselves are not in discipline and then they expect from us to be in discipline.
- Teachers' English is not clear and they expect from us to speak in English.
- Overall school is providing good facilities but some teachers have week teaching skills.
- Teachers should have good skills for making their students clear about particular concept.
- Both teachers and students play a major role in each other's life.
- Teachers are a very good support, so sometimes their exit does lead to a major problem.
- Teachers should let the child imagine by themselves.
- Teachers should know how to teach.
- Teachers should be excellent in teaching.
- A teacher's absence would make a difference if teacher is gentle and encouraging.

Box 8.2: Student's Comments on Management

- They should give the proper salary to the teachers and if they give the salary properly no teacher will leave the school.
- No increment to them because of that they leave the school, it should not happen.
- Management of school should provide facilities to respective teacher and main thing is they should give equal time for every subject.
- For teachers to leave it is not only counted as fault of teachers but also the students, training the students to get along with teachers method and explanation is what needed.

8.7 CHAPTER SUMMARY

Students of private schools were aware about the problem of high turnover of teachers in aided and unaided private schools and its impact on them. Their performance in studies got affected adversely. There were many cases in aided private schools, where students also changed their schools with teachers changing the schools. They considered teachers as a key factor to be considered while choosing a school for them. They shared special bond with their teachers. In many cases, they gave more importance to their teachers then their parents.

When a teacher leaves them in the middle of the year, they get affected negatively and they start disliking the subject ultimately. Students are the stakeholders who faces the highest difficulties with attrition of teachers. They strongly feel that qualified teachers should be retained in the school by adopting any measure. They also believe that their feedback on their teachers should be considered and steps should be taken accordingly. Students should be prime importance when making the decision pertaining to teachers' turnover. The impact of attrition is of long term on the students. The main reason behind deteriorating standards of education is unstable teachers in private schools. Students should also be a part of decision making pertaining to school or any stakeholder of the school.

CHAPTER 9

Summary, Conclusions & Policy Implications

9.1 INTRODUCTION

The chapter summarises whatever is inferred from the previous chapters. The problem high rate of attrition among teachers of private schools of Anand district is analysed and understood from the perspectives of management, teachers, parents and students. The problems and causes of the problem of high turnover of teachers among the teachers of aided and unaided private schools of the district are evaluated on the basis of various parameters. Information on not only demographic characteristics of the stakeholder but also information pertaining to schools, their management, their stakeholders, economic environment of schools were also taken in to consideration to highlight the problem. The study is so much in detail that it is a good reference for further study in any other part of the country or even in foreign countries.

The chapter is designed to recommend certain changes to the government in the form of policy implications. Efforts are also made to suggest remedial measures to management of private schools. Conclusion and inferences are drawn on the basis of all the discussions of the previous chapters. While doing the field research, Government officials and Management personnel have asked for the recommendations and policy implications of the study.

All the stake holders of the private schools are affected due to attrition of the teachers, as the ultimate impact of the attrition is on the quality of education. All the parties involved in the education understands the importance of the study as the problem is an economic problem for any nation. India is a country, which enjoys demographic dividend. But if they are not taught by competent, qualified and stable teachers; such demographic dividend is of no use and may become demographic liability.

Thus, all the stakeholders including government should consider inferences of the study to resolve the problem of high attrition of teachers in the private schools. With the help of few modifications in the whole education system, the causes of turnover of teachers can be handled positively.

9.2 SUMMARY OF THE STUDY

In the section, all the chapters discussed above are summarised. The study is conducted at aided and unaided private schools of all the eight tehsils of Anand district. Schools were selected from urban as well as rural areas of the district. Permanent as well as contractual teachers were covered under the study to understand scope of the problem of attrition in both the categories of teachers. Parents and students from secondary and higher secondary sections were surveyed for the purpose as they are matured enough to understand consequences of teachers' turnover. Almost all the students were from the schools, which have adopted English as medium of instruction as they can understand the schedule for study with its purpose.

All the schools selected under study were visited personally and all the stakeholders of every school were also interviewed personally to fetch necessary information from them. Prior appointments were fixed with each of the school and the survey was completed within the span of almost a month. Out of total private schools, 3 aided private schools and 19 unaided private schools were involved in the study from the district. Out of total schools, 8 schools are taken from Borsad tehsil, Petlad tehsil, Umreth tehsil, Tarapur tehsil, Sojitra tehsil, Anklav tehsil and Khambhat Tehsil of Anand district. Total 14 schools were taken from Anand district as number of schools are more in the tehsil with one education hub, Vallabh Vidhyanagar. From each school, 22 management representatives, 12 permanent and contractual teachers, 5 parents and 15 students were surveyed for the purpose of the study. The study was initiated to fulfil the following objectives:

1. To study pupil/student-staffing pattern in private schools of Anand district.
2. To study appointment patterns of teachers in private schools of Anand district.
3. To study problems in attracting competent teachers in private schools of Anand district.
4. To examine factors determining the healthy and positive relationship between different stakeholders (teacher-student-parent-management) in private schools of Anand district.

5. To find out reasons behind high attrition rate of teachers and its adverse effects in private schools of Anand district.
6. To suggest remedial measures to solve the problem of retaining good teachers for long time.

The Indian and international literature available in the form of books, articles, reports, articles and research papers were reviewed through objective wise analysis of developed, developing and underdeveloped countries on the subjects pertaining to the topic of the study. A number of books were analysed to understand various parameters related to attrition. Motivational theories and retention models were also reviewed to suggest remedial measures to management and government to resolve the problem of high attrition of teachers among private schools.

Pretested schedules were used to interview management, teachers, parents and students separately. Their responses were recorded and tabulated for evaluation. Schools having secondary and higher secondary sections were preferred as parents and students of those sections are targeted. Students of secondary and higher secondary schools were covered as they are aware about the problem of attrition in private schools and its implications on their studies.

As mentioned in previous chapter, there is craze among parents of getting their kids admitted in private schools and schools having English as medium of instruction. The trend towards private schools is due to failure of government schools in improving quality of education and infrastructure of school. There is mushrooming of private schools in district as many business entrepreneurs, social groups and political leaders have entered in to the field of education. But, again the question is on the quality of education. As such private schools provide state of the art facilities and all other amenities to the students, but they fail to retain qualified, competent, trained and experienced teachers.

The problem of high rate of attrition is more prominent in unaided private schools as they function on their own financial sources and fees collected from the students. Such schools cannot match up with the salary structures of that of public schools or aided private schools. Many a times they exploit their teachers. Contractual teachers are more likely to leave their self-financed private schools due to fixed pay and no job security. The problem of attrition is more prevalent among contractual teachers of self-financed schools of rural area of Anand District.

Therefore views of management personnel are recorded and analysed rigorously to understand how management of any school sees the problem of high turnover of teachers in private schools. Management personnel are interviewed personally with the help of pretested schedules and certain observations are recorded under field survey to check authenticity of their responses.

Management personnel of aided private schools covered under the study from Anand district do not find the problem of teachers' turnover applicable to their schools as they provide better facilities, higher pay and high job security to their teachers. Teachers of aided private schools are less likely to leave their schools before retirement.

As it is evident from the findings and discussions of responses of management representatives of unaided private schools of Anand district, the problem of high turnover of teachers is very prominent and it affects the schools adversely. They are working on remedial measures to be adopted like getting sign of the teachers on the bond of employment for some years, acquiring original documents of teachers at the time of joining, resolving any issues faced by the teachers etc. But most of such measures fail to provide solution to the problem of high attrition rate. Almost all of the management representatives feel that it is better to control attrition of qualified and competent teachers than to resolve its consequences.

There is also a rule of government on maximum fees to be collected by the unaided private schools in the district. That brings limit on the income, so to control expenses of recruitment, selection, training and development & replacement, the problem of attrition should be resolved. The problem can be analysed on a broader scale by involving teachers, parents and students in the survey.

Teachers are the main stake holders to understand causes, problems and remedies of the problem of attrition of teachers in private schools. 160 permanent and 104 contractual teachers from 3 aided private schools and 19 unaided private schools are involved in the study to get their responses on the parameters pertaining to them.

The problem of attrition is very common among teachers of unaided private schools than teachers of aided private schools due to less job security and low pay. Permanent and contractual teachers are always in need of adequate remuneration, good facilities, better incentives, trainings, development programs, pleasant working environment, supportive management, supportive peers, respect from students & parents, Job security and promotional opportunities.

Attrition of contractual teachers are higher than that of permanent teachers in unaided private schools. Number of female teachers surveyed is more than that of male teachers. Female teachers are more concern about their personal life, so to balance their personal and professional lives, they need flexi timing at work, leave provisions, counselling, safe environment and appropriate working hours.

From the discussions with teachers of unaided private schools, it can be summarised that teachers of private schools feel less important compared to students and parents of such schools. In many cases, teachers of private self-financed schools feel exploited as they have to work for more hours with less pay compared to government teachers. In many cases, teachers of unaided private schools leave their schools to get in to government schools. Many of the private school teachers continue in their schools and start taking tuitions for the students to support their livelihood.

Attrition is high among contractual teachers as they are on fixed pay, with no job security and also not entitled to benefits. They leave their jobs to get permanent employment in teaching profession or in any other profession. Most of the private unaided schools are dependent on contractual employees to reduce expenses. So when they leave, consequences are faced by other stakeholders. Management of private schools are getting used to attrition of teachers and teachers of unaided private schools also work there for short term till they get permanent or better opportunities. But implications on students and ultimately on standards of education are ignored by the private self-financed schools of Anand district.

Parents of private schools are aware about the problem of attrition among teachers of private schools and its implications on performance of their kids. They consider availability qualified and experienced teachers while choosing a school for their kids. Most of the parents from urban as well as rural areas of Anand district select private schools with English as a medium of instruction for their kids. They strongly believe that competent and stable teachers are required to improve education standards in aided and unaided private schools of Anand district. They are ready to help their kids to get adjusted to high attrition rate of teachers among private schools. But they seek solution to resolve the problem of high attrition rate among teachers of unaided private schools. Majority of the parents believe that teachers can be retained for long by providing better facilities to them.

Now a days, unaided private schools face problem of high attrition of students along with attrition of teachers. When the teachers are not stable and qualified, parents do not desire to continue in the same school. For majority of the students, qualified teachers and their style of teaching is the key parameter to be considered while selecting a school for admission. They get involved with their teachers emotionally, so their performance in studies gets highly affected due to turnover of teachers.

When a teacher leaves them in the middle of the year, they get affected negatively and they start disliking the subject ultimately. The impact is not only limited to their studies but it is also affecting their mental and psychological state. They also believe that their feedback on their teachers should be considered by the management and steps should be taken accordingly. The impact of attrition is of long term on the students. The main reason behind deteriorating standards of education is unstable teachers in private schools. Students should also be a part of decision making pertaining to school or any stakeholder of the school.

9.3 FINDINGS OF THE STUDY

After interviewing all the stakeholders of private schools of Anand district with the help of pre-tested schedules, their responses are recorded, tabulated and analysed in detail with the help of statistical tools. Responses of management personnel, teachers, parents and students are recorded and analysed separately. Major findings of the study from the perspectives of Management, Teachers, Parents and Students are as follows:

9.3.1 Findings Related to Management

- Out of total private schools covered under the study, 3 are aided private schools and 19 were unaided private schools.
- All the 3 aided private schools were established before 1980 and out of 19 unaided private schools, 89.47 per cent were established after 1980.
- Out of aided private schools, 2 have pre-primary, primary, secondary and higher secondary sections and 1 of them had only secondary section. Out of 19, 16 have all the sections viz. Pre-primary, primary, secondary and Higher Secondary. 1 of them all the sections except pre-primary and 2 of them have only secondary and higher secondary.

- All of the aided schools are affiliated to Gujarat State Education Board. Out of unaided private schools, 73.68 per cent are affiliated to Gujarat State Education Board and 26.32 per cent are affiliated to Central Board foe Secondary Education.
- All the three respondents of private aided schools were Principals of the schools, Out of 19, 14 respondents from unaided private schools were Principals, 4 were Campus Directors and one was Management representative.
- Management representatives of aided private schools are older than that of unaided private schools.
- All the three management representatives from aided private schools are male and out of total management representatives, 16 were male and 3 were female.
- Out of total management personnel, 63.63 per cent were B.Ed. graduates, 9.09 per cent possessed M.Ed., 9.09 per cent were Ph.D. holders and remaining had other qualifications.
- Work experience of management personnel of aided private schools was 28 years on an average and management personnel of unaided private schools had average work experience of 18 years.
- Average years of experience of management personnel from the unaided private schools in the current school was more than that of management personnel of aided private schools.
- The most important factor to be considered while selecting a teachers for majority of the management personnel was deep knowledge and with a higher qualification.
- The facility which was provided by the majority of the schools to their teachers as personal Lockers and the least provided facility was transportation facility by the private schools covered under the study.
- Festival celebration was done at the majority of the school under the head of incentives and the least given incentive was telephone allowances.
- Adequate salary was the most important factor to retain teachers for long for majority of the management personnel and the least preferred factor for retention was incentives by majority of the management personnel.
- The student teacher ratio found to be adequate in selected schools.
- In view of the most of the management, working conditions was the most important factor for retaining teachers.

- The most used recruitment strategy was newspaper advertisement for all the management personnel involved in the study.
- Qualification was the most important demographic characteristic of a good teachers as per majority of the management representatives.
- About 78.94 per cent of total management personnel believed that performance of teachers can be improved with the help of higher salary.
- The highest percentage of result as 92.33 per cent in aided private schools, and it was 96.18 per cent in case of unaided private schools.
- The most adopted practice to handle low scoring students by all the private schools under study is arranging Remedial classes.
- About 81.82 per cent of total management personnel believed that the most common impact of teachers' turnover is increased pressure on other staff members.
- About 91 per cent of the schools management considered the teachers' say on core issues related to education while remaining do not care about the same.
- Around three fifth of school management had conducted exit interview for the teachers leaving the school.
- About 77.27 per cent of total private schools under study gained feedback from teachers on facilities provided to them, while 52.94 per cent of those who gained feedback, did so for more than two times in a year.
- The most common practice to recognize contribution in aided private schools was through awards and certificate. The most adopted way to recognize efforts in unaided private schools was through performance appraisal.
- By most of the private schools involved in the study, the most adopted base for evaluation of teachers' performance was quality of teaching and the least considered factor is departmental audit.
- In around 63.15 per cent of schools involved in the study teachers could communicate with the management through direct meeting with the concern member of management.
- The most considered factor for promotion of the teachers in aided private schools was seniority and it was performance in case of unaided private schools.
- Around 84.21 per cent of schools covered under study, sought help from the existing teachers to deal with turnover of teachers.
- All the schools covered under study conduct planning and year ending meeting.

- Around 81.82 per cent of the surveyed schools had local management committee. Such LMCs met once or twice in a year in majority of the schools.
- Out of total sample private schools selected, 86.36 per cent conducted departmental audit. Out of them, majority conducted such departmental audit annually.
- Probation period for majority of the aided private schools was 5 years and it is 2 years in most of the unaided private schools.
- In around 86 per cent of schools, new teachers were trained with the help of Existing senior teachers.
- For around 2/3rd of the schools, notice period for confirmed teachers was 3 months and it was 1 month for teachers on probation in 55 per cent of total schools under study.
- The most used selection tool in the private schools under study was panel interview. Demo lecture was the second most used selection tool in aided private schools and the second most used selection tool in unaided private schools was reference check.
- Attrition was not common in aided private schools, but if it happens it was mostly to settle down to abroad. The reason for teachers' turnover in majority of unaided private schools was for government job.
- Most of the schools counseled teachers orally during notice period to control the attrition/turn over. They made adjustments in the salary also to stop going out of teacher.
- All the aided private schools and 63.16 per cent of unaided private schools ddi not lay off any of their teachers.
- In around 77.27 per cent of the schools involved in the study, decisions pertaining to teachers were taken by Management along with Principal.

9.3.2 Findings Related to Teachers

- It was observed that out of total selected sample teachers, around 62 per cent teachers were on permanent roll, while 34 per cent were full time contractual and remaining were part time contractual teachers.
- It was observed that permanent teachers were older than the temporary teachers.
- Out of the selected sample teachers, maximum share was of female teachers. It is very important to note here is that share of permanent teachers was almost the same across the gender of teachers.

- It was observed that about four fifth of selected teachers were found married. However, across gender, share of married permanent male teacher was higher than married permanent female teachers.
- It was observed that out of total sample teachers, three fifth teachers were having kids. Besides, education level of spouse of selected teachers was found to be at very high, i.e. of 17 years.
- It was observed that out of total sample teachers, three fifth teachers were from joint family, while remaining were from nuclear family.
- As far as education of teachers is concern, about 57 per cent of the total teachers hold B.Ed. degree and around 16 per cent hold M.Ed. degree, while remaining have other educational qualifications.
- The house of permanent teachers was located at much closer to schools as compared to contractual teachers. More than three fourth of selected teachers attend the school on their own vehicles, while remaining use the public and private transportations means.
- Almost all the teachers under study teach in the schools having all the sections of school education, (i.e. Preprimary, Primary, Secondary, Higher Secondary).Though selected schools has English language as a medium of instruction, most of the teachers uses combination of languages (local, i.e. Gujarati and English) while teaching the students.
- The distribution of teachers as per their school funding criteria, it was observed that around 88 per cent of the teachers teach in fully self-financed schools while remaining teach in private fully aided schools.
- All teachers of aided private schools teach in Gujarat State Education Board.
- From unaided private schools, there are more contractual teachers than permanent teachers who teach in Gujarat State Education Board & there are more permanent teachers than contractual teachers who teach in Central Board of Secondary Education.
- All the aided private schools are affiliated to Gujarat State Education Board.
- In unaided private schools 73.40 per cent of the teachers teach in the school having affiliation with Gujarat State Education Board, 26.60 per cent of the total teachers teach in the schools affiliated to Central Board of Secondary Education.
- Average teaching experience of permanent teachers was around 12 years, around 5 years with contractual and 4 years with contractual teachers.

- On an average, permanent teachers are in the same schools 9 years, full time contractual as well as part time contractual are in the same school since 3 years or so.
- Out of the selected sample teachers, for about two third of teachers, this is their second job, it means they had left their first job due to some professional or personal reasons.
- Out of those 63 per cent of the teachers, about half of them had left the earlier job due to less pay, more than one fourth of total teachers had left job because of marriage and remaining had left job due to inadequate working hours of previous job. Other important reasons were lack of promotional opportunities and for moving to be near family.
- Out of total teachers surveyed, majority of the teachers use lecture method as their style of teaching and the second popular method used by the teachers is Group Discussion.
- Out of the selected sample teachers, most of them got selected through Personal Interview and the second most used selection tool for teachers is Telephonic Interview.
- Out of total permanent teachers, Majority teachers draw monthly salary of rupees 10,000 to 20,000. Most of the contractual teachers draw salary of less than 10,000 rupees.
- Out of total permanent teachers, 60.63 per cent are satisfied with their current pay and 55.77 per cent of contractual teachers are not satisfied with their current remuneration as it is not sufficient.
- The facility which is enjoyed by most of the teachers is a facility of personal locker and the second facility which is which is enjoyed by many permanent and contractual teachers if of Canteen.
- Most of the permanent teachers get benefit of Provident Fund and most of the contractual teachers get benefit of Festival Celebration under the head of special incentive/perquisites.
- The most effective motivator for majority of permanent teachers is Working Environment and the most effective motivator for majority of contractual teachers is Relation they share with their students.
- Out of total permanent teachers, 91.25 per cent want to stay in the same school for 8.91 years on an average. Out of total contractual teachers, 81.73 per cent want to stay in the same school for 4.91 years on an average.

- Out of total sample teachers selected, majority of permanent and contractual teachers identify need for development by studying feedback of students on their performance.
- Out of total teachers, highest percentage of permanent and contractual teachers upgrade themselves in their respective subjects by reading books and magazines of their respective subjects.
- Schools of majority of permanent and contractual teachers conduct 1 to 5 training programs for the teachers per year.
- Out of total teachers involved in the study, majority attend 1 to 5 training and development programmes to upgrade their subject knowledge.
- The behavior which always has negative implication for permanent and contractual teachers is when they violate important rules and regulations laid by their schools. The behavior which never has any negative implication for permanent and contractual teachers is when they utilize school hours for personal work.
- Majority of permanent and contractual teachers completely disagree with the statement that image of teaching profession is lower than other professions in the job market. The statement which is completely agreed by majority of permanent and contractual teachers is Colleague's supportive behavior leads to positive work environment.
- Out of total permanent teachers, majority interact with their students for personal counseling and majority of contractual teachers interact with students for casual talks.
- Work pressures other than teaching were as exam duties, co-curriculum activities, assignment from management, parents-teachers association and the least from government assignments.
- Majority of the teachers manage their work related stress through effective time management, then by listening to music, going on outing with family and friends and through meditation.
- The most important professional factor which influences the permanent teachers to leave the job is pay scale/pay structure and the least important professional factor is too few responsibilities.
- The most important professional factor which may influence full time contractual teachers to leave the job is PAY and the least important professional factor is too few responsibilities and class size.
- The most important professional factor which may influence part time contractual teachers to leave the job is working on contractual

basis and the least important professional factor is too few responsibilities and school vicinity.

- The most important personal factor which may influence permanent teachers to leave the job is poor health and the least important professional factor is getting married.
- The most important personal factor which may influence full time contractual teachers to leave the job is poor health and the least important professional factor is age.
- The most important personal factor which may influence part time contractual teachers to leave the job is general dissatisfaction with teaching profession and the least important professional factor is age and getting married.
- The factor which would attract permanent teachers the most to the new job is higher salary and the factor which would attract the least is easier to get to.
- The factor which attract full time contractual teachers the most to the new job is higher salary and the factor which would attract the least is easier to get to.
- The factor which attract part time contractual teachers the most to the new job is better prospects and the factor which would attract the least is easier to get to.
- Out of total permanent teachers, 60 per cent are aware about Right to Education and 55.77 per cent of contractual teachers are aware about Right to Education Act. Remaining teachers have never heard about RTE, which is very disappointing.

9.3.3 Findings Related to Parents

- Average age of the sample parents selected was around 40 years.
- Out of total parents covered under study, 72.97 per cent were fathers of the students and remaining are mothers.
- Average qualification of 111 parents surveyed was of around 15.37 years.
- Majority of the parents involved in the study were teachers by profession.
- Majority of the parents had their kids studying in 12th standard.
- Around 74.77 per cent of parents had their kids studying in Gujarat State Education Board and kids of remaining parents study in Central Board for Secondary Education.

- Average distance from their residents to schools of kids was 7 kilo meters.
- The most considered factor by majority of the parents at the time of selecting a school for their kids was Qualified Teachers and the next most considered factor is reputation of school. The least preferred factor was Location of School at the time of their kids' admission.
- Around 91.89 per cent of the schools in the study conducted parent teacher meeting mostly four times in a year or two times in a year.
- Majority of the parents believed that they get better understanding of child's performance through parent teacher meetings.
- For majority of the parents, the most important factor considered in a teacher suitable for the kid was that teacher should have good communication skill, followed by style of teaching, understanding of the subject, years of experience, then discipline of the teacher and lastly interpersonal skills.
- Around three fifth of total parents mentioned that they were affected because of any teacher of the kid leave the school forever.
- While more than four fifth of total parents felt that study of their child was affected due to exit of any teacher in between.
- Majority of the parents felt that their child could not adjust with the new teacher. They also felt their kid lack interest in the subject concern due to teachers' turnover and then negative impacted on child's percentage while few felt that their kids may also got affected in all the ways.
- About two third of total parents opined that their kids faced difficulty in adjusting with the new teacher while remaining felt their kids adjusted with new teachers easily.
- Majority of the parents counseled their kids to adjust with the situation when any of their teachers leaving the school, then they also handled the situation with personal attention.
- When asked about the measures to prevent attrition of school teachers, majority of them felt that facilities provided to them was the most important measure and counseling was the least important measure to handle attrition.
- Around 73.87 per cent of the parents had never contacted the management for any issue.

- Parents had contacted management once or many a times in majority of the cases, and most of them got their issues resolved after such meetings with management.
- Only 10.81 per cent of parents gave donations at the time of admission of their kids. The amount of donation was 15,000 rupees in most of the cases. Amount of such donation was 100 per cent refundable for all of them.
- Majority of the parents purchased books, notebooks, uniform and shoes from outside the school.
- Around 42.34 per cent of the parents involved in the study has enrolled their kids in the school since last 1 or 2 years.
- In majority of the cases, parents have enrolled their kids in the school from Nursery or KG.

9.3.4 Findings Related to Students

- Average age of the students involved in the study was 15.53 years.
- Out of total students surveyed, 56.67 per cent were girl students and remaining are boy students.
- Out of total students covered in the study, majority were in standard 10th or 12th.
- Around 58.48 per cent of students study in schools affiliated to Gujarat State Education board and 41.52 per cent study in Central Board of Secondary Education.
- Out of total students, 55.76 per cent have one teacher as their favourite teacher. 35.5 per cent of them have two teachers as their favourite teachers. Remaining students do not have any teachers as their favourite teacher.
- In most of the cases, favourite teachers of students taught Mathematics and the favourite teachers of second majority teach English.
- Around 70.91 per cent of teachers recall some of the teachers, who have left the school. Out of them, 61.21 per cent want their teachers to come back whom they recall.
- Around 46.67 per cent of the students who recall their teachers, wanted them back because of their innovative methods and style of teaching.
- In majority of the cases, Students arranged bid farewell to their teachers by offering a gift on behalf of the class as a token of love.

- Around 46.97 per cent of the total students were in touch with the teachers who have already left their schools and 48.18 per cent of them do not keep any contact with left teachers.
- Around 73.64 per cent of the students involved in the survey, play active role in giving feedback to their teachers.
- Out of total students, 58.48 per cent of the students complained if they were unhappy with any of their teachers. In majority of the cases, such students complain to their principal and their Class Teachers.
- The factor which considered by majority of the students at the time of selecting a school for them was qualified teachers and style of teaching adopted by teachers of a school is the second most considered factor. The least considered factor was year of establishment of school by the students involved in the study.
- The most preferable quality of a good teacher for most of the students was knowledge of subject matter and then Innovative and effective style of teaching. The least preferable quality of a good teacher for majority of the students is Leniency and then approachability of teachers.
- Around 79.70 per cent of the students got affected by the exit of any of their teachers and remaining were indifferent to such turnover of teachers.
- The main and most important problem which students encountered with the exit of any teacher was that they face difficulty in learning and understanding the subject, followed by difficulty to cope up with the subject, their interest gets limited to specific topics, slowly develop poor Concentration, followed by feeling unprepared for the class, boredom and absenteeism.

9.4 CONCLUSIONS

The findings and discussions of responses of all stakeholders clearly indicate that problem of high turnover of teachers is very prominent in unaided private schools of Anand district and it affects the schools and studies of the student adversely. The problem of attrition is more prevalent among contractual teachers of self-financed schools of rural area of Anand District. Thus findings proved that:

1. There is high rate of attrition among temporary teachers due to job insecurity in private secondary schools in Anand district.

2. There is an effect of exit of teacher on education of students in Anand District.

9.5 MY EXPERIENCE OF THE STUDY

After many days of introspection and discussions with the experts I decided to study attrition of employees in any industry. On the basis of my experience in corporate Human Resources departments of various organisations and teaching experience in renowned educational institutes, I wanted to take up research topic which is a combination of Human Resources and Education. At last I could decide on topic of my study as "Attrition of Teachers in Private schools of Mumbai Suburban District: Problems, Causes and Remedies."

I presented my proposal to the Department Research Committee of Business Management Department of Sardar Patel University. I got registered under the guide ship of Dr. S.S. Kalamkar, Director, Agro-Economic Research Centre, Sardar Patel University. I find myself privilege to get guidance from such an industrious research expert.

After meeting my guide, I started with Review of Literature from India and abroad to find out presence of problem in developed, developing and under developed countries of the world. I enjoyed the phase of Review of Literature, as I started getting clarity of related aspects of the study. I with the consent of Guide decided research methodology to be followed for the study. Then, I with the help of guide prepared four different schedules for interviewing all the stakeholders of the schools separately. In depth schedules including all the parameters of the problem are prepared for Management, Teachers, Parents and students. I attended coursework organised by the department and I could relearn various topics of Research Methodology and Statistical Analysis on SPSS. The coursework was very fruitful from the point of view of my Ph.D. study.

For the purpose of field survey, I started visiting private schools of Mumbai Sub-urban district. I started data collection procedure and had encountered various problems in collecting data from private schools of Mumbai suburban district. In some schools, they didn't even allow me to enter the premises. In most of the cases, I failed to meet concerned personnel of management. I was not getting their responses to any of my schedules designed for collection of primary data. They were not even replying to any of my mails or calls. After considering the problems encountered, I had decided to change my area of study to Anand District. Thus, after approval from DRC of the Department my new topic of study is "Understanding Attrition of Teachers in Private Schools of Anand District in Gujarat: Problems, Causes and Remedies".

I enjoy the phase of data collection with the help of pre-tested schedules from all the stakeholders of schools from all different tehsils of Anand district. I traveled all over the district and collected data personally from all the sample aided and unaided private schools. I was so enthusiastic to cover 22 management personnel, 264 teachers, 111 parents and 330 students from 3 aided and 19 unaided private schools that hot climate could also not disturb my schedule. All the schools are studied in detail by recording responses of the stakeholders in the schedules and also recording all my personal observations. All the management representatives of the schools are very approachable and supportive. They made all the arrangements for discussions with the teachers, students and parents. I was really impressed with the kind of hospitality offered by almost all the schools. The stage of data collection was the best part of the study, where I could meet all noble and helping human beings. Till I reached this stage of recording the data in excel sheets, my personal engagements are taken care of by my mother and my husband.

The best part of the journey of this study is I conceived after registration of Ph.D., and completed all other stages of research while my baby was growing from an infant to a toddler. I was so much excited to enter new phase of my life that it could be reflected in my efforts in Ph.D. study. After tabulating all the responses of the stakeholders separately, I started analyzing the data. I was all thrilled to know that all findings are highlighting necessary parameters to draw conclusion. I presented the synopsis and got positive comments and suggestions for improvement. To support the findings of the study, Secondary data on status of education in Gujarat and Anand district was collected and characteristics of the stakeholders were studied in detail.

The journey throughout have added so much to my knowledge that I was converted to a hardcore researcher from a corporate personnel/academician. I am a more confident and organized professional. My way of looking at national and international issues has changed. I have been more focused, specific and analytical. I can help private schools in handling problem of high turnover of teachers on the basis of findings of my study. I would also like to recommend certain policy implications to government and management to improve quality of education with the help of competent and stable teachers. I have also prepared a project of Democratic School to handle the problems of deteriorating standards of education and low employability of Indian students.

9.6 RECOMMENDATIONS TO MANAGEMENT

On the basis of the findings of the study, following remedial measures are recommended to the management of private schools to handle the problem of attrition of teachers:

- Teachers of private schools should be given job security once they are confirmed. Such security can be in the form of letter for confirming their services till retirement with some conditions.
- Management of unaided private schools should reward their teachers adequately and also on time.
- Teachers of private schools should also be treated with respect and dignity. They should be treated as assets of the school.
- Teachers of private schools should be given attractive facilities to cope up with the salary standards of government teachers.
- Only qualified and competent teachers should be selected with the help of rigorous selection procedure.
- Proper induction programme should designed by the management with the help of experts to get them adjusted as per philosophy of the management.
- Experienced Human Resources professionals should be appointed to handle issues related to teachers with well-designed procedures.
- Teachers should be trained in all recent updates of their subjects. They should also be train in soft skills.
- The management should come up with the training calendar for on – going training programmes to get their teachers ready to face any challenges in their area of work.
- Development programmes for teachers should also be organised with the help of external experts to upgrade their knowledge and develop them as role models for future teachers.
- Past employment history of teachers should also checked to decide on the probability of their stability.
- Teachers should be recruited through existing teachers' referrals, as there will be someone to take care of retention of the new teacher.

- There should be less dependent on contractual teachers as when they complete the contract, they are more likely to leave the school.
- Suggestions of parents and students should be considered while handling attrition of teachers in self-financed private schools.
- If appointed teachers are not qualified, they should be given a deadline to acquire necessary qualifications.
- Management of unaided private schools should change their philosophy of handling teachers, as when they appoint teachers they should think of a long term association with the teacher.
- Facilities and perquisites should be same for permanent and contractual teachers.
- Management should interact with their teachers frequently, to resolve their problems in real time.
- There should be a special grievance handling cell for teachers to get their issues resolved.
- Management should involve teachers in decisions related to functioning of schools or decisions pertaining to them.
- Management should adopt cooperative approach while dealing with teachers rather than being commanding over them.
- Management should adopt practices like getting employment bond signed by the appointed teachers or asking for their original documents at the time of appointment.
- Teachers should be allowed to adopt innovative and creative practices to make their subjects more understandable for their students.
- Special contributions of the teachers should be recognised in an effective manner.
- More than anything else, the management should focus on improving quality of education with the help of qualified, competent and stable teachers.
- Efforts of management should towards controlling attrition of existing teachers than getting new teachers after they leave to handle turnover of teachers effectively.
- Management of schools should handle their teachers with transparency and without any discrimination and biasness.
- Management should create emotional bondage with their teachers to provide them with happy and healthy working environment.
- Teachers should be counsel to retain them after their resignation.

- Management should evaluate performance of teachers by involving all the stakeholders in the procedure and teachers should be rewarded accordingly.
- Teachers should be educated on the consequences of their attrition on students, parents and management.
- Monthly planning meetings should be organised to with teachers to assign them monthly duties to be performed.
- Teachers should be allowed to take decisions pertaining to their class and subjects.
- Teachers should be allowed to focus on their main duty of teaching and not be given extra pressures from the activities other than teaching.
- Teachers should be allowed to interact with students other than regular class to have emotional connect with the students.
- Teachers should be considered as a key stakeholder for sustainable success of any school.

9.7 POLICY IMPLICATIONS FOR GOVERNMENT

After understanding the problem of Attrition among teachers of private schools in Anand district and its problems, causes and remedies, following policy implications are suggested to the government.

- The chapter on "Attrition of teachers and its Consequences" should be included in the syllabus of B.Ed. and M.Ed. programs, to make them aware about the consequences of teachers' turnover on other stake holders.
- Government should intervene in deciding minimum amount of salary to be paid to teachers of private schools.
- Teachers should be allowed to complain to government officer in case they have any issues with the management of the schools. Their problems should be resolved by the government.
- Government should inspect functioning of aided and unaided private schools at primary, pre-primary, secondary and higher secondary sections in regular intervals.
- Teachers should also be covered under Labour Laws with special provisions for teachers in private schools.
- The guidelines for selection of teachers should be defined for public schools as well as aided and self-financed private schools by government.

- Syllabus of B.Ed. and M.Ed. courses should be updated with special weightage to rigorous internships to be undergone by the students at public or private educational institutions.
- Awareness about government initiatives in Education through programmes and acts like Right to Education should also be spread among teachers of self-financed schools.
- Teachers of unaided private schools should also be informed and allowed to attend trainings, development programmes and refresher courses organized by government.
- Teachers of government schools should be given job security with some conditions. If teachers of public schools are not performing up to expectations, there should be provision to layoff such teachers.
- Government should make provisions of Provident fund and Gratuity mandatory for unaided private schools also.
- As the Government of Gujrat is exercising its right to interfere in private schools through limiting maximum fees to be charged by private schools, they should also exercise such rights to decide on parameters pertaining to teachers.
- Government should come up with separate Grievance Handling Cell for self-financed schools to handle grievances of teachers of self-financed schools pertaining to exploitation, discrimination, harassment at work.

References

[1] Baah Y., Otoo K.N. and Osei-Boateng C. (2009). *Teacher Attrition in Ghana: Results of a Questionnaire Survey.* The study commissioned by Ghana National Association of Teachers (GNAT) and Teachers & Educational Workers (TEWU) of Ghana, Trades Union Congress.

[2] Badubi R. (August, 2017). *Theories of Motivation and Their Application in Organizations: A Risk Analysis,* International Journal of Innovation and Economic Development, ISSN 1849-7020 (Print) ISSN 1849-7551 (Online) URL: http://dx.doi.org/10.18775/ijied.1849-7551-7020.2015.33. 2004, Volume 3, Issue 3, Pages 44–51, DOI: 10.18775/ijied.1849-7551-7020.2015.33.2004.

[3] Basteyns B., IBF International Consulting (April, 2013). *Study on Policy Measures to improve the attractiveness of teaching profession in Europe: Volume I.* European Union: Luxembourg, 2013. ISBN 978–92-79-27887-7, DOI 10.2766/40827

[4] BC (2015). Annual Report, 2014–15 The British Council, (available at https://www.britishcouncil.org/sites/default/files/annual-report-2014–2015.pdf).

[5] Bhattacharya S., Tiwari K., Gautam V. and Das C. (2016). Educational Statistics At A Glance, Government Of India Ministry Of Human Resource Development, Department Of School Education & Literacy, New Delhi.

[6] Boniface R., (2016). *Teachers' Retention in Tanzanian Remote Secondary Schools – Exploring Perceived Challenges and Support,* Linnaeus University Dissertation No 240/2016, Linnaeus University Press, 351 95, ISBN: 978-91-87925-97-9.

[7] Boyd D., Lankford H., Loeb S. and Wyckoff S. (2006). *How changes in entry requirements alter the teacher workforce and affect student achievement,* American Education Finance Association.

[8] Buchanan, J., Prescott, A., Schuck, S., Aubusson, P., Burke, P. and Louviere, J. (2013). *Teacher Retention and Attrition: Views of Early Career Teachers.* Australian Journal of Teacher Education, 38(3).

[9] Calvin Y. (October, 03, 2016). 5:00 AM SGT, *5,000 teachers leave service over 5 years,* The Straight Times, Singapore.

[10] Dhavan H. (2013). *Enrolment in schools rises 14% to 23 crore,* Times of India, Jan 22, 2013, 01:08 IST.

[11] Getahun T., Tefera B. and Burichew A. (2016). *Teacher's Job Satisfaction and Its Relationship with Organizational Commitment in Ethiopian Primary*

Schools: Focus on Primary Schools of Bonga Town. European Scientific Journal May 2016 edition vol.12, No.13 ISSN: 1857 – 7881 (Print) e - ISSN 1857- 7431. doi:19044/esj.2016.v12n13p380.

[12] GOG (2010). The Gujarat Elementary Education Rules, Education Department, Government of Gujarat.

[13] GOG (2017). Socio-Economic Review, Gujarat State, 2016–17, Government of Gujarat.

[14] Gupta A (October, 2013), *Education Status Report – Gujarat (Primary, Middle and Secondary Education)*, Center for Education Innovations, Catalyst Management Services (CMS) | CEI – India, P 8.

[15] Ingram D. (2009). *Motivation Theories & Employee Turnover,* Chron, retrieved from http://smallbusiness.chron.com/motivation-theories-employee-turnover-11785.html.

[16] Karsenti T. and Collin S. (2013). *Why are New Teachers Leaving the Profession? Results of a Canada-Wide Survey.* Education 2013, 3(3):141–149. DOI: 10.5923/j.edu.20130303.01

[17] Kaur R. (2017). *Employee Retention Models and Factors Affecting Employees Retention in IT Companies, International Journal of Business Administration and Management.* ISSN 2278-3660, Volume 7, Number 1, © Research India Publications http://www.ripublication.com.

[18] Keigher, A. (2010). *Teacher Attrition and Mobility: Results From the 2008–09 Teacher Follow-up Survey* (NCES 2010–353). U.S. Department of Education. Washington, DC: National Center for Education Statistics. Retrieved from http://nces.ed.gov/pubsearch.

[19] Khanka S. (2009), Human resource Management (text and cases), S. Chand and Company Limited, New Delhi2009, p146.

[20] Kohli N., (2015) 17:05 IST, *Not in the class: A story of India's missing teachers,* Hindustan Times, April, 06.

[21] Kothari M. and Chavan P. (2015), *Attrition in Schools: A New Trend,* ASM's International E-Journal on Ongoing Research in Management and IT with E-ISSN-2320-0065, Page no. 213–217.

[22] Kothari M. and Chavan P. (2015), *Attrition in Schools: A New Trend,* ASM's International E-Journal on Ongoing Research in Management and IT with E-ISSN-2320-0065, Page no. 213–217.

[23] Kothari M. and Chavan P. (2015), *Attrition in Schools: A New Trend,* "ASM's International E-Journal on Ongoing Research in Management and IT" with E-ISSN-2320-0065, Page no. 213–217.

[24] Manduku J., Koech Z. and Chepkirui P. (2016). *Stress Management Strategies and their Effects on Teachers 'Commitment in Primary Schools in Sabatia District, Vihiga County, Kenya.* Education Research Journal Vol.

6(1): Pg. No. 1-12, ISSN: 2026–6332. Retrieved from *http://resjournals.com/journals/educational-research-journal.html.*

[25] McKinnon M. & Walker L. (January, 2016), 6.14am AEDT. *Teachers are leaving the profession – here's how to make them stay*, The Conversation AU.

[26] Memoria, C. and Rao, V. (2012), Personnel Management Text and Cases, Himalaya Publication, Chapter No. 13, pp. 251.

[27] Memoria C. and Gankar S. (2010), Personnel Management, Text and Cases, Himalaya Publication House, 21st revised Edition, p273.

[28] National Policy on Education (April, 2016). Ministry of Human Resource Development, Report of the Committee for Evolution of the New Education Policy, Government of India, P 1.

[29] NCERT (2006). Seventh All India School Education Survey, National Tables on Schools, Physical and Ancillary Facilities, A Joint Project of National Council of Educational Research and Training and National Informatics Centre, New Delhi, National Council of Educational Research and Training, New Delhi.

[30] NUEPA (2007). District Report Cards, 2006–07, *Elementary Education in India, Where do we stand?* National University of Educational Planning and Administration.

[31] NUEPA (2011). *Elementary Education in India: Progress towards UEE,* National University of Educational Planning and Administration, International Print-o-Pac Limited.

[32] OECD (2009). *Education at a Glance-2009,* OECD Indicators. Organisation for Economic Co-Operation and Development.

[33] Oke A., Ajagbe M., Ogbari M. and Adeyeye J. (2016). *Teacher Retention and Attrition: A Review of the Literature*, Mediterranean Journal of Social Sciences, MCSER Publishing, Rome-Italy, Vol 7 No 2, ISSN 2039-2117 (online) ISSN 2039-9340 (print) DOI: 10.5901/mjss.2016.v7n2s1p371

[34] Peter D. and Welch D. (2010). International Human Resource Management, 4th Edition, Managing people in Multinational Context, Cengage Learning India Private Limited, New India, p196.

[35] Piramal A. (2014). *Educate the Educator for economic growth*, Hindustan Times, January 21, 2014, 23:22 IST.

[36] Prasad L. (2011). Human Resource Management, Sultan Chand and Sons Educational Publications, New Delhi, pp 563–569.

[37] Ramchandran V. (2005). *Why School Teachers Are Demotivated and Disheartened, Economic and Political Weekly*, May 21.

[38] Rana N. and Dave H. (2017). *Survey Raises Red Flags About Quality of Education in Gujarat*, Ahmedabad Mirror, January 19, 02.00 am IST.

[39] Rasheed M. , Humayon A., Awan U. and Ahmed A., (2016). *Factors affecting teachers' motivation: An HRM challenge for public sector higher*

educational institutions of Pakistan (HEIs), International Journal of Educational Management, Vol. 30 Issue: 1, pp. 101–114 DOI: *http://dx.doi.org/10.1108/IJEM-04-2014-0057.*

[40] Shah T. (2014). *Secret of Creating High Performing Knowledge Institutions,* AERC Foundation Lecture 2014, Agro-Economic Research Centre, Sardar Patel University, Vallabh Vidyanagar, July.

[41] Sindhi S. (2012). *The Plight of Non Government Teachers in India,* International Journal of Humanities and Social Science Invention with ISSN (Online) No.: 2319–7722, ISSN (Print) No.: 2319–7714, Volume 1, Issue 1, December, PP 45–49.

[42] Sindhi S. (2012, December). *The Plight of Non Government Teachers in India,* International Journal of Humanities and Social Science Invention with ISSN (Online) No.: 2319–7722, ISSN (Print) No.: 2319–7714, Volume 1, Issue 1, PP 45–49.

[43] Subba Rao P. (2012). Essentials of Human Resource Management and Industrial Relations (Text, Cases and Games), Himalaya Publishing House, Fifth Revised edition, Chapter no 30, pp 667–669.

[44] Summiya Y., Raghavendra S., Raghupathi H., Nehru A., Pandit V., Srivastav A. and Chatterjee G. (2008). Country wide Report on *Dismaying teacher shortage in Indian academia,* June.

[45] Thomas D. and Hammond L. (2017, August 16). *Teacher Turnover: Why It Matters and What We Can Do About It,* Learning Policy Institute, USA.

[46] U-DISE (2016). School Education In India, Flash Statistics, U-DISE 2015–16, National University of Educational Planning and Administration, New Delhi, Department of School Education and Literacy Ministry of Human Resource Development, Government of India, September.

[47] UNESCO (2006). *Teachers and Educational Quality: Monitoring Global Needs for 2015,* UNESCO Institute for Statistics, 2006.

[48] UNESCO (2018). UNESCO Institute of Statistics, Report- 2018 (available at http://uis.unesco.org/).

[49] UNESCO (2015). Education for All Global Monitoring Report, Policy Paper 19, *The challenge of teacher shortage and quality: Have we succeeded in getting enough quality teachers into classrooms?,* UNESCO, April.

[50] UNESCO-UIS (2006). *Teachers and Educational Quality: Monitoring Global Needs of 2015,* UNESCO Institute for Statistics, Canada.

[51] USAUD (2011). School Dropout Prevention Pilot Program on Dropout Trend Analysis: India, submitted to United States Agency for International Development Washington, DC and prepared by Creative Associates International, Inc. Washington, DC.

[52] Vankatesh K. (2016, March). *Job Satisfaction among Primary School Teachers With Respect To Age, Gender and Experience,* The International Journal of

Indian Psychology, ISSN 2348-5396 (e) | ISSN: 2349-3429 (p) Volume 3, Issue 2, No.10, DIP: 18.01.183/20160302 ISBN: 978-1-329-99963-3 http://www.ijip.in | January–March, 2016.

[53] Varma S. (2014). 04:03 AM IST, *Teachers' Day: Most teachers get a pittance for pay*, TNN, September 5.

[54] Vimala R., Pal M., Jain S., Shekar S. and Sharma J. (2008). *Teacher Motivation in India.*

ANNEXURE I

Schedule for Management

1 For Management

Dear Sir/Madam,

I, (Mukti Patel), a Ph.D. Scholar registered at Sardar Patel University, Vallabh Vidyanagar, Anand (Gujarat) have designed this schedule to get response from school management on selected parameters to be used for Ph.D. research work purpose on the topic "**Understanding Attrition of Teachers in Private Schools of Anand district of Gujarat: Problems, Causes and Remedies**". The data will be used purely for academic and research purpose only and confidentiality of respondent would be maintained.

(Mukti Patel)
Ph.D. Scholar (Management)
Sardar Patel University,
Vallabh Vidyanagar, Anand (Gujarat)

Sign of Respondent with Stamp with Date: ______________________

1. Name of the School: ______________________________
2. Year of Establishment: ____________________
3. Type of School Funding:
   A. Private fully-aided ☐ B. Private self-financed ☐
4. Standards in the School: Class ____________ to ____________
5. Board:
   A. State Board ☐ B. CBSE ☐
   C. ICSE ☐ D. IB ☐
6. Name of the Respondent: ____________________________
7. Designation: ____________________________________
8. Age (years): ____________________________________
9. Gender: A. Male ☐ B. Female ☐
10. Qualification: __________________________________
11. Years in Service:__________________________________
12. Years in the School: ______________________
13. Contact No.: ____________________________
14. What is the student-teacher ratio in the school?

Standard	*No. of Students*	*Student/Teacher Ratio*	*Male Teachers*	*Female Teachers*
A. IX				
B. X				
C. XI				
D. XII				

15. What factors does the school consider while selecting a teacher? (Rank the following factors from 1-Most Important to 8-Least Important)

Factors	
A. Friendliness and Congeniality	
B. A Good Personality	
C. Confidence and Perfection	
D. Deep Knowledge and a Great qualification	
E. A Good Communicator	
F. A Good Listener	
G. A Good Sense of Humor	
H. Kindness	

Any other, please specify____________________________________

16. Tick before the facilities provided by the school: (you may tick on more than one option)

A. Canteen		B. ICT [Information and Communication Facility]	
C. Counseling Centre		D. Rest Room	
E. Personal Lockers		F. Separate Staff cubicles	
G. Transportation		H. Teachers Resources Center	
I. Medical Facilities		J. Recreation Centre	

Any other Facility: ____________________________________

17. Tick before the perquisites/incentives provided by the school: (you may tick on more than one option)

A. Flexi Timing		B. Staff Credit Co-op. Society	
C. Provident Fund		D. Housing	
E. Gratuity		F. Telephone Allowance	
G. Medical Allowances		H. Study Leaves	
I. Festival celebration		J. Privilege Leaves	
K. Gifts		L. Staff picnic	
M. Health Insurance		N. Paternity Leaves	
O. Maternity Leaves		P. Sport Events	
Q. Coupons		R. Performance Recognition	

Any other Facility: ________________________________

18. What are the characteristics of school most likely to be successful in retaining teachers? (You may tick on any one from the following options)

A. Salaries ☐ B. Incentives ☐

C. Support system ☐ D. Timings ☐

E. Pleasant environment ☐ F. Training ☐

G. Attachment with students ☐

Any other, please specify________________________________

19. What factors does the school consider for retaining teachers?
(Rank the following factors from 1-Most Important to 9-Least Important)

Factors	
A. Working Conditions	
B. Induction & Monitoring Programs	
C. Recruitment Strategies & Policies	
D. Performance Appraisal	
E. Motivation	
F. Recognition	
G. Decision making involvement	
H. Role and Responsibilities	
I. Facilities	

20. What strategies does the school adopt for the recruitment of teachers?
A. Online Recruitment Practices ☐
B. Recruitment Consultancies ☐
C. Referral Programs ☐
D. Newspaper Advertisement ☐

21. What accounts for demographic of the current population of the teachers?
A. Age ☐ B. Qualification ☐
C. Past experience ☐

22. Does offering higher salary increase the quality of teachers who are recruited & retained?
A. Yes ☐ B. No. ☐

23. What is the level of percentage in your School?
A. Highest (%) ______________ B. Lowest (%) ______________

24. How do you handle low scoring students?

Ways	
A. Through counseling	
B. By arranging remedial classes	
C. Supporting students by admitting them in special school for slow learners.	
D. By taking help of parents for understanding the child's behavior outside school	
E. Advising parents to admit their kids too there school	

25. In what ways does the school get affected due to teacher's turnover? (You may tick on more than one option)

Ways	
A. Disturbance in the time table	
B. Negative impact on the annual results	
C. Disturbance in the functioning of school	
D. Increased pressure on other staff members	
E. Pressure of hiring a new teacher	

26. Do you consider teacher's say on the core issues related to education?

A. Yes ☐ B. No ☐

27. Does the school conduct exit interview for the teachers?

A. Yes ☐ B. No ☐

If yes, what new policies/changes do you implement in accordance with the feedback receive? ____________________

28. Does the management follow any procedure for gaining feedback regarding facilities provided to the teachers on duties?

A. Yes ☐ B. No ☐

If yes, how often?

A1. Once a year ☐ A2. Twice a year ☐ A3. More than twice a year ☐

29. In what ways are the contributions of a teacher recognized by the management?

    A. Incentives ☐

    B. Rewards and recognition ☐

    C. Awards and certificate ☐

    D. Performance appraisal ☐

30. On what basis is the performance of teachers evaluated?

Factors	
A. Quality of the teaching	
B. Relation with student	
C. Annual result of student	
D. Relation with other Teachers and Management	
E. Departmental Audits	
F. Performance of school in inter-school competition	

Any other, Specify ____________________

31. In what ways teachers can communicate with the management?

    A. Through a telephonic call or text messages ☐

    B. Suggestion box ☐

    C. Writing letter at your postal address ☐

    D. Through formal or informal meeting ☐

    E. Directly meeting with concern officer/member of management ☐

32. Do you conduct planning meeting and year ending meeting with teachers?

    A. Yes ☐ B. No ☐

33. Do you have Local Management Committee (LMC)?

    A. Yes ☐ B. No ☐

    If yes, how many times does it meet in a year? ________________

34. Do you conduct Departmental Audit?

A. Yes ☐ B. No ☐

If yes, how often?

A1. Quarterly ☐ A2. Half yearly ☐

A3. Annually ☐

35. From the given factors which one is mainly considered while promoting teachers?

A. Seniority ☐ B. Qualification ☐

C .Performance ☐ D. Any other, specify _____

36.How do you deal with the turnover of an efficient and reliable teacher?

A. By evaluating the exit forms ☐

B. By seeking help from the existing teachers ☐

C. By hiring volunteers ☐

D. By arranging extra classes for left out portion ☐

37. Do you take student's feedback on the performance of teachers?

A. Yes ☐ B. No ☐

38. Any Suggestion/Opinion on handling Attrition of Teachers in Private Schools:

____

____

____

39. What is probation period for newly appointed teachers before they get confirmed?

A. 6 months ☐ B. 1 year ☐

C. 2 years ☐ D. No Probation ☐

E. Any other arrangements: _______________________

40. How do you train new teachers to fit your school? *(you may tick on more than one option)*

A. Existing Senior Teachers ☐ B. External Experts ☐

C. Government Trainings ☐

D. Through CBSE Workshops ☐

E. Any other way, specify:_______________________

41. What is Notice Period to be served by the Teachers, when they want to leave the School?
    A. For Confirmed Teachers: ____________________
    B. For Teachers on Probation: ____________________
42. Tick the tools used for the Selection of Teachers from the given below: *(you may tick on more than one option)*
    A. Subject Knowledge Test ☐ B. Psychometric Test ☐
    C. HR Interview ☐ D. Panel Interview ☐
    E. Telephonic Interview ☐ F. Demo Lecture ☐
    G. Reference Check ☐
43. Why do teachers mainly leave the school? *(you may tick on more than one option)*
    A. For Government Job ☐ B. For Getting Married ☐
    C. For Settling down to Abroad ☐
    D. For Transfer of Spouse ☐ E. For Better Prospects ☐
    F. Any Other: ____________________
44. Do you try to convince teachers to stay back during Notice Period?
    A. Yes ☐ B. No ☐
    If Yes, then how? ____________________
45. Do you lay off any teacher from your side for any reason?
    A. Yes ☐ B. No ☐
    If Yes, then why? ____________________
46. Who takes decisions pertaining to Teachers? *(you may tick on more than one option)*
    A. Management ☐ B. Principal ☐
    C. Campus Director ☐
    D. Specially appointed Management Representative ☐
    E. Please specify if anybody else:____________________

47. How your school is different from other schools? (List down all special features of the school)

Personal Observations:

ANNEXURE II

Schedule for Teachers

2 For Teachers

Dear Sir/Madam,

I, (Mukti Patel), a Ph.D. Scholar registered at Sardar Patel University, Vallabh Vidyanagar, Anand (Gujarat) have designed this schedule to get response from Teachers on selected parameters to be used for Ph.D. research work purpose on the topic "**Understanding Attrition of Teachers in Private Schools of Anand district of Gujarat: Problems, Causes and Remedies**". The data will be used purely for academic and research purpose only and confidentiality of respondent would be maintained.

(Mukti Patel)
Ph.D. Scholar (Management)
Sardar Patel University,
Vallabh Vidyanagar, Anand (Gujarat)

Sign of Respondent with Date: ______________________________

1. Name: Mr./Ms./Dr. ____________________
2. Age (in years): ____________________
3. Gender:
   A. Male ☐ B. Female ☐
4. Marital Status:
   A. Married ☐ B. Single ☐
   C. Divorcee ☐ D. Widow ☐
5. No. of Kids:
   A. One ☐ B. Two ☐
   C. More ☐
6. Education of spouse: ____________________
7. Occupation of spouse: ____________________
8. Type of family:
   A. Nuclear ☐ B. Joint ☐
9. Education:
   A. B.Ed. ☐ B. M.Ed. ☐
   C. Ph.D. ☐
   Any other, specify____________________
10. Distance from School (km): ____________________
11. How do you attend school?
   A. Self–vehicle ☐ B. School transportation ☐
   C. Railway ☐ D. Bus ☐
   E. Auto Rickshaw ☐ F. Cab ☐
   G. Walk ☐
12. Residential address: ____________________
13. Contact No.: ____________________
14. Home Town: ____________________
15. Name of the School: ____________________
16. Address of the School: ____________________

17. How many education sections does the school have?
    - A. Pre–schooling (Play Group, Nursery, KG 1 &2) ☐
    - B. Primary schooling (1 to 8) ☐
    - C. Secondary schooling (9–12) ☐
18. What is the medium of instruction used in the school?
    - A. English ☐ B. Gujarati ☐
    - C. Hindi ☐ D. Other ____________
19. Type of School Funding:
    - A. Private fully-aided ☐ B. Private self-financed ☐
20. Type of employment:
    - A. Permanent ☐
    - B. Full time Contractual ☐ C. Part-time ☐
21. Type of board you teach: (you may tick on more than one option)
    - A. State Board ☐ B. CBSE ☐
    - C. ICSE ☐ D. IB ☐
22. Which of the following board school have?
    - A. State Board ☐ B. CBSE ☐
    - C. ICSE ☐ D. IB ☐
23. How many years of experience do you have in teaching?:
    ___________ years
24. Since how long have you been in this school?: __________ years.

25. Is this your first job? A. Yes ☐ B. No ☐, if not, why did you leave the earlier job?

B1. Professional Reasons		***B2. Personal Reasons***	
A. Working on contractual basis		A. Getting married	
B. Less Pay		B. Expecting a child	
C. Working hours		C. Moving to be near partners job	
D. Too many responsibilities		D. Moving to be near family	
E. Too few responsibilities		E. Poor health	
F. Lack of promotion opportunity		F. Disability	
G. Lack of training/ professional development		G. Age	
H. Experience of discrimination/harassment		H. General dissatisfaction with teaching profession	
I. Class size		I. Caring for relatives	
J. Pupil behavior		J. For reasons connected with education of own kids	
K. Parental behavior		K. High Cost of buying accommodation	
L. Behavior Policy of Management		L. High cost of renting accommodation	
M. School- i. Environment (e.g. buildings)		M. Commuting - inconvenience/time taken	
ii. Resources		N. Cost of transportation per week	
iii. Colleagues			
iv. Reputation			
v. Vicinity			
N. Management - lack of support		Any Other,	
O. Management - lack of direction			

26. Which of the following is your Style of teaching? (You may tick on more than one option)

A. Lecture	☐	B. Group discussion	☐
C. Role playing	☐	D. Case study	☐
E. Laboratory	☐	F. Demonstration	☐
G. Activities and games	☐	H. Visit	☐

Any Other, ______________________________

27. What was the selection tool used for your appointment? (you may tick on more than one option)

A. Personal Interview	☐	B. Group discussion	☐
C. Written Test	☐	D. Telephonic Interview	☐
D. Class Demo	☐	E. Panel Interview	☐

F. Any Other, ______________________________

28. What is your Monthly Pay?:

Rs. ____________________

29. Are you satisfied with your current pay scale?

A. Yes	☐	B. No	☐

If no, why? ______________________________

30. Tick before the facilities provided by the school:(you may tick on more than one option)

A. Canteen		B. ICT [Information & Communication Facility]	
C. Counseling Centre		D. Rest Room	
E. Personal Lockers		F. Separate Staff cubicles	
G. Transportation		H. Teachers Resources Center	
I. Medical Facilities		J. Recreation Centre	

Any other Facility: ______________________________

31. Tick before the perquisites/incentives provided by the school: (you may tick on more than one option)

A. Flexi Timing		B. Staff Credit Co-op. Society	
C. Provident Fund		D. Housing	
E. Gratuity		F. Telephone Allowance	
G. Medical Allowances		H. Study Leaves	
I. Festival celebration		J. Privilege Leaves	
K. Gifts		L. Staff picnic	
M. Health Insurance		N. Paternity Leaves	
O. Maternity Leaves		P. Sport Events	
Q. Coupons		R. Performance Recognition	

Any other Facility: ______________________________

32. Rank the following motivators as per your preference. (What motivates you the most?)(1-Most Effective Motivator and 10-Least Effective Motivator)

A. Work environment	
B. Pay	
C. Relation with colleagues	
D. Positive attitude of management	
E. Relation with students	
F. Recognition	
G. Decision making involvement	
H. Role and Responsibilities	
I. Facilities	
J. Good Feedback Ranking	

33. Do you want to stay in the same school?

A. Yes ☐ B. No ☐

If yes, for how long? ____________ Years

34. How do you identify the need areas for your professional development? (you may tick on more than one option)

A. Attending courses on teaching	
B. Having your own teaching observed and commented upon	
C. Observing others' teaching (Learning by example)	
D. Studying students' feedback	
E. Mentoring by experienced colleagues	
F. Discussion about the performance with the experts	

Any other: ______________________________

35. How do you upgrade yourself in your respective subjects? (you may tick on more than one option)

A. Attending Seminars	
B. Attending Conferences	
C. Attending subject related workshops	
D. Attending Refresher Courses	
E. Reading books/magazines	
F. Surfing e-resources on the subject	
G. Updating through news	
H. Interacting with subject experts	
I. Regular visit to Library and books reading	

Any other: ______________________________

36. How frequently does the school conduct on-the job/off-the job, specific/general training programs for the teachers per year?

A. Not at all ☐ B.1–5 ☐

C. 6-10 ☐ D.>10 ☐

37. How many training & development programs do you attend every year?

    A. Not at all ☐ B.1–5 ☐

    C. 6–10 ☐ D.>10 ☐

38. Is there any negative Implication (penalty/punishment) for the following behavior? (Tick before the appropriate options)

Behavior	*Always*	*Sometimes*	*Never*
A. For not being on time to school			
B. For violating important rules & regulations			
C. For conflicting behavior with peers			
D. For misbehavior with students			
E. For not meeting the deadlines			
F. For utilizing school hours for personal work			
G. For using school property for personal task			

39. Read the following statements and tick before the appropriate options.

	Statements	*Completely Disagree*	*Partially Disagree*	*Neutral*	*Partially Agree*	*Completely Agree*
1.	Involvement in work related decisions may lead to high morale.					
2.	Colleague's supportive behavior leads to positive work environment.					
3.	Working environment affects work commitment.					
4.	Job satisfaction may reduce attrition.					

	Statements	*Completely Disagree*	*Partially Disagree*	*Neutral*	*Partially Agree*	*Completely Agree*
5.	Teaching at the same place for a longer period gets monotonous.					
6.	Jump in early career is necessary for career growth.					
7.	Lack of acknowledgement may cause inefficiency in work.					
8.	Long term job security is a key to retaining teachers.					
9.	Image of teaching profession is lower than other professions in the job market.					
10.	Personal family issues do play a vital role in the performance of teachers.					

40. Do you interact with students other than regular class?

Yes ☐ No ☐

If YES, how:

A. Mentoring ☐ B. Counselling ☐

C. Causal talks ☐ D. Personal counselling ☐

Any other: ____________________

41. What kind of work pressure do you handle other than teaching?

A. Co-curriculum activities ☐

B. Government assignments ☐

C. PTA ☐

D. Assignment from management ☐

E. Exam duties ☐

Any other: ____________________

42. How do you manage work related stress? (you may tick on more than one option)

Ways	
A. Break down your work into smaller tasks	
B. Try not to take things too seriously at workplace	
C. Through effective time management	
D. Meditation	
E. Talking about your problems	
F. Through Exercise	
G. Indulging in your favorite hobby	
H. Ask for help with the jobs you dislike	
I. By taking adequate sleep	
J. Planning an outing with family and friends	
K. Listening to uplifting music	

Any other: ______________________________

43. Read the following PROFESSIONAL factors that may influence your decision to leave this job, and rate them using a number from 1 to 3.

Factors	*Very Important 1*	*Important 2*	*Not Important 3*
A. Working on contractual basis	1	2	3
B. Pay	1	2	3
C. Working hours	1	2	3
D. Too many responsibilities	1	2	3
E. Too few responsibilities	1	2	3
F. Lack of promotion opportunity	1	2	3

Factors	*Very Important 1*	*Important 2*	*Not Important 3*
G. Lack of training/professional development	1	2	3
H. Experience of discrimination/harassment	1	2	3
I. Class size	1	2	3
J. Pupil behavior	1	2	3
K. Parental behavior	1	2	3
L. Behavior Policy of Management	1	2	3
M. School i. Environment (e.g. buildings)	1	2	3
ii. Resources	1	2	3
iii. Colleagues	1	2	3
iv. Reputation	1	2	3
v. Vicinity	1	2	3
N. Management - lack of support	1	2	3
O. Management - lack of direction	1	2	3

44. Read the following PERSONAL factors that may influence your decision to leave this job, and rate them using a number from 1 to 3.

Factors	*Very Important 1*	*Important 2*	*Not Important 3*
A. Getting married	1	2	3
B. Expecting a child	1	2	3
C. Moving to be near partners job	1	2	3
D. Moving to be near family	1	2	3
E. Poor health	1	2	3

Factors	*Very Important 1*	*Important 2*	*Not Important 3*
F. Disability	1	2	3
G. Age	1	2	3
H. General dissatisfaction with teaching profession	1	2	3
I. Caring for relatives	1	2	3
J. For reasons connected with education of own kids	1	2	3
K. High cost of renting accommodation	1	2	3
L. High Cost of buying accommodation	1	2	3
M. Commuting - inconvenience/ time taken	1	2	3
N. Cost of transportation per week	1	2	3

45. If you would move to another job, either in teaching or elsewhere, please indicate in the list below what factors would attract you the most to the job, using a number from 1 to 3.

Factors	*Very Important*	*Important*	*Not Important*
A. Higher salary	1	2	3
B. Better prospects	1	2	3
C. Looks more interesting	1	2	3
D. Wanted a change	1	2	3
E. Easier to get to	1	2	3
F. Better benefits	1	2	3
G. Fits better with my family circumstance	1	2	3
H. Better reputation of the School	1	2	3
I. Important job profile	1	2	3

46. What about the Right to Education? What are the merits and demerits of it?
    A. Have you heard about RTE: Yes/No, if yes, source ___________
    B. What are the merits of RTE: ___________________________
    ____
    C. What are the demerits of RTE: ______________________
    ____

47. Any suggestion/opinion to handle attrition of teachers in private schools:
    ____
    ____
    ____
    ____
    ____
    ____
    ____

48. Personal Observations:

ANNEXURE III

Schedule for Parents

3 For Parents

Dear Sir/Madam,

I, (Mukti Patel), a Ph.D. Scholar registered at Sardar Patel University, Vallabh Vidyanagar, Anand (Gujarat) have designed this schedule to get response from parents on selected parameters to be used for Ph.D. research work purpose on the topic **"Understanding Attrition of Teachers in Private Schools of Anand district of Gujarat: Problems, Causes and Remedies".** The data will be used purely for academic and research purpose only and confidentiality of respondent would be maintained.

(Mukti Patel)
Ph.D. Scholar (Management)
Sardar Patel University,
Vallabh Vidyanagar, Anand (Gujarat)

Sign of Respondent with Date: ______________________________

1. Name: ____

2. Age (years): __________________

3. Gender:

   A. Male ☐ B. Female ☐

4. Qualification: _________________

   Profession: ______________

5. Pupil's Standard:

   A. IX ☐ B. X ☐

   C. XI ☐ D. XII ☐

6. Pupil's Board:

   A. State Board ☐ B. CBSE ☐

   C. ICSE ☐ D. IB ☐

7. Residential Address: ___________________________________

8. Distance from School (kms): _______

9. Contact No.:___________________________

10. Which of the following factor/s do you consider while choosing a school for your kid/s (you may tick on more than one option)

Sr. No.	*Factors*	*√ (tick)*
1.	Reputation of school	
2.	Qualified teachers	
3.	Teacher-pupil ratio	
4.	Principal of school	
5.	Management of school	
6.	Board availability	
7.	Infrastructure	
8.	Facilities provided to students	
9.	Co-curricular activities	
10.	Fee structure	
11.	Location of School	
12.	Achievements of school	

Sr. No.	*Factors*	*√(tick)*
13.	Sports activities	
14.	Style of teaching	
15.	Timing of school	
16.	Year of establishment of school	
17.	Uniform of school	
18.	Quality of students	
19.	Class size	
20.	Track record of School in Board result	

Any other: ____________________

Does the school conduct Parent Teacher Meeting?

A. Yes ☐ B. No ☐

If yes, how often?

A. Once a year ☐ B. Twice a year ☐

C. Thrice a year ☐ D. Four times a year ☐

E. More than Four Times ☐ F. Every Month ☐

12. How are you benefitted from such meetings? (You may tick on more than one option)

Benefits	√ *(tick)*
A. Better understanding of child's performance	
B. Able to know the teacher well	
C. Getting idea about different facilities provided by the school	
D. Involvement in decision making regarding important aspects	
E. Getting to know if everything is as per expectations	
F. Guidance on good parenting from teachers	
G. Report of Grievances no proper teaching	
H. High Teacher turnout and its impact on leaning of subject by student	

Any other: ____________________

13. What factors do you consider in a teacher suitable for your kid?
    A. Years of experience ☐
    B. Interpersonal skills ☐
    C. Good communication ☐
    D. Understanding of the subject ☐
    E. Style of teaching ☐
    F. Discipline Teacher ☐
14. If your child discusses with you about one of his/her teacher leaving the school forever. How you would be affected by the given situation?
    A. Highly affected ☐ B. Affected ☐
    C. Least affected ☐ D. Not affected ☐
15. Do you think that study of your child would be affected due to the leaving of any teacher in between?
    A. Yes ☐ B. No ☐
16. How is your child affected by teacher's turnover? (You may tick on more than one option)
    A. Difficulty in learning & understanding ☐
    B. Unable to adjust with the new teacher ☐
    C. Negative impact on child's percentage ☐
    D. Lack of interest in the subject ☐
    E. All of above ☐
17. Would your child face any difficulty in adjusting with the new teacher?
    A. Yes ☐ B. No ☐
18. In case of the above situation, how would you deal with your child's changing behaviour towards his Studies?
    A. Counseling him/her ☐
    B. Personal Attention ☐
    C. Talking to the new teacher ☐
    D. Taking help of the teacher who left ☐
    E. Taking help of child's friends ☐
    F. Any Other: ____________________

19. According to you what measures should be adopted by the school to prevent growing attrition rate of school teachers? *(You may tick on more than one option)*

Measures	√ *(tick)*
A. Structured induction for beginning teachers	
B. On-the-job observations and coaching in the classroom	
C. Conducting mentoring programs for the teachers	
D. Peer Assistance and Review Programs	
E. Timely pay to the teachers	
F. Facilities provided to them	
G. Through effective evaluation of student feedback report	
H. Through Counseling	

20. Have you contacted the Management ever?

A. Yes ☐ B. No ☐

A1. If yes, how many times? What type of action they have taken?

21. Whether the following facilities are provided by school or you have to buy it?

A. from Schools:

Books ☐ Notebooks ☐

Uniform ☐ Shoes ☐

B. From Outside School:

Books ☐ Notebooks ☐

Uniform ☐ Shoes ☐

22. Did you give any donation at the time of admission?

A. Yes ☐ B. No ☐

A1. If yes, how much? How much of the amount is non-refundable?

Total: ______________________

Non-refundable: ______________

23. Since how long your child is enrolled in this school (in years) and from which standard? (Years: ________________ Standard: From __________to __________)

No. of Years		*Standard*	
A. 1		A. Play Group	
B. 2		B. Kindergarten (K.G.)	
C. 3		C. Junior K.G	
D. 4		D. Senior K.G.	
E. 5		E. I	
F. 6		F. II	
G. 7		G. III	
H. 8		H. IV	
I. 9		I. V	
J. 10		J. VI	
K. 11		K. VII	
L. 12		L. VIII	
M. 13		M. IX	
N. 14		N. X	
O. 15		O. XI	
P. 16		P. XII	

24. Any other suggestion:

25. Personal Observation:

ANNEXURE IV

Schedule for Students

4 For Students

Dear Sir/Madam,

I, (Mukti Patel), a Ph.D. Scholar registered at Sardar Patel University, Vallabh Vidyanagar, Anand (Gujarat) have designed this schedule to get response from Students on selected parameters to be used for Ph.D. research work purpose on the topic **"Understanding Attrition of Teachers in Private Schools of Anand district of Gujarat: Problems, Causes and Remedies"**. The data will be used purely for academic and research purpose only and confidentiality of respondent would be maintained.

(Mukti Patel)
Ph.D. Scholar (Management)
Sardar Patel University,
Vallabh Vidyanagar, Anand (Gujarat)

Sign of Respondent with Date: ________________________

1. Name: ______________________________

2. Age (years): __________

3. Gender:

   A. Male ☐ B. Female ☐

4. Pupil's Standard:

   A. IX ☐ B. X ☐

   C. XI ☐ D. XII

5. Pupil's Board:

   A. State Board ☐ B. CBSE ☐

   C. ICSE ☐ D. IB ☐

6. Address: ______________________________

7. Contact No. : ______________

8. Who is your favorite teacher? Which subject does he/she teach?

   ____

9. Have any of your teachers left since last 1 year?

   ____

10. Do you want any of your teachers who have left to come back?

    A. Yes ☐ B. No ☐

    If yes, why ______________________________

11. How do you bid farewell for your teachers?
    (You may tick on more than one option)

    A. By presenting a gift individually to the teacher ☐

    B. By offering a gift on behalf of the class as a token of love ☐

    C. By organizing a party ☐

    D. Giving away an Admiration Speech ☐

12. Are you in contact with any teachers who have already left?

    A. Yes ☐ B. No ☐

13. Do you play active role in giving your feedback for teachers?

    A. Yes ☐ B. No ☐

14. Do you complain if you are not happy with the teacher?

A. Yes ☐ B. No ☐

If yes, to whom?

A1. Class Representative ☐ A2. Class Teacher ☐

A3. Supervisor ☐ A4. Principal ☐

A5. Management ☐

15. Which of the following factors appeal to you while choosing your school? (You may tick on more than one option)

Factors	
A. Reputation of school	
B. Qualified teachers	
C. Teacher-pupil ratio	
D. Principal of school	
E. Management of school	
F. Board availability	
G. Infrastructure	
H. Facilities provided to students	
I. Co-curricular activities	
J. Fee structure	
K. Location of School	
L. Achievements of school	
M. Sports activities	
N. Style of teaching	
O. Timing of school	
P. Year of establishment of school	
Q. Uniform of school	
R. Quality of students	
S. Class size	

16. What are the qualities you look for in a good teacher?
(Scale: 1-Most preferable quality to5- Least preferable quality)

Qualities of a good Teacher	*1*	*2*	*3*	*4*	*5*
A. Good Personality					
B. Innovative and Effective style of Teaching					
C. Clear Objectives for Lessons					
D. Excellent Discipline Skills					
E. Good Classroom Management Skills					
F. Good Communication skills					
G. Strong Rapport with Students					
H. Calm and Patient towards students					
I. Leniency					
J. Knowledge of Subject Matter					
K. Approachability					
L. No Biasness					

17. Would your performance in the class get affected by the exit of your teacher?
A. Yes ☐ B. No ☐

18. What problems/difficulties you are likely to encounter with the exit of your teacher? (Tick before any one of the following options)
A. Poor concentration ☐
B. Interest limited to specific topics ☐
C. Boredom ☐
D. Difficulty in learning and understanding ☐
E. Feel unprepared for the class ☐
F. Absenteeism ☐
G. Difficulty to cope up with the subject ☐

19. Personal Observation:

____

ANNEXURE V

Case Study 1

Teacher's View on Attrition

Introduction

Attrition of teachers in the private schools is the biggest problem of the day. The increasing interest of the parents in the private schools for the better future of their students has attracted the attention of a large group of the people towards this problem. There are many problems that cause attrition of teachers in the private schools. Let us examine a teacher's view on attrition who thinks of leaving the school where he works.

Analysis

A teacher named, Chirayu Virendrabhai Patel, found that attrition of the teachers in the private schools causes a psychological problem for the students. Citing his own example, he informed that the teachers working in the private schools are not satisfied with their jobs to a great extent. They face different problems like "students' attitude", "students' psychological effect", "parents' coordination", "school management coordination", and "limitation of the school management". His views make it clear that apart from the management problems, the "parents' coordination" is also one of the significant cause of the teachers' attrition. He observed that the most of the students behave properly in the class, even though it seemed that they are also very much conscious about their "social structure" or "social status". During his six and half years' service in the school wherein he has been employed as a higher secondary teacher of Economics, he found the problem of coordination at the management level. These problems are the lack of coordination among the trustees of the school and the lack of coordination between the principal and the managing trustee. Chirayu found that the school management has failed to understand certain problems of the teachers and as a result this causes a problem on the academic side. Many problems of the teachers can be resolved through a sympathetic attitude of the management towards its teachers which is unfortunately missing. Chirayu made it clear that these problems of the teachers are not the personal problems always. Majority of these problems are the academic problems – the product of the biases created by the school management. The school management has created the rivalry among the teachers nourishing the favouritism. Some teachers are given good 'treatments' by the management, whereas as the others are treated indifferently. This has aroused a feeling of discrimination among the teachers. Salary is also one of the reasons for the higher attrition rate in the private schools. In most of the schools, teachers are not given the salary according to the government's wage rule. They expect, as Chirayu informed, around ₹ 15,000 to ₹ 20,000 salary per month but they are not given this much salary in most of the schools. This economical exploitation makes the teachers indifferent towards teaching and the duties they are assigned with. Many teachers continue their jobs despite of this exploitation only because of their family commitments. Hence, whenever the teachers come across any better opportunity, they leave their jobs and go somewhere else where they are given better salary. However leaving a school is often followed by a critical thinking on the various aspect of the school wherein the teachers see a better chance. They often consider the reputation of the school. If the school is comparatively reputed they may leave the current school for the new. If the school is not reputed enough, they may not leave their current school even if they are offered better salary. Chirayu also informed that the government have also introduced the different aptitude tests for the teachers like TAT and TET. Those who do not have good merit in these tests are forced to work wherever they get jobs and working in the private schools also gives a good experience to those who have scored well and are waiting for the government jobs. There are teachers, like Chirayu, who weigh the private job over the government. For them the only reason for getting into the government job is the security. If the private school provides them the job security and good salary (equivalent to the government job), there are many teachers ready to serve the same school life time. Chirayu told that due to the increasing competitions among the private schools and their increasing numbers, it may happen that after five years the private schools may find the risk of less numbers of the enrolled students. In this case also, some teachers would like to leave their current school for a better opportunity. Chirayu, during his interview, told that the teachers of the private schools have an expectation from the government that it should form certain concrete rules to stop the uncontrolled mushrooming of the private schools. This would ensure the quality of education and would stop the competition in the field of education ensuring to the teachers of the private school risk-free career. The teachers expect that the management should give them good reasonable salary that may attract them for serving the school for a long time and stop them working for tuition classes. Chirayu informed that the teachers and students have emotional relationship. When a teacher leaves the job, this emotional attachment is also broken down. This emotional bonding takes place after a long time when a new teacher is employed at the place of one who has left. So, attrition also causes a problem of emotional bonding with the student. Some teachers also expect that the management should standby the teachers in an event of teachers-students' struggle on certain issues.

Case Problem

The teachers working in the private schools seem to have four basic problems that often result in the attritions of the teachers. These problems are: (i) low salary, (ii) lack of job security, (iii) favouritism created by the management, and (iv) the lack of the support by the management. This also makes it clear that the private schools are more inclined towards the profit-generations motives than the quality of education. In their craving for the profit, they exploit teachers and invite the problem for the students.

ANNEXURE VI

Case Study 2

Teacher's View on Attrition

Introduction

There are many factors responsible for the attrition of teachers in the private schools. These factors are: heavy workload, unequal work distribution, administrative corruption, low salaries and other benefits, lack of professional development programmes, and social and economic problems. In a country like India, where the population is increasing day-by-day and the country needs more teachers for schools, the problem of the high attrition rate of the teachers from the private schools needs a close inspection. Let us examine a teacher's view on the causes of attrition. This is a teacher who left private school of urban area to join public school of rural area.

Analysis

A teacher named, Dharmendrasinh Navalsinh Gohel, a teacher of Economics at a government school in one the villages of Anand District, says that he has left the school, the private school, where he worked earlier for around ten years because of the administrative problem and job security. He told that in the private schools there are frequent changes in the administrative policies and the board of trustees. Hence, it may be possible that with coming of a new administrator the policies change abruptly. Since the new administrator does not have any rapport with the existing teachers he will take such decisions which are problematic for the existing teachers. He may have his own men as the teachers in the school. So, this administrative shifts and corruption make teachers ponder about their future seriously. And this often results in attrition of teachers. He also informed that in the private school, there is always the problem of the strength of the students in the class. This is another reason that makes a teacher serious about getting a new opportunity. Dharmendra acknowledged that the private schools provide more facilities than the government schools but only because of the job-security he decided to leave the school where he worked earlier as an in-charge Principal. Dharmesh found that the students from the rich families majorly opt for the private schools, hence in the private schools there are fewer numbers of the students who come from the poor families. He said that he finds satisfaction in working at the government job because he can serve the students from the poor families which he missed at the private school. He also found the students of the village government school more humble than the students in the private city-area school. He experienced that in the government schools the students give importance to the teachers and show their interest in different activities, whereas the students in the private schools think that they can learn the things from tuition classes or from some other resources hence do not give much importance to the teachers.

Dharmendra said that financial exploitation and uneven work distribution are also important factors for the attrition of the teachers from the private schools. Exploitation of the teachers in the private schools is found in every school, though at varying degree. Dharmendra would not have gone any other school from the school where he worked even he would have offered better salary because he found the exploitations of the teachers in other schools in a greater degree than his own school. Dharmendra was given better salary in the private school than his current government job. But it is because of the 'family pressure' he opted for the government job. It makes clear that the private schools have the tendency of firing teachers when their performance ceases. So, the teachers like Dharmendra prefer the government schools over the private schools. Even family also plays important role in the process. Since the families of the teachers want to have a constant flow of income in the homes, they sometimes pressurise the teachers for leaving a current school for a better prospect. Government jobs provide good salary and other perks that always fascinate the teachers for the jobs.

Dharmendra opined that the private schools should introduce certain schemes to increase job-satisfaction among the teachers. They should hire teachers for more years with friendly terms and conditions. Dharmendra also confessed that he would not have left his private school job, if the management had ensured him service till the age of retirement in writing. Dharmendra says that to stop the attrition of the teachers from the private school the government should interfere in the policies of the private schools. The way the government has introduced the measures of controlling the fee in the private school, similarly the measures for the appointment, work-hours, and salary can be introduced by the government in the private school. This will create the trust among the teachers and all other stake-holders.

Dharmendra shared his experience that the students do not easily accept a new teacher in the classroom. When he joined the government school he also faced the same problem. A teacher creates a rapport with his students which is always based on the mutual understanding. When a teacher leaves the private school, this mutual relationship is broken up and it mentally haunts the students. So, he said that attrition of teachers in the private school also causes the mental agony for the students. He is a teacher of a public school, but he visits the previous private school regularly after working hours as he shares special bonding with the private school, from where he started his career.

Case Problem

A teacher who has already left a private school where he worked for nearly about ten years says that security of the job is the main cause of the attrition in the private schools. The government should take some measures in ensuring the job-security to the teachers who are working in the private school. The government has whole-heartedly given permission for the opening of the private schools but without any policy control is major draw-back on the part of the government. If the teachers are offered job-security, they will definitely serve for a longer time in the private schools.

ANNEXURE VII

Case Study 3

Principal's View on Attrition

Introduction

Growing population of India has caused a problem of providing education to all for the government. The public has turned towards the private schools thinking that they are the good sources for educating the children. On one hand, the demand of the private schools is increasing day-by-day, and on the other, the teachers of the private schools are leaving their job due to varied reasons. This attrition of the teachers has caused the problems for the students and the parents. Let us understand what a Vice-Principal of a school thinks about this.

Analysis

Mr. Kartikey, a Vice-Principal of a school, informed that he works both as a teacher and an administrator. Mr. Kartikey is a teacher of English and has been teaching in the same school for last twelve years. He has also worked in some other schools for three years previously. He received many opportunities from other schools while working in the current school. Mr. Kartikey has ignored all these offers because he is satisfied with his current job. He informed the reasons for his satisfaction: 'job security' and 'family-like atmosphere of the school'. According to him, this 'family-like atmosphere' is supported by the teachers and the administration. This has happened because of the administration's support for the development of the teachers. Mr. Kartikey, as an administrator, said that their prime concern is the 'stability' of their teachers. They think that "if the teachers are stable, the students, parents and administrators would be stable." Mr. Kartikey informed that they take care of the dignity of their teachers in the terms of respect and salary. This is the result why they could create the family-like atmosphere.

Attrition is common everywhere. Though Mr. Kartikey and their team have created a healthy atmosphere, they do come across some cases of the attrition of the teachers. He said that "when a teacher leaves the job during the mid-term, only students have to suffer." Since attrition has become a problem for the administrators, they have started employing different strategies. Mr. Kartikey's school has adopted a bond-system. They sign a bond with the teachers at the time of appointment clearly stating that they will not be allowed for leaving the school during the mid-term without any genuine reason. They have to serve the notice period of three months before leaving the job. Mr. Kartikey was happy to inform that he has not seen any case of attrition since his appointment in his current school. And the credit of decreasing or stopping the rate of the attrition goes to the 'family-like atmosphere'. Mr. Kartikey informed that it is better to do something to sustain the current teachers in the school instead of recruiting some new teachers at their places. Recruiting the students of the same school as teachers is another strategy that Mr. Kartikey's school has employed. Since these teachers are accustomed to the atmosphere of the school and they have a homely attitude towards the school, it becomes easy for the administrators to work with them smoothly.

According to Mr. Kartikey, the main reason behind the attrition in the majority of the school is the salary of the teachers. Though the private schools charge very high fees and have good infrastructural facilities, they pay less salary to their teachers. On another hand, the government school provides good salary to their teachers. So the difference in the salary fascinates the teachers to opt for the government schools over the private schools. Mr. Kartikey also thinks that the government should interfere in the matter of salary. Mr. Kartikey has also observed that many private schools exploit their teachers since these schools are profit-oriented. If the government implements any policy for the salary of the teachers working in the private schools, this problem of attrition can be easily addressed. Mr. Kartikey said that many private schools offer the salary around ₹ 4000–₹ 10000 per month to their teachers which is too less to survive. This low salary makes the teachers disinterested in their work. It makes them to think about the better opportunity constantly. This is the reason why the teachers engage themselves in other businesses apart from teaching.

Mr. Kartikey does not feel insecure in his school though his school is private. He believes that performance is the key to success. "If you perform well, you will automatically survive for a long time". Job security haunts those who do not work or have doubts regarding their potential. Mr. Kartikey opined that in the government school the teachers are not satisfied with the work and infrastructure, they primarily work for the salary. Whereas the teachers in the private schools are performance-oriented, they primarily work for job-satisfaction.

Mr. Kartikey upheld that the 'stability' of teachers and good 'management' can stop the problem of the attrition. If a school-management takes care of the stability of its teachers, the rate of the attrition will automatically be reduced. Instead of allowing the teachers to leave the school, the school management should counsel them and try to sort out their problem.

Case Problem

Though attrition is a great challenge, it can be solved out by the management. This problem is caused by the profit-oriented nature of the school. Many school-managements do not consider the condition of the teachers. The school-management should focus on the development of the teachers. Many schools do not realise the importance of the teachers. The day they will realise the situation, the problem of the attrition will be solved to a great extent.

ANNEXURE VIII

Case Study 4

Principal's View on Attrition

Introduction

The ratio of teachers' attrition in the private school is increasing day-by-day. This fact hints at certain problems that have remained either unnoticed or unattended by the school management. Though it may seem a superfluous matter, it is one of the major challenges of the current education system. It is a major challenge because it is directly associated with the country's future. All the stakeholders of the education system have their own perspectives on this problem. Let us understand how a principal as a component of the administrative processes looks at this problem.

Analysis

A lady-Principal, Ms. Nandini, who is a Principal of a private school for six years says that through attrition of the teachers in the private schools is a grave prove problem, it does not affect all the schools. Citing the example of her own school, she says that only 'two-three' teachers have left the school in the last six years. She says that these teachers have left the job because of their personal problems and not for any academic reason. Ms. Nandini says that they could control the rate of attrition in their school by making the teachers participate in the decision making process. The school has both senior and junior teachers. The school has taken care of their views and aspiration and has created a healthy atmosphere for the teachers to work together.

The school, wherein Ms. Nandini has been working, has provided the facility of teachers' quarters to the teachers and the hostel for the students. So, the teachers can live with their family in the school campus only and even the students can interact with the teachers apart from the school-hours. This has created a family-like atmosphere in the school. Since the school management also helps the teachers by focusing on their needs; the school has not yet encountered the problem of attrition. Ms. Nandini, as a principal, also counsels the teachers regularly regarding their academic and family needs. During her counselling of the teachers, she has not yet encountered any case where the teacher is intending to leave the school.

By retaining the teachers in the school for a long time has also proved fruitful for the school-management. The teachers are familiar with everything regarding the school, policies, and culture of the school. It has also increased the mutual understanding between teachers and students. Ms. Nandini opines that recruiting new teachers on and not retaining the current teachers in the school makes no sense. Hence, it is advisable to retain the current teachers only than recruiting and training the newer ones. Recruiting teachers needs a lot of investment not in terms of money but in terms of understanding, training, and time. Ms. Nandini also informs that the teachers who have left the school because of their personal reasons in the past have re-joined the school. It clearly suggests that they have succeeded in retaining the teachers better than others. Certain problems of the teachers cannot be solved by the management, in that case Ms. Nandini's school allows them to leave the school and they have also made the policy of re-recruiting such teachers when they come back.

While answering a question on the treatment of the teachers in the school, Ms. Nandini suggests that since the teachers are thinking human-beings they must be respected. Respecting teachers in the school encourages them to work with a school for a long time. Those schools that allow their teachers to leave the schools without addressing their problem, according to Ms. Nandini, should make attempts to retain the teachers first. As she already said, it is always better to retain the current teachers instead of looking for the newer ones and repeating the long time-consuming process of recruiting and training. Ms. Nandini believes that showing his or her own importance of the teacher who is willing to leave school instils the pride in him or her and in this way also one can control the attrition rate in the school where he or she is working.

In certain cases where the teachers have to leave the school, then they plan his or her exist from the school in such a way it does not affect the academic session. Since the teachers themselves understand the problem of leaving the school in-between and the problems that students may face, they resign during the vacation, if it has to be. In certain cases, Ms.

Nandini has also observed that the teachers themselves train the new teachers before they leave the school. This has also proved beneficial for the school management.

Case Problem

Though attrition is a serious problem, it can be resolved. To solve this problem, the school management does not require the investment of money but what they require is the handing the problems of the teachers in a more serious way. Understanding a teacher and his needs and addressing his problems makes the teacher committed and this inspires him to work for the school for a long time.

ANNEXURE IX

Case Study 5

Teacher's View on Attrition

Introduction

Addressing the problem of attrition of the teachers in the private schools, one needs to know why the teachers leave the schools. What instigates them for leaving the schools they are working with? In a country like India where the government has indirectly indicated that the government no more can provide financial assistance to the schools in the times of growing population and a growing need of the teachers, it is crucial for us to understand the root of the problem. Let us understand what a teacher says on this issue.

Analysis

RaziaVhora, a twenty-eight-years experienced teacher of English who has an experience of working with four school says that she started her career as a kindergarten teacher. She has an ambition of moving ahead in her career so she started teaching in the primary section and so on. As a kindergarten teacher, her salary was insufficient to afford a good life. By changing the standards and the classes, she started earning a good income. So, according to her the reason for leaving the school was primarily salary she was offered to. Another reason, as she acknowledges the malpractices of the management. She also finds that women teachers are not paid well in comparison to the male teachers. Unequal distribution of the work is also distressing problem for the teachers.

As RaziaVhora says, some schools are very much religion-conscious. In one of the school, she was asked to reign during the midterm because she belongs to a religious-minority community. Razia tells that the private schools do not have any fixed policy for the termination of the teachers. This is also one of the reasons why teachers leave the private school in search of a better prospectus. Razia informs that once she was terminated from a school without any reason. Later, she realised that she was forced to leave the school because of her religion. Razia has also an experience of working with a minority school of her own community. But she finds that the school was too traditional to welcome any change. They even did not provide any liberty to teachers to carry out any experiments in teaching patterns or to introduce any new learning activity. Razia finds that those private schools which take care of teachers and their families can easily retain the teachers in their schools for a long time. The school management's positive indulgence in the lives of its employees for their betterment ensures the teachers of the management's positive approach to them and thus it results in emotional bonding. Razia gets comparatively less salary but she is happy with her work and the environment of her workplace. She also informs that she has very good colleagues and they aspire to live the school. The reason for their aspiration is that the government job provides a life-long security. But they are quite sure that until they get government jobs they will work in the same school.

Razia opines that encouragement is a powerful key to retain the teachers in the private school for a long time. Most of the private schools do not encourage their teachers for academic or any kind of change. As a result, the teachers feel that their liberty and their rights as teachers are in danger and they live the school in a search for a new. Apart from good salary, the teachers want respect, encouragement, motivation, and support of the school in the problematic situation. If a private school succeeds in providing these things to the teachers, it is sure that the school will succeed in retaining the teachers. She finds that all the teachers have their own style and way of teaching. They create an emotional bond with students. So when a teacher leaves the school, nobody else can replace his or her personality. Even the irregularity of the teachers, in terms of appointment and termination of the teachers, also affect the students psychologically.

Case Problem

Razia's view on the attrition clearly suggests that big problems are big if they are solved out strategically. For the private schools, attrition is a great challenge nowadays. If the private schools wish, this problem can be solved out by the schools by indulging in the lives of the teachers positively and by creating a bond of trust. The attrition occurs because of the threat of security of the job and the challenged relationship between the school management and the teachers. If the private schools succeed in ensuring the long-term security to the teachers, the problem of the attrition can be solved easily.

Annexure X

Case Study 6

District Education Officer's View on Attrition

Introduction

District of Anand has majorly 3 types of schools, 1. Government Schools 2. Private Aided Schools 3. Private self-financed schools. The data shows that the number of student enrolling in the private self-financed school is the highest among all three. The District Education Officer (DEO) looks after the education on several parameters in the district and holds responsibility and authority of better education. DEO of the district of Anand Mr M. B. Sharma was interviewed personally to get his inputs about the issue of teacher's attrition among the private schools to understand the perspective of the government administration's perspective on this issue.

Analysis

Mr. M.B. Sharma is the DEO of Anand and looks after the all schools including the private aided and self-financed schools along with 13 government schools. He was in the position since May 18, 2017. According to him, the advent of private school is due to failure of the government schools. About the teacher's issue he had the view that the government schools have strict qualification requirements for the recruitment of teachers whereas no such strict guidelines or norms are there for the private schools. This leads to well-known phenomena of "Head-hunting". The well to do teachers from one private schools are offered good positions with hike at competitor school which leads to attrition of good teachers. He informed that the government does not have much say in the private schools other than fee structures.

In the district of Anand, good locations such as urban areas have seen transition of teachers to tuition classes as easy availability of students and high monetary benefits. Citing the example of Jawahar Navoday Vidhyalay he informed that the school has facilities far better than any private school but due to job security and high earning of the teachers at government schools are leading to lack of interest for the government schools. An important point drawn by him also suggests that many private science schools managements have private colleges as well. Many students and parents prefer them due to favour in the admission in the colleges after schooling. The DEO also mentioned about the shocking tie up of the Govt. of Gujarat with other states like Andhra Pradesh, Karnataka and Tamil Nadu to provide student s to the universities of those states. The business is estimated of Rs. 425 Cr.

According to him, out of all the good private schools approx. 20-25 % have shown exploitation of teachers even if run by good trusts. In public schools the ratio of teachers to classes is 1:1.5 where as in private schools the ration of teachers to students is 1:(20–25). The private schools also have edge over public schools due to the involvement of counsellors to help the students. Discussing about the scenario of the public schools, he informed that there are 13 public schools in the district and high job security and salary is a problem with government schools.

The parents shall be considered responsible for the wrong usage of private schools. There is a mechanism to redress complaints from parents about the private schools but they are not followed or never explored. Teachers of private schools do have a channel to complaint about the managements but they mostly refrain from practicing it due to fear of management sacking them. Many rules levied by the government are not followed by parents, teachers and schools. To incorporate private schools in quality of teachers, common training for public and private schools are held. The teachers from private schools are involved in the functioning other than teaching also. When asked about his comments on the privatisation of education, he refrained from answering it qualitatively.

He has shown interest in receiving policy implication of this study. He suggested a policy of transferring government teachers to other districts, who are not up to the mark in their work. He further added that the attrition of teachers is not much prevalent in the public schools as teachers have good incentives there.

Case Problem

Measures to be undertaken by government to resolve the problem of attrition should be highlighted. There a trend among the parents of the district to get their kids enrolled in private schools. DEO strongly believes that the trend is because of failure of government schools to improve quality of education in the district. He strongly feels that parents and teachers of private schools should complain to the DEO office in case of any problems with private schools. Teachers of private schools should also participate in the training and development programmes organised by the government.

Annexure XI

Glimpses of School Visits

S-1: V&C Patel English School

S-2: Zen School

S-3 Bavis Gam Vidhyalaya

S-4 J.P. Thakkar High School

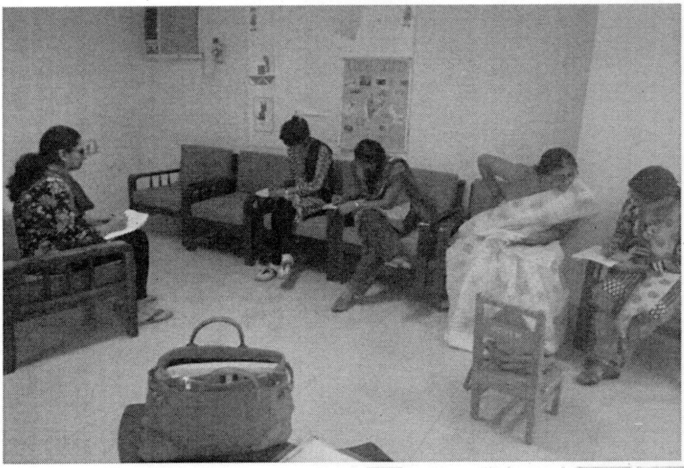

S-5 Charotar English Medium School

S-6 Laksh School of Science (Khambat)

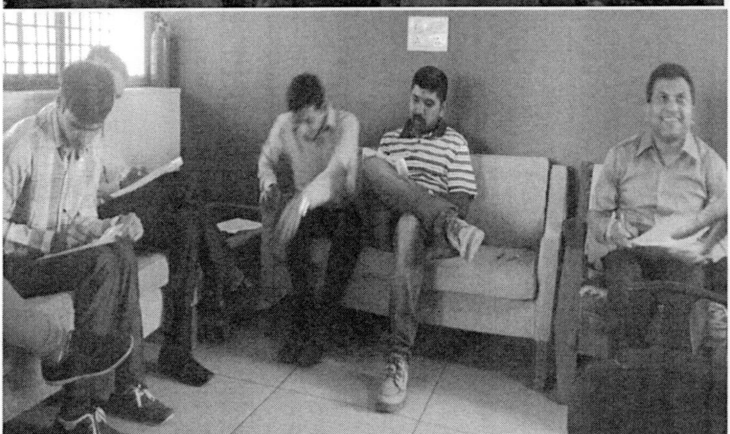

S-7 Adharshila Vidhyalaya (Aaklav)

S-8 Shri C.B. Patel English Medium School

S-9 Knowledge High School

S-10 Thamna Education Institute (Umreth)

S-11 BAPS Swaminarayan Vidyamandir

S-12 Swaminarayan Vidyapith

S-13 I.B. Patel English School

S-14 D.Z. Patel Higher Secondary School

S-15 Excellent English Medium School (Borsad)

S-16 S.J. Patel English Medium School (Tarapur)

S-17 Shree Swaminarayan English Medium School

S-18 T.V. Patel Higher Secondary School

S-19 Vrajbhoomi International School

S-20 Angel English Medium School

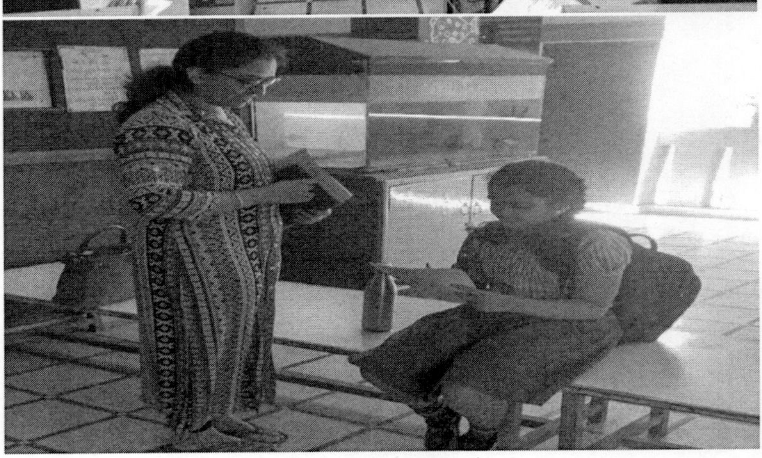

S-21 H.M. Patel English Medium School (Petlad)

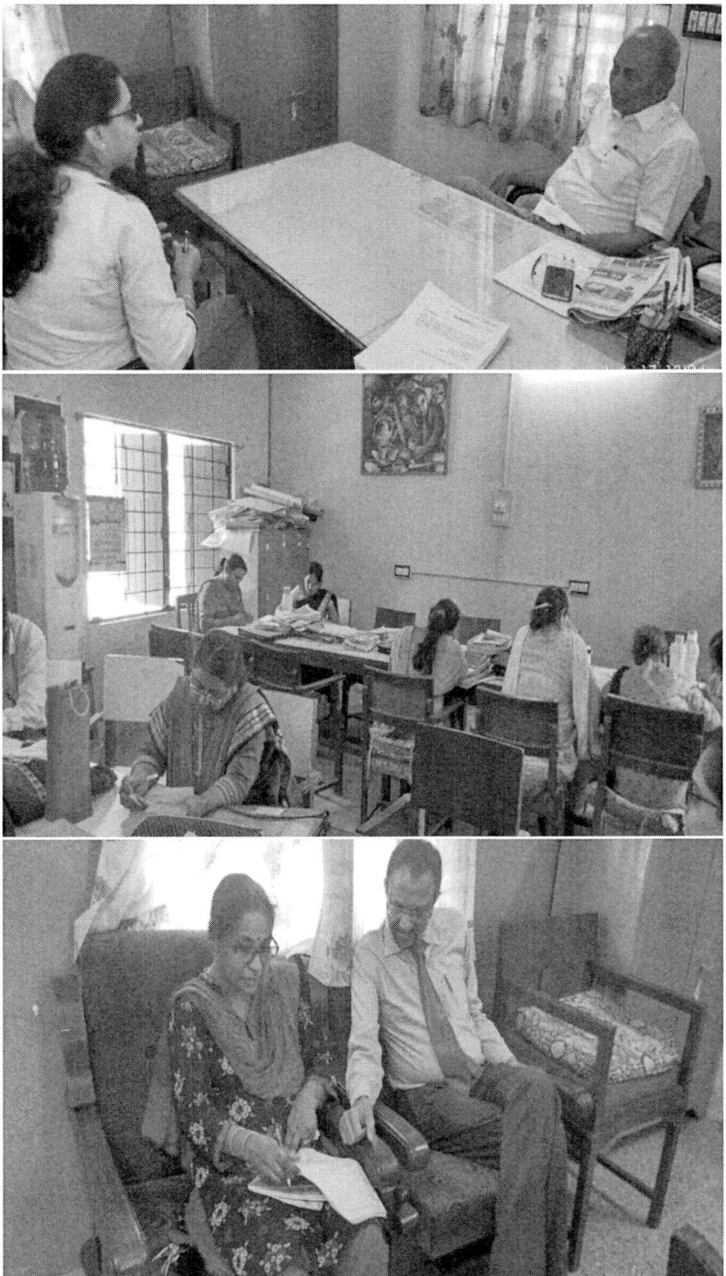

S-22